AUG - 5 1971

D0407619

IN PRAISE
OF
YIDDISH

by
MAURICE SAMUEL

COWLES BOOK COMPANY, INC.
NEW YORK

Cowles Book Company, Inc.
A subsidiary of Cowles Communications, Inc.

Published simultaneously in Canada by
General Publishing Company, Ltd.
30 Lesmill Road, Don Mills, Toronto, Ontario

Printed in the United States of America

First Edition

Acknowledgments

In my autobiographical *Little Did I Know*, 1963, I promised to write a book to be called *The Charm of Yiddish*. It was to open with a detailed side by side comparison of Stutshkof's magnificent *oytser fun der yidisher shprakh* (*Treasury of the Yiddish Language*) and *Roget's Thesaurus of the English Language*. I intended to show how the number and variety of words and idioms gathered round particular objects and ideas in the respective languages mirror the differences in the modes of thinking and of historical experience. Other plans intervened and I was the better part of a decade getting down to the enterprise, for which I had much relish but no model, not even the beginnings of a guide.

I was reawakened to the idea by the manuscript of Leo Rosten's *The Joys of Yiddish*, of which he says in the Preface, "*This is not a book about Yiddish*" (his italics). I found it for the most part a fascinating compendium of words (some of them unknown to me) that have worked their way from Yiddish into a lively and predominantly low form of English. It certainly is not, to quote Mr. Rosten again, "written for students of Yiddish," but it may very well move some of them toward making a beginning, for which all thanks are due.

My second encouragement—it was like an admonition *zikh nemen tsu der arbet*, "to get cracking"—came from the immensely erudite Mr. Yudl Mark, and my third from the late Dr. Solomon Bickel. Without these two devoted spirits I should never have got off the ground. With Yudel Mark I worked systematically; with Solomon Bickel, a man of the widest reading and utmost delicacy of style, and with his gifted wife, Mrs. Yetta Bickel, I enjoyed frequent and absorbing conversations ranging over the subtleties and intimacies of Yiddish.

Two other outstanding scholars gave me the benefit of systematic readings, Dr. Mordkhe Schaechter, the ardent modernizing Yiddishist,

v

and the late Dr. Solomon Simon, whose command of Bible, Talmud, and Jewish-Yiddish tradition helped me through many knotty passages.

To Professor Dov Sadan, Professor Emeritus of Yiddish at the Hebrew University at Jerusalem, and master lexicographer in Yiddish (as well as Hebrew, Russian, and other languages), I am indebted for several conversations—more exactly, discourses—during his recent visit to America.

I have, in addition, laid under tribute scores of listeners, and I restrict mention to a few lest too many become none. Miss Dina Abramowicz, librarian of the Yivo Institute for Jewish Research, was infinitely patient in suggesting and tracing sources, and Dr. Shlomo Noble, of the same institute, was continuously at my disposal for similar services. Dr. Samuel D. Freeman, of the Jewish Center Lecture Bureau, was the first to read my manuscript for popular Yiddish appeal. I have sought advice from the poet, Jacob Glatstein, from the distinguished Yiddish columnist, Ben Zion ("B.Z.") Goldberg, from Professor Elias Tartak of the New School for Social Research, and from many others.

The thorough and ingenious index to this book is the work of Mrs. Helene Fineman, formerly assistant editor of the Franklin Papers at Yale University; I hope it will be useful for browsing as well as reference.

I am especially grateful to my wife, Edith, for her editorial skill, her inexorable patience, and her inexhaustible helpfulness.

To Abram L. Sachar, founder and now chancellor of Brandeis University, and my friend of close on half a century, I owe, for this book and for so much of my previous writing, a continuity of encouragement equally memorable for warmth and duration.

The completion of this book was made possible by a grant from the Philip W. Lown School of Judaic Studies at Brandeis University.

A Note on Sources

Writing in English on the character of the Yiddish language is very meager; it can be summed up in parts of the three volumes of *The Field of Yiddish: Studies in Yiddish Language, Folklore and Literature* (ed. Uriel Weinreich), New York, 1954 and 1969, The Hague, 1965; publications of the Linguistic Circle of New York; and the fourteen volumes of the *Yivo Annual of Jewish Social Studies*. There are also occasional essays difficult of access and, like the foregoing volumes, seldom getting down into the heart of the language itself.

Of direct use are of course the dictionaries, of which I list three:

1. Alexander Harkavy, 22nd edition, 1881. English-Yiddish, 759 pp., Yiddish-English, 364 pp. A classic in its day and still frequently reprinted, though now old-fashioned in many parts.

2. Paul Abelson, *English-Yiddish Encyclopedic Dictionary*, 1915, 1748 pp. With numerous illustrations, large format, still very useful but out of print and hard to come by.

3. Uriel Weinreich, *The Modern English-Yiddish Yiddish-English Dictionary*, 1968. English-Yiddish, 370 pp., Yiddish-English, 420 pp. Completely modernized, with many new terms and old revised ones, a pioneering work with far-reaching influence on the language.

To those who have a working knowledge of Yiddish I recommend, in addition to the Yiddish sections of the first and third dictionaries above mentioned, the two following as indispensable:

1. Nokhem Stutshkof, *der oytser fun der yidisher shprakh, The Treasury of the Yiddish Language*, edited by Max Weinreich, 1950, 932 pp. Covers and adds greatly to the proverbs, locutions, idioms, etc. that have been collected by Ignacz Bernstein and others. I estimate that more than a quarter of my material is drawn from Stutshkof and could not have been obtained elsewhere. A thorough reworking of Stutshkof in English would be a large and invaluable enterprise.

2. *Groyser verterbukh fun der yidisher shprakh, Great Diction-ary of the Yiddish Language.* See p. 275 of this book.

In a class by itself is Uriel Weinreich's *College Yiddish: An In-troduction to the Yiddish Language and to Jewish Life and Culture.* Yivo Institute for Jewish Research, New York, 1949. Frequently re-printed and revised.

To round out the treatment of my present volume, I have oc-casionally drawn on material from *The World of Sholom Aleichem, Prince of the Ghetto,* etc.

Pronunciation of Yiddish

The Yiddish I use throughout this book is very close to the system that has been worked out by the Yivo Institute for Jewish Research. In pronunciation it is nearest to what is commonly known as Lithuanian or Litvak Yiddish, and in its latest development is written almost phonetically. I have tried to approximate the transliteration to standard American English, but there are some deviations, noted below.

Vowels and Diphthongs

a as in fAther

e as in pEt

> When two *e*'s follow each other they are pronounced separately, with or without the glottal stop; thus *gE-Efent*, "opened."

i as in sIn, inclining to sEEn, but short

> When *i* is followed by *e*, the two letters are pronounced separately, as in *mI-En*, "to exert oneself." Usually there is a carryover in sound, so that *mI-En* is actually pronounced *mI-YEn*.

o as in pOrt

u as in fUll, not as in mUd

ay like UY in bUY

ey like EY in prEY

oy like OY in plOY

Consonants

g as in Give, not as in Gin

> Gn is pronounced as two letters, as in Agnon, Agnes, etc.; thus *GNoteven*, "to oppress," and *liGNay*, "adversely."

h as in Head, always breathed

k as in Kin

Kn is pronounced as two letters, as in nicKName; thus *KNaker*, "braggart." *Kh* is the gutteral approximating to the German *ach*. Attention must be paid to a *kh* following a *k*; thus *haK-KHoshe*, "denial," and *laK-KHenen*, "to steal, swipe."

r as in Roll, not as in the English poRt, toRn, etc.

In the Yiddish words *poRn*, "to pair," *toRn*, "to dare," etc., the *r* is rolled in such fashion as to make a second syllable, in the same way as the Scottish *r* in *bairRn*. But in *poRt*, "pairs" (verb) and *toRt*, "dares," though the *r* is rolled, there is only the sound of one syllable.

s as in Silent, never as in riSe

Care must be taken to read the *s* and the *h* separately when they occur as in *oyS-Hoykhn*, "to breathe out," and not to confuse them with the English *sh* as in SHabby; so with *oyS-Hitn*, "to guard against." The English *sh* is written as one letter (*SHin*) in Yiddish. When this letter is preceded by *s*, the two sounds must be carefully kept apart, as in *oyS-SHpayen*, "to spit out," *oyS-SHrayen*, "to cry aloud"; but in ordinary diction, the two sounds are run together, making the words sound like *oySHpayen*, etc. Care must also be taken not to run together a *z* following an *s*, as in *oyS-Zen*, "appearance," *oyS-Zukhn*, "to seek out," etc. Attention is drawn to the *s* preceding a *ts*, as in *oyS-TSien*, "to draw out."

ts is the equivalent of the Yiddish *TSadik*, the German *z*, the Russian *TSeh*, etc.

tsh is like the English *ch* in CHip, but softer

zh is like the *z* in aZure

The English *x* is transliterated as *ks*

y is read as in Yarn, Yap, etc., never as in bY

All other consonants pronounced as in English

What is written as *pn*, e.g., in *khaPN*, "to snatch," etc., is pronounced in the Yiddish original and the English transliteration as *pm*. It is as though the speaker were too lazy to pronounce *khaPEN* as written (though not so pronounced) in unmodernized Yiddish, and said *khap*, followed by the release of the epiglottis, the lips remaining closed. The *e* similarly disappears in *fayfn*, "to whistle," *zogn*, "to say," *lakhn*, "to laugh," *hitl*, "hat," *metupl*, "burdened," though the lips are not closed. In all cases the suppressed *n* constitutes a syllable in sound. The suppressed *e* in *hitl, metupl*, etc., duplicates the suppressed pronunciation of *e* in the English word shovEl, usually pronounced as "shovl."

Yiddish is written and printed without capitals. To avoid awkwardness I have used capitals in the transliteration at the beginnings of sentences.

When there is more than one syllable in a Yiddish word, the accent usually falls on the last but one; but the exceptions are numerous and must be learned by heart.

The reader may find himself confused at the outset by the difference between my transliteration of Hebrew or Hebraic Yiddish words and those Hebrew words that have passed into standard English. As a rule, the Anglicized Hebrew words copy the current Israeli Sephardic for transliteration. The same word will appear in two forms according to whether it is quoted in the English text (*The Random House Unabridged Dictionary*), or whether it is transliterated from my Yiddish text. Thus, "Yom Kippur" is English, *yom kiper*, Yiddish; so with "siddur" and *sider*; "Chassid" (plural "Chassidim") and *khosid* (*khasidim*.) Similarly with names, it is "Sholom Aleichem" in the English text, *sholem aleykhem* in the Yiddish, and so on.

Kheyder (plural *khadorim*) is used rather than the italicized English "*cheder*" (*cheders*).

When all these instructions are followed, the reader will obtain a reasonable approximation to the sound of Yiddish. Certain important nuances are nevertheless absent, such as the distinctions between the light and soft *l*, the hard and soft *k*, etc. It is difficult to convey these without oral instruction.

Explaining the Book

The task I have set myself in this book is to convey to the English reader the inside feel of the Yiddish language. I do not want merely to describe, I want to induct. Nevertheless this is not a textbook; it is an intimate introduction with inserts of illustrative folklore and occasional helpings of history, etymology, anecdote, and personal memories. It is a book with a special bias toward certain features and elements in the language. It is not the book of a scholar and is not intended for scholars; but it is not, I hope, unscholarly.

A certain amount of technical exposition is, as a matter of honest dealing, unavoidable, but the main effort is to transmit the peculiar Yiddish intellectual-spiritual experience. A minimal knowledge of the language is assumed for most readers. But this book is written also for those with sufficient interest but no knowledge of Yiddish at all.

A cautionary word is in place here for those who harbor a sentimental but uninstructed affection for Yiddish as a quaint patois which has somehow produced a number of gifted writers and has attracted the condescending attention often bestowed on "vanishing" or "minority" cultural phenomena. I address the same admonition to those Jews whose vestigial Yiddish is of the kind cultivated by borsht-circuit comedians posing as experts. Yiddish is neither a "quaint" nor "cute" nor "funny" language. The mutilated fragments of it that float about in the popular Jewish novels* no more indicate an intimacy with Yiddish than a sprinkling of *acushlas* and *arrahs* in an "Irish" story indicate a knowledge of Erse. Yiddish is a full-blooded language which unless acquired naturally in childhood must be mastered with the same exertions as one devotes to French or German or Russian. Jews innocent of Yiddish but acquainted with Jewish history have some advantage in getting at the interior enjoy-

---

* *I make an honorable exception of Mr. Saul Bellow, whose Yiddish is authentic and sensitive.*

ment of it; the few words and phrases they have picked up from Yiddish transmuted into English slang will be of no help.

The reawakening of a popular interest in Yiddish has also given birth to a misplaced and misleading indulgence. It is gratuitously assumed that Yiddish, being merely a patois, can dispense with strict forms and usages; part of its appeal is supposed to lie in a happy-go-lucky grammatical and syntactical laxity which makes error impossible and everyone knowledgeable. Nothing could be further from the truth.

This notion may have been fostered by the varieties of Yiddish pronunciation, which have little or no effect on written Yiddish. But the differences are not much greater than in other languages. An educated Liverpudlian may speak with a heavy Lancashire accent which brings a smile to the lips of an educated Londoner but they use the same spelling. An educated Breton and an educated Auvergnois may feel uneasy carrying on a conversation, but they write the same French. So in Yiddish conversation *kigl** and *kugl* are equally correct for "pudding," depending on whether you come from Warsaw or Vilna.

Alas, I have already stumbled into a mare's nest of cultural differentials. *Kugl* is no more "pudding" than *shoyfer* (Heb) is "ram's horn," though it is precisely and literally that. In Merrie England "Christmas pudding" may have been laden with sentimental values as rich as, if quite different from, those associated with a *shabesdik* or "Sabbath" *kugl* in the old Yiddish world. But in the modern English-speaking world, "pudding" does not inevitably call up "Christmas," while in Yiddish *kugl* still calls up *shabes* (Heb). For that matter, Sabbath no more resembles *shabes* than "pudding" resembles *kugl*. The Sabbath of the Christian world was never the sanctuary of the *shabes*. I use sanctuary here in its two related senses, a holy place and a refuge from enemies, a turning to the kindness of God and a forgetting of the cruelty of man.

Now "ram's horn," the literal translation of *shoyfer*, has no sentimental charge whatsoever, while *shoyfer* explodes with it. On the High Holidays—*rosh hashone* (Heb), usually pronounced *rosheshone*,

---

* Where not otherwise indicated, the Yiddish words are of Germanic origin. The abbreviations Heb (Hebraic), Slv (Slavic) will be used.

"New Year," and *yom kiper* (Heb), "Day of Atonement"—the sounding of the *shoyfer* belongs to the tense moments of the services, and a Jew whose religious affiliations have dwindled to these two days of the year is still moved and troubled by those mysterious unmusical petitionary announcements before the gates of heaven. And again, even Jews with but a smattering of Yiddish know the Hebraic-Yiddish phrase *shoyfer shel meshiekh* (Heb), "ram's horn of the Messiah," which sums up millennial hopes and millennial patience.

The proper phrase is, of course, "the trumpet of the Messiah," but a familiar Jewish story hinges on the inadequacy of this rendition, too. A *bal-tekie* (Heb), "blower of the ram's horn," ignorant of English, sued a congregation for a breach of contract. As soon as the trial opened the judge asked for the meaning of the word *shoyfer*. The court interpreter said, "Your Honor, a *shoyfer* is—is—a *shoyfer*."

Judge: The court cannot accept that definition. Please be more specific.

Interpreter (desperately): Your Honor, a *shoyfer* is—a—a what shall I say—a *shoyfer*.

Judge: The case will be adjourned if an intelligent definition is not immediately forthcoming.

Interpreter (in a panic): Your Honor, your Honor, a *shoyfer* is a trumpet.

Judge: Why did you not say so in the first place?

Interpreter (helplessly): I ask your Honor, *is* a *shoyfer* a trumpet?

Contents

IN PRAISE
OF
YIDDISH

CHAPTER ONE

The Character
of Yiddish

1.

More than most languages Yiddish is a ciphered history of the people who created it. Less than a thousand years old and based largely on Germanic dialects, Yiddish reaches back through its powerful Hebraic component through another twenty-five hundred years. One might call Hebrew the "classical" element in Yiddish, but whereas the Latin and Greek origins of words and phrases in English, French, or Italian belong to "etymology," the words and phrases of Hebraic origin in Yiddish are as fresh today as when they were minted.

Everyday Yiddish echoes with the voices of the Patriarchs, the Egyptian bondage, the Kings, and the Prophets. The effect is quite different from the biblical suffusion of the language in, let us say, puritanical England of the seventeenth century. The secular Yiddish vocabulary of the home and the street, the idioms and locutions of unspecialized discourse, is rich with unstudied resurrections of the far-off past. "The wisdom of Solomon," "the strength of Samson," "the still, small voice," "my brother's keeper," and hundreds of other biblical phrases are current in English, but it is a slightly superior English, the English of conscious quotation. When not associated with a religious atmosphere, the phrases have a literary—sometimes stilted—flavor; they will not be heard in the shop and factory, in careless gossip, or a street-corner quarrel. In Yiddish they are completely unaffected. Many examples will be offered in the following pages; here I offer a few as a prelude.

2.

Reporting the effects of a hurricane, one might make the simple declarative statement *es hot ongemakht a khurbn* (Heb), "It did a tremendous amount of damage," literally, "It made a destruction." The first four words of the sentence are Germanic and without a special flavor; the last word, *khurbn*, written in Yiddish exactly as in Hebrew, is heavily loaded with history and emotion. The simplest, all but illiterate Yiddish-speaking Jew knows that *der ershter khurbn*, "the First Destruction," refers to the end of the Judaic kingdom and the First Temple, before the Babylonian Exile, and *der tsveyter khurbn*, "the Second Destruction," to the fall of Jerusalem to the Romans. *Khurbn* is therefore a word with two identities, a general (destruction at large), and a special (the Destruction), passing easily from one to another, the general never free from the heavily loaded special.

Someone describing the grief of his family at the death of a beloved member might say, *in shtub iz geven tishebov* (Heb), "The home was plunged into mourning," literally, "In the home it was *tishebov*." But *tishebov*, though pronounced differently, is written exactly like the Hebrew *tesha b'av*, "the ninth of Ab," the traditional date of the destruction of both Temples, sometimes known as the Black Fast.

Of the credulous simpleton one says *bay im iz es toyres* (Heb) *moyshe*, "For him it is the Law of Moses," which is something like "He accepts it as gospel truth." Neither English phrase implies that the person referred to is a believing Jew or Christian. But *toyres moyshe*, transferred without a change in spelling from the Hebrew to the Yiddish, calls up in other contexts the ancient records of the Jewish people, the obstinate fidelity in persecution, the words of the first prayer

.

a mother taught her child as soon as it was able to lisp—all with a vividness that the word "gospel," even in its gravest usage, does not approach.

At the same time, *toyres moyshe* leads us into an illustration of the Yiddish propensity for intramural self-mockery. *Toyres lokshn* (Slv), substituted for *toyres moyshe*, is a nonsense phrase (*lokshn*, "noodles"), that may be used to designate a person or a theory.

Of a man who is forever doing things out of season, it is usual to say, *a gants yor shiker* (Heb) *purim* (Heb) *nikhter*, "all year drunk, on Purim sober." Now since Jews have a merited reputation for abstemiousness, a Jewish drunkard is rarity enough; that he should choose to play the teetotaler on the one day of the year when to become drunk (in theory) is meritorious if not mandatory, bespeaks an unusual strain of perversity. He refuses to rejoice with his people over the doing-in of Haman, the archanti-Semite, twenty-odd centuries ago. He is therefore known as *a moyshe kapoyr*, "a Moses upside down," a masculine "Mary, Mary quite contrary." The companion word to *shiker* is *lot*; *shiker vi lot*, "as drunk as Lot," refers to the unedifying nephew of Abraham, who in his drunkenness begot sons on the two daughters who put him in that condition for that purpose. Other biblical figures might have qualified as the prototype of the toper—Noah, for instance, or Ahasuerus; but Noah did after all perform a notable service for mankind, and enjoys retroactive honorary membership in the Jewish people, while Ahasuerus, the imperial dope (*melekh tipesh* in Hebrew) is, drunk or dry, a stranger.

An article appearing for sale in the shops is bought up with lightning rapidity; the proper phrase is, *me hot es tsekhapt* (Slv) *vi matse-vaser*, "It was snapped up like matzo water." Matzo, the unleavened "bread" of the Passover, is an accepted English word; *matse-vaser*, "matzo water," is the special and guarded spring water used by superpious Jews in the dough for ritually superpure Passover matzos. The English idiom is "sold like hot cakes."

To be sure, while every Yiddish-speaking Jew knows the phrase *tsekhapt vi matse-vaser*, nine out of ten will not know exactly what *matse-vaser* means; they are nevertheless aware of its mystical place in the perfect celebration of the immemorial ritual.

3.

More particularly, Yiddish is a mirror of the total Jewish condition of the last two thousand years. It is a *goles* (Heb) or "exile" language, one of the many (Bialik enumerates sixteen, but who can be sure that some have not flourished and perished without a trace?) that Jews have fashioned in various lands and ages since the *khurbn* of the Second Temple, and even before. Wherever Jews have lived their segregated— but never insulated—lives, they have remodeled for intra-mural use the local language, adapting it to their peculiar psychological needs, and seasoning it with the ever-persistent Hebrew. It may be said that the Jews of the Second Commonwealth already spoke, in their own homeland, an exile language, Aramaic, which they had picked up in Babylonia; but the close kinship between Hebrew and Aramaic permits us to lump them together, and words from either language transmuted into Yiddish are listed in this book as Hebraic. Contemporaneously with the Jews of the Second Commonwealth, those of Persia spoke Judeo-Persian and those of Alexandria either Coptic or Greek (Koine). Since then we have had, among others, Judeo-Arabic, Judeo-French, Judeo-Spanish (also known as Ladino and, more scientifically, as Dzhudezmo), the last of which still lives on the lips of thousands of Sephardic Jews.

4.

Yiddish is the most important of all the exile languages. It has been spoken by far larger numbers than any other; at its prime, a generation ago, by some eleven millions, which is probably five or six times as many as ever spoke ancient Hebrew. It is the only one to have spread as a lingua franca to all the five continents, and the only one to have produced a solid literature, unless we consider the Talmud a Judeo-Aramaic work. A great many more Jews understand Yiddish than can speak it or write it. A generation ago it was fashionable among "modernized" Jews to pretend not to understand it; today it is the fashion to make unfounded claims to a knowledge of it.

The function of Yiddish, as of every other Jewish *goles* language (and here I would emphasize that "Jewish," the general descriptive adjective meaning "related to the Jews," is not the same as the noun "Yiddish," the language: "I can talk Jewish" is not English), has been to provide expression for the mode of life adopted by the Jews for the preservation of their folk identity. What was that mode? The essence lay in what might be called an ingenious charade, which governed their religious life, which in turn interpenetrated their secular life. They pretended they were still living in their ancient homeland; they continued to celebrate its seasonal holidays at the formerly appropriate times, with largely unchanged prayers and symbols, irrespective of the calendar and customs of their actual environment. They prayed for rains suitably spaced for the Holy Land, hundreds or thousands of miles away, while the learned among them continued to study assiduously the sacrificial rites prescribed for a temple long a ruin and the duties, mostly lapsed, of a hereditary priesthood without a certified lineage.

They did all these things while remaining acutely aware of the total disparity with their environment, natural and human. Few of them were farmers, but since their welfare depended on that of their neighbors they no doubt rejoiced to have the local weather behave seasonably; their prayers, however, implored it to do the same in the distant Holy Land, partly no doubt because Jews lived there, too (there was never a time without Jews in Palestine), but mostly because it *was* the Holy Land, which they would return to some day, please God. Perhaps they did not want it to get into bad meteorological habits.

When Yiddish was beginning to crystallize into a separate language, the condition of the Jewish people was at a low ebb. It was the time of the first Crusades. The stamp was set on a long period of special anti-Jewish rage. The Jews were gradually pushed out of whatever foothold they had on the soil, and they never became part of the craft guilds. It is probable that Yiddish absorbed more of a sense of frustration than any other exilic language, and the Yiddish vocabulary reflects both the external privations of Jewish life and the internal compensations which made it livable and creative.

5.

Throughout its existence Yiddish has been an exilic language in a double sense: It has been the language of a people in exile, and it was long in exile among the elite of that people. To the gentile world the Jew was often a substandard human being; to the educated Jew, *i.e.*, the Bible- and Talmud-trained Jew, Yiddish was a substandard language. The strange parallel goes further. The Christians looked down on the Jew but used him whenever they needed him; some even developed a genuine liking for him. The learned Jew looked down on

Yiddish but among his own people could not get along without it. Hebrew was for prayer, study of religious literature (there was no other kind in Hebrew), and written communication with other learned Jews. Business accounts might be kept in Hebrew by those with a sufficient command of the language, but oral communication with other Jews was in Yiddish, even among the learned. A sneaking affection for Yiddish was apt to develop here and there even when it had to be despised in principle.

An elementary Hebrew education was mandatory for boys; all that a girl had to know was the little group of prayers accompanying her ritualistic duties, such as the blessing of the Sabbath candles and the sacrifice of a piece of dough from every baking. A higher Hebrew education for women was more remote from the classical Yiddish world than votes for women in eighteenth-century Europe. The *sefer ha-khasidim* (Heb), "the Book of the Righteous," a medieval morality book, affirms that "He who teaches his daughter the Torah, it is as if he taught her frivolity," and until a century or so ago the ruling was accepted by the vast majority of orthodox Jews. There was no prohibition as to Yiddish, but no one "learned" Yiddish anyhow. Statistics are not obtainable, but it cannot be doubted that a hundred years ago the majority of women could not read or write Yiddish. This was certainly the case in my grandfather's world, though Roumanian Jewry, to be sure, was backward by comparison with Lithuanian and even Polish Jewry. Nevertheless there was a devotional Yiddish literature, and literature of a more worldly kind, intended chiefly for women, especially after the introduction of printing.

As a child—one might say infant—a Jewish boy was at home, with his mother, his sisters, and his younger brothers. There he spoke Yiddish, that is, *mame-loshn* (significantly, *mame* is Germanic, *loshn*, Hebraic), "mother tongue," which was that in a peculiar and poignant sense foreign, for instance, to English. It was the mother's particular contribution to the

9

crystallization of the child's mind; it was set apart from Hebrew, in spite of the overlapping vocabularies, which was the domain of the father and the grown-up masculine world. The beginnings of the "study" of Hebrew (Hebrew was never *studied* as a language, it was absorbed via oral, singsong translations into Yiddish), the initiation of the boy into the life of the *kheyder*, the one-room Hebrew school (*kheyder* is actually the Hebrew for "room"), was a tremendous childhood event, attended by rites more solemn and appealing than (until recently) those of the *bar mitzvah*. One learned to write Yiddish incidentally, once the Hebrew alphabet was mastered, and the knowledge of it was taken for granted, attended by no distinction. However, a sprinkling of Hebrew and Aramaic tags from Bible, Talmud, Midrash, etc., like similar sprinklings of Latin tags in English conversation and correspondence at one time (*cf.* Boswell's *Johnson*, etc.), was *de rigueur* for educated Jews whenever they used Yiddish.

With the entrance of the boy into *kheyder* life a curious relationship developed between him and his mother. The Hebrew he was beginning to learn was the status language to which she had no access. The more he acquired of it, the higher he rose above her intellectual reach. The bonds of affection were not weakened, for the mother delighted in the progress of her son, and the son reciprocated with enjoyment of her happiness. But there intruded into the relationship an element of unalienating distance. We are inclined to look for a parallel in the case of a simple and illiterate modern mother whose son has achieved high academic distinction. However unimpaired their love for each other, the mother cannot share in the friendships of her son, or do more than listen in awed, uncomprehending silence to the conversations at which she is sometimes present. But the parallel is faulty. The Jewish mother had a particular partnership in the learning of her son (as of her husband); the terms of the partnership were religious and the dividends other-world and eternal.

10

She had, indeed, an exalted status of her own quite unlike that of the simple mother of a Nobel Prize winner; she was a sort of prize winner in her own right.

But the role of Yiddish among learned Jews must not be misunderstood, and we must distinguish between the attitudes of different periods and groups. Before modern times one could not speak of specific hostility toward Yiddish on the part of the learned. They spoke Yiddish with enjoyment, and they enriched it with innumerable words, phrases, and turns of speech drawn from Hebrew and Aramaic sources, thereby bringing the common folk into the vestibule of scholarship. But the common folk, too, familiar with the *sider* (Heb), the daily prayer book, the *makhzer* (Heb), the festival prayer book, the Pentateuch with Rashi's commentaries (the staple of the *kheyder* education), the enchanting Haggadah, the special liturgical "handbook" of the Passover, also made their contribution. Thus Bible, Talmud, and Midrash (the earliest collections of exegesis and legend), all in Hebrew or Aramaic, mingled with the familiar and popular devotional books, also in Hebrew and Aramaic, to turn Yiddish into something other than a European language.

But even with this rich infusion, Yiddish could not rid itself of the exilic stigma. It remained the symbol of the great Jewish humiliation. Its earliest literary productions, most probably devotional, were ersatz for the unfortunate who were deficient in Hebrew; or, if they went into non-Jewish and non-devotional themes, and imitated the popular fictional literature of the gentiles, were furiously denounced as impious, bordering on apostasy. Until the secularization of Jewish life, no scholar dreamed of producing a learned work in Yiddish, any more than an early medieval scholar would have written in the barbarous dialect of his locality. Nevertheless, there was a world of difference between this relegation of Yiddish to a secondary role and the systematic denigration, hatred, and contempt toward it that have appeared in modern times.

11

In the learned orthodox circles of a century ago or even less, no one thought of comparing Yiddish with any European language to the detriment of the former, for the good reason that orthodox Jews did not study European languages. Given its secondary role, Yiddish was, after all, the language of the Jewish people, and as such had its acknowledged merits and functions. It was at least the transition language for the young to scholarly attainment. Better for a simple Jew to speak Yiddish, with its Hebrew interweave, than a gentile language devoid of Hebrew. But by certain modern movements Yiddish was rejected without qualification.

There were various grounds. The men of the Jewish Enlightenment (Haskalah) despised Yiddish as an uncouth jargon, a sort of pidgin German, in which a modern education could not possibly be acquired. It was poor, shapeless, antiquated, unadaptable to the contemporaneous world. Apart from these crippling intrinsic defects it was obscurantist in spirit, drenched in superstition, incurably infected with the "debasement" of the Chassidic movement. From another point of view, Yiddish was attacked by part of the Zionist movement as a language deformed by the exilic life in which it had been born and for which alone it was fit.

In most of what is now Israel, many early settlers carried on harsh public campaigns against the use of Yiddish while the old-time Yiddish-speaking pietists roundly cursed the pioneers for degrading Hebrew into a workaday language. There was also a pathetically schizophrenic group aspiring to complete Hebraization but tied by habit and inclination to Yiddish. I have seen Yiddish-speaking pioneers (this was nearly fifty years ago) enduring agonies of frustration in order to "pass" completely into Hebrew. At the communal table they would point dumbly to what they wanted—knife, apple, kettle—waiting to be reminded of the Hebrew *sakin, tapuakh, kumkum,* rather than utter the Yiddish *messer, epl, tchaynik* (Slv).

There were distinguished Zionist leaders completely bilingual in the written use of both languages but as speakers fluent only in Yiddish, while they sometimes spoke Hebrew only with sustained and unnatural concentration. It used to be said among them: "To speak Hebrew is like riding on a noble horse; at first exhilarating, then rather uncomfortable, and finally a torture. Dropping into Yiddish is like getting off the horse onto your own two feet. What a *mekhaye!*" (*Mekhaye*, amusingly enough, is Hebrew for "joy, relief, pleasure, refreshment.") Writers of the first order such as Sholom Aleichem and Mendele Moycher Sforim, who were not Zionist leaders, were equally at home in the written form of both languages, but did not make a practice of trying to converse in Hebrew. Both took their first steps as writers in Hebrew and turned to Yiddish for folk audiences. Mendele, whom Sholom Aleichem called the *zeyde* (Slv), "grandfather," of modern Yiddish literature, was a creator of modern Hebrew literary form not less than of Yiddish.

In the Israel of today these tortuous relationships have disappeared; Hebrew is the natural language of the majority. Most young people are as ignorant of Yiddish as their parents or grandparents were of Hebrew, while among some, as we shall see, there is actually a nostalgic hankering for Yiddish as the language of the exile experience. Hostility to Yiddish has practically disappeared; the tens of thousands of immigrants who have brought that language with them, and, lacking the heroic self-discipline of the earlier pioneers, continue in it comfortably, are no longer liable to be rebuked in public with the cry, *goy dabeyr ivrit,* "Gentile! Speak Hebrew." There is a successful Yiddish newspaper in the country and a Yiddish theater, while the Yiddish quarterly *di goldene keyt, The Golden Chain,* published in Tel Aviv and read throughout the Diaspora, is the finest publication of its kind in the world.

It is only of late that the hostility toward Yiddish, wherever it remains, is a specialty of people completely ignorant of the language. As recently as fifty or sixty years ago one could, with enjoyment, read denunciations of it written by masters of the language; there were of course other opponents of Yiddish who were not thus qualified, in fact had no qualifications at all, and they alone have survived in this field, queer relics of a bygone age.

There has remained imbedded in Yiddish, like old battle scars, the reaction of the masses to their exclusion from the exalted company of the learned. Though they stood in genuine awe of the scholar, and were grateful to learn from him, behind his back they worked off their frustrations in disparaging locutions. Acknowledging that *loshn koydesh* (Heb), "the holy tongue," was the proper medium for prayer and scholarship, they would refer to it sarcastically as *loshn koyletsh* (Slv), or *lokshn koydesh*, nonsense phrases: *koyletsh* is another name for *khale* (Heb), the special braided white loaf of Sabbath and festivals; *lokshn* (Slv) is "noodles." They would quote such Hebrew tags as they knew by heart and append either a disrespectful mistranslation or add a humorous comment: *odem yesoydoy meofer vesoyfoy leofer*, "Man's foundation is the dust and his end is dust" (classic quotation), *un beyni leveyni* (both Heb) *iz gut a trunk bronfn*, "and in between whiles a drink of whiskey is a good thing." We shall see how Sholom Aleichem turned this type of humor into a high art.

The Yiddish masses were strangers to the earthy joys that lightened the lives of their gentile neighbors. Their consolations were to a large extent of the imagination, and therefore their language, besides serving a normal need, had an esoteric function unimaginable to their neighbors. All languages have their peculiarities and impenetrable privacies, but where the lives of contiguous peoples follow similar patterns (religious, occupational, etc.), the mutually exclusive areas are relatively small. The overall spirit of Yiddish sets it apart from contiguous languages. The difficulty of translating Yiddish into English, French, or German lies far less in the absence of corresponding vocabularies than in the Jewish-Yiddish conception of the meanings of life and the destiny of the people.

This is brought out with special clarity in the relationship of Yiddish to German. Something like 80 percent of the Yiddish vocabulary is an easily recognizable form of German. Yet it is harder to translate Yiddish into German than into English or French. Just as the memory is blocked by a word resembling the one we are trying to recall, so the physical similarity, often amounting to identity, between Yiddish and German reinforces the disparity, often amounting to incommensurateness, between them.

In a larger framework, the difficulty of translating Yiddish into any Western language lies in the misleading similarity between Judaism and Christianity, obscuring the nature of the difference between Jewry and Christendom. We may say that Yiddish at its most secular cannot divest itself of the centuries of religious and Messianic fixations. Its unique coloration corresponds to the uniqueness of the Jewish experience.

CHAPTER TWO

The Strata of Yiddish

1.

The oldest words in Yiddish are taken directly from the Bible, the Talmud, the Midrash, and the various prayer-books—daily and festival—the last two overlapping a great deal with the first two. These words, as we have seen, retain an evocative sacred or historical flavor, and even in completely secularized contexts lead the memory back to their origins.

One of the oldest and best known prayers in the *sider* and *makhzer* is the *shiminesre* (so pronounced though written in its Hebrew form of *shemoyne-esreh*). The words mean "eighteen," a not quite accurate count of the "blessings" it contains, more exactly, of the beneficent acts it attributes to God, reminding Him, as it were, to continue them. The *shiminesre* is also known technically as the *amidah* (Heb), "standing," because it must be repeated in that posture— also in complete silence, or in a tense, barely audible murmur —while turned in the direction of the Holy Land. A pious Jew repeats that prayer over a thousand times in the course of the year, at home and in the synagogue, and it is the core of his daily devotions. Even those laxest in synagogue attendance, who never or very infrequently pray at home, have some familiarity with it. From it alone dozens of words have passed into Yiddish.

Malbesh, "dress, garment," occurs in the benediction *malbesh arumin*, "clother of the naked." *Ikh vel mir koyfn a nayem malbesh*, "I will buy myself a new suit of clothes," is everyday Yiddish.

Meysim, "dead men, corpses," occurs *in mekhaye mey-sim*, "resurrector of the dead"—and we have already noted *mekhaye* as good Yiddish with a related meaning. *Tsvey*

19

meysim geyn tantsn, "Two corpses are going to (join in a) dance," is a popular saying that describes two persons of equal incompetence engaging in a common enterprise, *e.g.,* two tone-deaf old ladies opening a music school.

Royfe khoylim, "healer of the sick," splits in Yiddish into its two component parts, *royfe,* "doctor, healer," *khoyle,* "sick man, patient."

In the Friday evening *kidesh,* "sanctification," repeated by the father of the family when he returns from synagogue, there are, similarly, many phrases that have passed into Yiddish. *Zikorn,* "memory," "memorial," *zekher,* "reminder," occur in the *kidesh,* the first in connection with the Creation, the second in connection with the Liberation from Egypt. *Er hot a gutn zikorn,* "He has a good memory," and *fun zayn gants farmegn iz nit geblibn keyn zekher,* "Of his large fortune not even a reminder was left," have no religious connotation whatsoever, but *zikorn* and *zekher* retain a glimmer of the Friday evening candles, though all the other words in the two sentences are Germanic.

Without necessarily being aware of it, the Yiddish-speaking Jew has the solid beginnings of a Hebrew vocabulary; of the 20 percent or so of Yiddish words that are not Germanic, the larger part is Hebraic. One is tempted to say "Hebrew" instead of "Hebraic," since most Hebrew words enter Yiddish without any change of form though sometimes with a change of usage.

The following words have the same meaning, spelling, and pronunciation in both languages:

Meyvn, "one who understands"; *shoykhet,* "ritual slaughterer"; *novi,* "prophet"; *mase,* "burden"; *mizmer,* "song"; *mazl,* "luck"; *soyne,* "enemy."

When there are changes, they are rarely serious enough to obscure the origin. In the prayers, the Hebrew for "head of the household" is *bal habayis;* in the Yiddish it is pronounced, and sometimes written, as *balebos,* and has the extended meaning of "boss, master, owner." *In DEM shtetl bin ikh der balebos*, "In *this* village I'm the boss," the boast of the local tyrant, is the Yiddish equivalent of *l'état c'est moi. Balebateven*, "to boss people, throw one's weight around," shifts even further from the Hebrew original. Similarly, *meyvn* becomes almost lost when it merges into *bahavnt*, "expert."

Most Hebrew verbs enter Yiddish by taking the German *zayn*, "to be," as auxiliary, leaving the Hebrew stem unchanged in spelling; this subject is explored at length in a later chapter. But some Hebrew verbs enter Yiddish by assuming a Germanic form, adding an *n* or *en* for the infinitive, and going through the conjugations like Germanic verbs. Thus *shekhtn*, "to slaughter" (*cf. shoykhet*, above), *masern*, "to report, denounce (to the authorities)," etc.

Unlike Yiddish, Hebrew is written without vowels, which sometimes (altogether so in poetry) are supplied by various dots and dashes beneath, above, and beside the consonants. What is pronounced in Hebrew as *shoykhet* is written *shkht*; similarly *moyser*, "denouncer," is *msr*. Until very recently the Hebrew words that had turned into Yiddish by means of prefixes and suffixes were separated from those additions by apostrophes; thus *geshokhtn*, "slaughtered," would be written *ge'shkht'n*, *gemasert*, "denounced," as *ge'msr't*. Now the apostrophes are being dropped, but the Hebrew roots, still without vowels, stand out strikingly, even admonishingly, from the rest of the Yiddish text, which, as we have seen, is written phonetically. (See section on Pronunciation, p. ix.)

It can hardly be doubted that this insulation of the Hebrew-Yiddish words from their Germanic and Slavic-Yiddish environment had a cultural-spiritual purpose. The conscious motive may have been purely pietistic, a revulsion from the dejudaization of the Hebrew word. Certainly the effect was to keep Hebrew partly alive in the daily intercourse of the unlearned masses and just as certainly the successful resuscitation of Hebrew in Israel after two thousand years was thereby greatly facilitated. This far-flung "program," as it may justly be called, has no parallel in history.

There have been proposals for the merging of the Hebraic elements in Yiddish with the non-Hebraic, whereby the phonetic system would be applied uniformly. It would then be impossible for a non-Hebraist to identify the Hebrew words. Such proposals have of course come mostly from secular and "advanced" spirits; they have never achieved a popular following. It remained for the communist governments to turn this proposal into something like law. Such Yiddish publications as appear behind the Iron Curtain apply the phonetic spelling system throughout; the result is that the average Yiddish reader outside the Iron Curtain must often struggle to recognize the Yiddish words of Hebrew origin, so outlandish have they become to the eye. A sense of forcible denaturalization rises from the printed page. Behind the Iron Curtain, Yiddish-reading Jews have of course become accustomed to the new forms, and are thus permanently protected from reminders of Bible and ritual.

2.

The next oldest layer in Yiddish is an extremely meager one, almost obliterated between the more powerful lower Hebraic and the more massive upper Germanic. Romance in character by way of Old French and Old Italian, it is little more than a curiosity, but a highly instructive one. Its few nouns and proper names have been so completely assimilated, their flavor has become so peculiarly Yiddish, that they have taken on the validity and authenticity of ancient Hebraic sources.

Tsholent (*cf.* modern French *chaud*, "warm," and *chaleur*, "heat") is one of the most *heymish*, "homey," words.

Heymish, in turn, though Germanic, itself has an inside flavor which removes it entirely from its non-Jewish origin. Now *tsholent* is the common name for the Sabbath dish kept warm in the oven from the previous day because the lighting or use of fire is forbidden on the Sabbath. When the poet Heine, half universal revolutionary, half homesick Jew, falls into one of his nostalgic Jewish moods, he sings rapturously and at length (in his *Prinzessin Sabbat*) of *tsholent*. He spells it *schalet*, and calls it "God's kosher ambrosia." He gives it a charming history of his own invention: Moses, he says, learned the secret of its preparation, along with the rest of the Oral Law, during his forty-day sojourn in the heavens above Sinai, and passed it on to the succeeding generations together with the Written Law, the Torah.

Formally, Heine, the baptized Christian, had only a smattering of Jewish knowledge, picked up in childhood and later from Jewish scholars to whom he was drawn; spiritually he responded to it with the sensitivity of genius. He was entirely inventive when he attributed to Moses, and through Moses to God Himself, the recipe of the dish. But deep insight led him to understand that whatever the recipe, it does not account for the incomparable flavor of *tsholent*, unless we think of the Sabbath itself distilled into it as its chief ingredient. For *tsholent* is redolent of the Sabbath, of leisure, of escape from the grind, the coarseness, the debasement of daily life; it is fragrant with the suggestion of original human dignity, and of that Sabbath of Sabbaths which will be ushered in by the Messiah.

All this resides in *tsholent*, which is perhaps the equivalent of the Negro idea of "soul food," but it does not explain why a Romance word was chosen instead of, say *khamin*, a good Aramaic word for a warm dish.

In discussing the Germanic side of Yiddish, we shall find many "sanctifications" of imported words (*heymish*, already mentioned, is one of them). It is true that, as might be ex-

23

pected, Hebrew dominates the religious area of Yiddish, but non-Hebraic terms have penetrated into the very heart of the religious life. It is equally puzzling that outside the religious vocabulary many words have remained obstinately Hebraic though perfect synonyms have offered themselves in vain from the Germanic and Slavic.

Davnen, "to recite one's prayers," is one of the oddities of intimate assimilation, and is therefore mentioned here though not of Romance origin. Astonishing as it may seem, there is no Hebraic-Yiddish word that can be substituted for it. The nearest to it is *mispalel zayn,* "to pray (for someone)." *Ikh vel mispalel zayn far aykh* means "I will pray for you (your welfare)," but *ikh vel davnen far aykh* is a nonsense sentence, similar to "I will breakfast for you."

Davnen is in much more frequent use than *mispalel zayn.* Among religious Jews, the majority till recently, the recitation of the set prayers every day was not less a part of life than eating, begetting children, and struggling for a livelihood. We hear people say, "If I don't read the morning paper I feel as if I hadn't brushed my teeth." The analogy faintly hints at the condition. A pious Jew who had missed his morning prayers would be walking about as in an evil trance. The role of the Hebrew prayers in the life of the average Jew of three or four generations ago can hardly be imagined by his descendants. He attended synagogue once or twice daily, spent there the Sabbath morning and part of the afternoon, repeated the grace after every meal and the regular night prayer before he turned to sleep; and then there were the festivals and High Holidays and the numerous benedictions and rituals at home. That part of the prayers that he did not understand word for word was not just gibberish to him; he became so familar with the sound of Hebrew that the repetition of the words affected him in a special way, like the syllables of long and familiar incantations, comforting, allusive, reassuring, interspersed with stretches of intelligibility and, on the dread days of the

New Year and of Atonement, heavily charged with his personal destiny and that of his people.

Davnen remains an etymological mystery. It is neither Hebraic nor Romance; only the suffix is Germanic. It has been variously traced to the Persian *divan*, meaning a collection of poems, the path of its entry being via the *loshn knaan* of Russia (see below), and to the German root of the modern *tönen*, "to sound," via the late medieval Yiddish of a group in northern Italy. One may say of *davnen*, as of *tsholent*, that it belongs to the class of *geyrim* (Heb), "converts," the memory of whose non-Jewish origin has passed out of our awareness so completely that we rank them with the patriarchal section of the language brought down from Canaan.

Bentshn is of that company. It has two principal meanings: (1) saying of grace (*i.e.*, thanks, *cf.* Italian *grazia*) after meals, (2) bestowing a blessing (as in *yankev hot gebentsht zayne zin eyder er iz geshtorbn*, "Jacob blessed his sons before he died").

Bentshn sounds a loftier note, as a condition of grace, in the lines of Ch. N. Bialik:

> *Gliklekh iz der un gebentsht zol er vern*
> *Vos vet fareybign ayere trern*
> Happy is he, and blessed shall he be,
> Who will immortalize your tears.

Bentshn derives from the Latin *benedicere*, "to bless," and came into Yiddish via Old French or Old Italian (the languages grouped as Laaz by Max Weinreich). It has in some usages displaced the original Hebrew word *bareykh*. The formal call to grace after a meal is *raboysay lomir bentshn*, of which the first word is Hebrew, "gentlemen," and the second Germanic, "let us." It is, however, also proper to use Hebrew throughout, *raboysay nevoreykh*, the second word not having passed into Yiddish.

25

For the short *ad hoc* benediction on taking a drink of water, or a bite of bread (the latter either at the opening of a meal or independently of one), or hearing the sound of thunder, or answering the call of nature, or seeing a royal personage, or encountering a person of rare beauty, or catching sight of a freak, in short, on any occasion calling for attention, the proper phrase is *makhn*, "to make," *a brokhe* (Heb), "benediction." *Brokhe* is also used in a phrase like *a brokhe oyf dayn kop*, "a blessing on your head," but "God bless you" can only be rendered by *got zol dikh bentshn*. How deeply the Romance word has penetrated into the Jewish world may be gauged from the fact that the phrase for the Sabbath and festival lighting of candles, *likht bentshn*, literally, "to bless the candles," lingers among nonobservant Jews as a hallowed evocation long after the practice has disappeared. *Likht*, Germanic and commonplace when standing by itself, is in this phrase exalted by its companionship with *bentshn*, and so linked the two words are a piece of Jewish life unrivaled for sanctity.

In the Yiddish world of my childhood two words competed for "to read," *leyenen* and *lezn*, the first from the Latin *legere*, again through the Romance, the second direct from the Germanic. There was a curious difference in their usage. *Lezn* meant ordinary reading, but for reading aloud from the Torah at services *leyenen* was obligatory. It was not until I was grown up that I ever heard anything but *lezn* for a newspaper, or a letter, or a book. But *lezn* is rejected in standard use, and does not appear in the Weinreich dictionary.

Both Old French and Old Italian, which were not as highly differentiated as modern French and Italian, were brought into the Rhine Valley from their respective territories at some period round the beginning of the eleventh century, and though Jews are mentioned in the annals of Cologne as far back as the reign of Constantine, little is heard of them in the interim. The largest immigration was, however, from

French territory, where there was a considerable Jewish population with a high level of scholarly activity. Rashi (Solomon ben Isaac, 1040–1105), the greatest of the Bible and Talmud commentators, and his followers, used thousands of French words, transliterated into Hebrew, to elucidate the Hebrew and Aramaic texts. Old French, in various dialects, was obviously the common language of those Jews who migrated into Germanic-language territory, but almost nothing of it remains. A few words like *pultsl*, "young girl" (*cf. pucelle*), *orn*, "to pray" (*cf. orrare*), *prayen*, "to request, beg" (*cf. prière*), survived on German soil but ultimately disappeared.

Names of persons have fared a little better, and three of them have moved as far from their original and alien flavor and as intimately into the Yiddish aura as *bentshn*. Whatever *Esperanza* might have suggested besides "hope" to speakers of a Romance language a thousand years ago, it cannot resemble what *Shprintse* suggests in Yiddish—a lively good-natured daughter of an orthodox and unpretentious household scattering grain among the clucking fowl in the backyard. Very different is *Yente*, the coarsened descendant of Gentile: Her voice is loud in the house and market place and her husband is a refugee in the *besmedresh*, the "study house" (the Hebrew form is *bes hamidrash*). *Fayvish*, too, has fared badly; his lineage is of the highest, Phoebus (Apollo) no less, but he is an irreclaimably comical and inconsequential figure (at least it was so in our parts, where a *yukl fayvish*—I have not been able to trace the first half—was the generic name for a nincompoop). Names have their destinies no less than books. Who would suspect that John, that sturdy, red-blooded English name (John Bull) is a form of *Yokhanaan*, "God has been gracious"?

There seems to be no explanation for the practically complete disappearance of the Old French and Old Italian element from the Jewish vernacular. Every *kheyder* boy comes across the words when he learns *khumesh* and Rashi; the

German commentators did not substitute early Yiddish words for them in the text. Some five thousand useful Romance words, covering domestic, business, and nature terminology, have been carefully preserved—as in amber. One would have thought that their association with the most revered and most studied of the Bible commentators would assure part of them a permanent place in the Yiddish vocabulary. What has happened is without logic.

The merchants, peddlers, craftsmen, and moneylenders who left Paris and the Provence to settle in Triers, Mainz, Worms, and Cologne dropped their French very easily and passed to German dialects for their intramural use and ultimately for their study of Bible and Talmud. This is in sharp contrast with the behavior pattern of those Jews who in later centuries left German-speaking areas for Poland, Russia, and the Ukraine. These immigrants did not take up the Slavic languages as a base; they clung to their early Yiddish and enriched and embroidered it till it became the instrument of a Sholom Aleichem. The Slavic languages certainly exerted a powerful influence on Yiddish, both grammatically and by way of vocabulary, but the Germanic base was not disturbed quantitatively. According to one theory, the small Jewish groups to be found on Russian territory before the immigration from the west spoke the local language known as *loshn knaan*, "the language of Canaan."

"Canaan," or *knaan*, has a peculiar significance here; it refers to the biblical phrase *eved knaani*, "Canaanite slave," which has the idiomatic force of "slave of slaves" or "slave *par excellence*," because of the curse laid by Noah on Canaan, the son of Ham. But, as we know, the word "slave" is only another form of "Slav," a memorial of the time when high numbers of that people were slaves in Europe. So instead of saying *loshn slav*, "language of the Slavs," the Jews reverted to Hebrew and called it *loshn knaan*.

There were Jewish communities on the northern shores of

the Black Sea more than two millennia ago; they were Greek-speaking. Jews preceded Russians in the Ukraine, as did the Jewish kingdom of the Khazars, converted Finno-Ugrians and Turks, in the seventh and eighth centuries. What the *loshn knaan* was like we shall never know, for nothing remains of it but the name. However, it is possible, even probable, that some of the Slavic words today found in Yiddish also occurred in *loshn knaan*, but since there are no documentary remains of the period there is no way of identifying them.

One factor in the disappearance of *loshn knaan* from among Jews must have been the cultural backwardness of early Russian Jewry. It had no schools of its own and sent its young men to the west, to France and Germany, to obtain a Jewish education, just as pious American Jews used to send their sons to European yeshivas forty and fifty years ago. "From the German mother country," writes Simon Dubnov, "the Polish Jews received not only their language, a German dialect . . . but also their religious culture and their communal organization."

The question still remains why the French Jews, with their rich and centuries-old culture, did not impose their vernacular on the German environment. The only memorial of the onetime dominance of Romance Yiddish, as we might call it, is a word which has passed from Rashi into the vernacular, *belaaz*, an acronym from the Hebrew *bilshon am zar*, "in the language of the stranger people." Rashi inserts it parenthetically whenever he uses an explanatory French word. In the vernacular *belaaz* now has a humorous connotation. If a Jew speaking Yiddish has to fall back on an English word he may, with an apologetic smile, add *"belaaz!"* just as when a Jew speaking English, and falling back on a Yiddish word, may add as a cute aside, "If you'll pardon my French."

CHAPTER THREE

Sanctifications

1.

Until modern times Hebrew remained the Jewish language of prayer in the Diaspora throughout all migrations and all changes of vernacular. There were a few important exceptions, like the *kadish* (the glorification of God in memory of the dead), the *kol nidre* of the Eve of the Day of Atonement, and a few others. These, in the cognate Aramaic, may be also called Hebraic. One would therefore expect that the religious vocabulary of Yiddish would be almost exclusively Hebraic, but such is not the case. A considerable portion of it is Germanic while little of it is Slavic, for reasons noted above. Only certain sections of it have remained obstinately Hebrew.

There are no Germanic designations for the following important key words:

Khumesh, "the five," for the Pentateuch (itself containing the Greek for "five"); *tanakh*, the Jewish Bible, an acronym of *toyre* (here meaning the *khumesh*), *nevi'im*, "prophets," *ksuvim*, "writings," the three constituents of the collection of sacred Book of Books (meaning not only "book" *in excelsis*, but the "book made up of a number of books"); the *tsenerene*, once a highly popular devotional book for women (as the form, feminine plural imperative of "go forth and see," indicates), based on the Bible, Midrash, legends, and pietistic exhortation, now little used.

In Yiddish the Talmud and the Midrash have only Hebraic names. Hebraic also is the *shulkhn orekh*, the standard code of religious laws and practices compiled in the sixteenth century by Joseph Caro, the Palestinian mystic. It has become so symbolic of orthodoxy and conformity that it has passed into (slightly facetious) secular use. It is good idiomatic Yiddish to say *loyt dem marksistishn shulkhn orekh volt badarft zayn punkt farkert*, "According to the orthodox Marxist theory (or practice) it ought to be the exact opposite."

Without Germanic equivalents are:

Shabes, "Sabbath"; *yontev* (Hebrew *yomtov*), "festival"; *peysekh*, "Passover"; *rosheshone*, "New Year"; *yom kiper*, "Day of Atonement"; *tishebov*; *shvues*, "Pentecost" (Festival of Weeks); *purim*, "Lots"; *khanuke*, "Rededication" (Festival of Lights); *sukes* (Festival of Booths).

Similarly there are no Germanic equivalents for *di oves*, "the Patriarchs" (Abraham, Isaac, and Jacob); *yoym ha-din*, "Day of Judgment"; *tkhies hameysim*, "Resurrection of the Dead"; *yetsies mitsrayim*, "the going forth from Egypt" (Exodus); *halokhe*, "ritualistic and religious law and lore of Judaism" (the word itself connotes "the going, the way one should go"); *luekh*, "calendar" (for Jewish dates only, otherwise *kalendar*); *tume*, "impurity" (primarily ritualistic but extending into the moral field); *pshat* "literal interpretation of texts," etc.

2.

It is when we come to ritualistic objects and practices that the monopoly of Hebrew begins to break down. *Tales*, "prayer shawl"; *mezuze*, "door post scroll"; *esreg*, "citron"; *lulev*, "palm branch" (the last two used during *sukes*), are all Hebraic without Germanic equivalents. But it is the synagogue of all things that has no commonly used Hebraic name. *Shul* is of Germanic derivation, originally from Latin and Greek (*schola, schole*) for "school," the synagogue being not only a *beys-tfile* (Heb), "house of prayer," but a *besmedresh*, "house of study." *Shul* is as thoroughly Yiddish as *gan-eydn* (Heb) "paradise," literally, "Garden of Eden."

Tales, we have just seen, has no Germanic equivalent, but *tales-kotn*, "small *tales*," the ritualistic sleeveless fringed garment worn by males under the outer garment (also called by the Hebraic name *arbe-kanfes*, "four wings"), has a curious Germanic synonym, *laybtsudekl*, "body coverlet." This name came about as a mispronunciation of the correct half-Germanic, half-Slavic *laybserdak*, meaning a dress worn on the breast. But *tsitsis*, the ritualistic fringes on the *laybtserdak* for the sake of which the garment was invented, has no Germanic name. *Laybserdak* was also corrupted into *laybserdrak*, an expression of contempt.

As if to balance *shul*, of pagan origin, *kheyder* is one of the Hebraic words that have become more Jewish in Yiddish than in the original language. The *kheyder* was often remembered as the setting of childhood's most extreme miseries and frustrations—born of the confinement, the discipline, and, paradoxically, the formlessness of the institution; added was, often enough, the harshness and pedagogic ineptitude of the *melamed*, "teacher" (another irreplaceable Hebraic word, the Germanic *lerer* being associated exclusively with secular subjects). The *kheyder* was usually cramped, unclean, and reeking of poverty; corporal punishment of a humiliating kind was regarded as in the natural order of things. The *melamdim* were resentful of their profession, their wretched pay, and their low status, for *melamed*, when applied to anyone but a *melamed*, was synonymous with "poor stick, bungler, helpless creature." Nevertheless, the miraculous capacity of children for wringing happiness out of the most disheartening circumstances cooperated with the equally miraculous transforming power of time, and "the *kheyder* years" is a sentimental phrase, like "schooldays."

Besides, there were also cheerful *kheyders* (strictly, *khadorim*) and kindly *melamdim*, and as children usually passed through several *kheyders* between induction and *bar mitzvah*, some of their memories were intrinsically happy. The *kheyder,* with all its defects, was hallowed as the instrument of folk survival. One of the most popular of Yiddish songs—it has achieved the status of an anonymous folk song, and the name of its author, Y. Y. Varshavsky, is scarcely remembered —is one that depicts the warm, cosy room, the fire dancing in the stove, and the little ones learning the *alef-beys* in the traditional singsong.

Kheyder is therefore a key word in Yiddish. It is also used figuratively. *Er iz gegangen in bundishn kheyder,* "He went to school to the Bundists," might mean that he never went to a *kheyder* at all. The Bund, once much more powerful than today, is a leftist, Yiddishist, antireligious movement founded at the end of the nineteenth century in the same year as the World Zionist Organization.

Toyre as meaning either the Five Books of Moses or sacred writing generally has no Germanic equivalent, but *di toyre* as the physical scroll of the Pentateuch has a marvelously created word, *di reynikeyt,* "the Purity," which is just as reverential and loving as *toyre.* Now the ordinary Germanic Yiddish word for "purity, cleanness," is *reynkeyt,* and that is never used for the Torah scroll. *Di reynikeyt* (the article and the added *i* are obligatory) means only one thing, and this monopolization, this focusing, has given the word great power, not surpassed by any Hebrew term. To a sensitive ear the phrase *di reynikeyt in orn,* "The Torah scroll in the ark," has a special charm because of the melodic counterpoint between the Hebraic *orn,* which is superior in age, and the Germanic *reynikeyt,* which is not inferior in sanctity. (*Orn,* "ark," must not be confused with the obsolete *orn,* "to pray.")

It is strange that the commonest Yiddish word for "holy" should be the Germanic *heylik,* though for "Holy of Holies" the only phrase is the Hebrew *kodshe-kdoshim.* But perhaps the most surprising linguistic turn is the sanctification of the Germanic *got,* for God. It has been suggested that this came about because of the prohibition against the utterance of the

Tetragrammaton YHWH; but there is no prohibition against the use of the Hebrew *adonoy*, "Lord," the conventionalized substitute for the Tetragrammaton, or against *eloyhim*, an alternative name, though neither of these have passed into Yiddish. *Reboyne-shel-oylem*, "Arbiter of the world," *boyre*, "Creator," and *hakodesh-borkhu*, "the Holy One blessed be He," are Hebrew and Yiddish, and both are used freely. Nevertheless, *got* is by far the commonest appellation, side by side with the affectionate diminutive *gotenyu*.

The commandment "Thou shalt not take the name of the Lord thy God in vain," now translated, "You shall not swear falsely by the name of the Lord your God," was taken to mean that one must not invoke God's name lightly or frivolously. In that sense, *gotenyu* is a very frequent offender. It may be used seriously and prayerfully as an endearment, in wheedling supplication, and then it has much tenderness; but far more often it occurs in the most absurd contexts, and is then about as reverential or as meaningful as "holy smoke!" Of a simple, half-witted woman one might say, *gotenyu iz dos a shtik beheyme*, literally, "darling little God, is that a lump of a cow." In its serious usage *gotenyu* will be linked with other similar homely references to God, such as *tate* (Slv), "father," *tate-foter* being a repetitive form used only in addressing God.

There are elaborate Germanic periphrases for the divine name, a kind of pious hovering on the outskirts of the ineffable; such are *der vos ikh bin nisht vert tsu dermanen zayn nomen*, "He that I am not worthy to mention (remember) His name," and *der vos ikh hob di hent nisht gevashn*, "He that (for whom) I have not washed my hands (and am therefore unfit to mention by name)." In the Germanic phrase *a dank zayn libn nomen*, "thanks to His dear Name," we have an echo of the Hebrew *hashem yisborekh*, "the Blessed Name." Another pious German periphrasis is *der vos lebt eybik*, "He that lives forever." More direct and more popular is *der eybershter*, "the All-Highest," while *der almekhtiker*, "the Almighty," and *der bashefer*, "the Creator," are slightly more formal, also slightly old-fashioned. The Slavic *bog*, "God," never achieved the slightest foothold in Yiddish, which is quite remarkable, since at least the phrase *bozhe moy*, "my God," though it never became Yiddish, was certainly known in the Yiddish-speaking world.

Actually there are more Hebraic than Germanic forms of reference to God, but the Hebraic are more heavily loaded with concepts, while the Germanic, especially when linked with *got*, are more popular. Taken direct from the Hebrew are: *di hashgokhe*, "providence," implying a philosophy of direct divine supervision of human affairs, while *di shkhine* hints at the difficult and mystical idea of "Indwelling" or "Immanence of the Divine," for which the English has no equivalent. A complex word is *kavyokhl*, current in pious and scholarly circles; literally it means "as if it could be," or, "as if one could say it," and is a remote way of rejecting anthropomorphism. In current usage these subtle values do not come into play; *der kavyokhl* is simply a synonym for "God," sometimes under the aspect of omnipotence.

3.

The complete conversion of Germanic words, one might almost say their circumcision and adoption into the Covenant, is happily illustrated in a large number of technical terms relating to sacred Jewish studies (but all Jewish studies are sacred), and the outstanding instance has to do with the very concept of study, or the acquisition of learning.

The Germanic *lernen* means both "to learn" and "to teach," and unless the context specifically points to a secular subject it implies only the sacred Jewish field. If one says of

38

a man *er ken lernen,* "He knows (how) to learn" (itself an idiom for "He is a man of learning"), only the sacred books are implied, that is to say, all Jewish books ultimately related to Jewish thought on God and man. The question *ir hot amol gelernt?,* "Did you at one time learn?", means "Did you at one time attend a yeshiva (or receive equivalent instruction)?" If directed at secular subjects—and even general ethics would come under that heading—the Germanic *shtudirn* is in order, and the question would be *ir hot amol shtudirt?,* "Did you at one time study?", meaning, "Did you at one time attend a university?" One may, however, say *er lernt (zikh) frantseyzish,* "He is learning French," as well as *er shtudirt frantseyzish,* but one cannot say *er shtudirt bobe metsiye* (a popular tractate of the Talmud).

Many idioms relating to sacred studies have been formed by an intimate bonding between a Germanic and Hebraic word, and here one may best observe the permeation of the Jewish masses by the atmosphere of scholarship, or what I have called their induction into the vestibule of learning.

These idioms embody distinctions that in English strike one as academic and sophisticated; in Yiddish they are wholly of the folk. No Yiddish-speaking Jew with a simple *kheyder* education would make a misstep among the seemingly technical terms that follow.

When reference is made to Rashi's commentaries on Bible and Talmud, the only correct phrase is *rashi makht,* "Rashi observes, comments, says." While *makhn* means literally "to make," it is used idiomatically in the foregoing senses just as, in English, "to have" acquires another meaning in "Rashi has it that . . ." We do not know why only *makht* can be used with Rashi.

Similarly, for the Midrash, the phrase is, "*der medresh brengt,* "The Midrash brings (adduces)," which is to say, "The Midrash has this contribution on the subject"; and so strongly is this figure lodged in the popular mind that it is impossible to put *makht* or *zogt*, "says," in place of *brengt*. Concerning the Talmud, one may say *di gemore lernt*, "The Talmud teaches," or *es iz do a gemore*, "There is a Talmud (passage)." (The Talmud is most frequently referred to as the *gemore*, "completion," because that is the main body of the "completing text," in Aramaic, built round the core, called the Mishna, which is Hebrew. Strictly speaking the Talmud is both the Mishna and the vast development round it.)

When one quotes the Sages of old, the correct introductory phrase is *di khakhomim zogn*, "The Sages say," or *di khakhomim hobn undz gelernt*, "The Sages have taught us." There is an interesting difference between the singular and plural uses of the word. *Khokhem* is an everyday word; it applies to any man who is wise, clever, profound, etc. (also used ironically, see below), but *di khakhomim* means only "the Sages of old." Also current is *es iz do a maymer khazal*, "There is a saying of *khazal*" (an acronym of the Hebrew *khakhomim zikhroynom levrokhe*, "The Sages, their memory be a blessing").

When the *rebe*, "teacher, rabbi," is about to hold forth to his disciples, we announce, *der rebe vet zogn toyre*, "The rabbi will 'say' Torah." It is correct to announce *der rebe vet lernen toyre*, "The rabbi will teach Torah," but it lacks intimacy.

If one were to say in Yiddish company *di khakhomim brengen*, "The Sages adduce," or *di gemore makht*, "The Talmud has this comment," or *rashi lernt*, "Rashi teaches," an indefinable uneasiness would be created; the meaning would be perfectly clear, but the listeners would look at each other with a wild surmise: in what undiscovered region had this Jew learned his Yiddish?

Khokhme (written *khokhmah*), "wisdom," as used in biblical Hebrew, is a serious and even solemn word. We read: "The beginning of *khokhmah* is the fear of the Lord," "God gave Solomon *khokhmah* and understanding," "For the price of *khokhmah* is above rubies," "The Lord by *khokhmah* founded the earth," etc. *Khokhmah* approximates to the *logos*, preexistent to the world, the plan according to which the world was created. But in Yiddish, *khokhme* has uses undreamt of by the biblical writers. It can be used seriously, of course, though it never has the biblical solemnity; it comes closer to "cleverness" than "wisdom." It also means "wit," usually of a facetious kind. But mostly it is used in a slightly derogatory sense, of a joke, a trick, not of a high order. A popular story tells of a Jew who arrived at the railroad station well ahead of time as he thought, and seeing his train standing, went into the men's room. He emerged just as the train was pulling out, and exclaimed between anger and contempt: "A *khokhme!*"—as much as to say "wise guy!" (Another version makes the exclamation "*antisemit!*") Similarly, *khokhem* may mean its own opposite: *khokhem eyner*, addressed to a person, and meaning literally "you wise man," never means anything but "dope!"

The Germanic *makhn*, "to make, do, fare," already noted in connection with Rashi, has become indispensable over a wide range of special circumstances.

Makhn shabes, "to make, observe, celebrate the Sabbath," is enshrined in the lament of the poor man, *ikh hob nisht mit vos tsu makhn shabes*, "I haven't with what to make the Sabbath"; he lacks the wherewithal to lift the seventh holy day above the commonplaceness of the other six. Say what one will, it is not enough to free one's mind from care, exalt it in contemplation of everlasting values; something ceremonial must be added, be it ever so small a change; a drop of wine for the *kidesh* or sanctification, a slice of white bread to supplement the rye, a white tablecloth, an extra dish. Wretched indeed is his lot who cannot greet the Sabbath Queen with some tiny worldly token of his loving homage. In the privacy of his home he may conceal his poverty from the rest of the world, but how shall he come before the

41

All-seeing Eye without so much as a beggar's gift? All of this is condensed in the cry *ikh hob nisht mit vos tsu makhn shabes*. And marvelously enough, the All-seeing Eye, which might at least have seen to it that the wherewithal should be there, is never reproached!

A totally different spirit pervades the phrase *makhn shabes far zikh*, "to make Sabbath for oneself," that is, separately, ignoring everyone else. It is not related to the Sabbath at all, but describes one who goes his own way, indifferent to the conventions and the community pattern.

We have considered *makhn a brokhe*, to make the *ad hoc* benediction for special occasions. A meal opens traditionally with the *brokhe* over bread, for Him "who draws forth bread from the earth," in Hebrew *hamoytsi lekhem min hoorets*, whence one says *makhn a moytse*. Similarly, *makhn a shehakl* (usually pronounced *shakl*), from the Hebrew *shehakol niye bidvoroy*, "that everything became at His word," is the *brokhe* for a drink of water taken apart from a meal.

The water benediction is mystically appropriate, since life began in water, but the *shakl* is also attached to a drink of whiskey. To be sure, it is also the proper benediction for any fruit juice but grape, and for anything eatable not otherwise provided for, but the association with a distilled liquor is uppermost in the Yiddish mind. *Makhn a shakl*, "to make a *shakl*," means in fact to take a drink of whiskey, and if Reuben were to say to Simon, *kum, lomir makhn a shakl*, "Come, let's make a *shakl*," and offered him a glass of pineapple juice, Simon would have grounds for action, or at least complaint. Reuben might defend himself on a technicality, but the Yiddish saying is *a min(h)eg* (Heb) *brekht a din* (Heb), "Custom breaks (overrides) the law." The secular salutation over an alcoholic drink of any kind is, of course, *lekhayim* (Heb), "to life," and the response is, in Hebrew, *lekhayim toyvim ul'sholem*, "to good life and to peace." *Lomir makhn a lekhayim*, "Let's make a *lekhayim*," is a general invitation to a drink, to express satisfaction at the conclusion of a bargain, or joy in a reunion, or *stam* (Heb) *azoy*, "just like that," for no reason at all.

Makhn a bris, "to make a 'covenant,' " is to celebrate a circumcision ceremony with the accompanying festivities. (*Bris* is the Hebrew *b'rith* or *b'rit*, as in B'nai B'rith, "Sons of the Covenant.") But if you ask your newly married friend —you would not ask it of a mere acquaintance—*nu*, *ven makhstu a bris?*, "When are you making a *bris?*", you mean "Well, when are you going to present the Jewish people with a male child?"

Another Germanic word, *oprikhtn*, "to perform, celebrate," runs *makhn* a close second as the inseparable companion of a Hebrew word in set ritualistic phrases. *Oprikhtn a seyder*, "to perform the *seyder*," rings the right note for the elaborate and charming home rituals of the first and second evenings of the Passover. I do not remember ever having come across *makhn a seyder*, though it would be technically correct. On the other hand, when speaking of the *havdole*, "division," the beautiful and haunting home ceremony for separation from the Sabbath, the passage from sanctity to earthliness, *makhn* is again the correct word—*makhn havdole*, not *oprikhtn havdole*.

But again, *oprikhtn* is the only way of referring to the practice—found in almost all great religions—of performing the penance of exile, of purifying one's soul, especially in old age, by leaving hearth, home, and friends to wander as a beggar, eating the sour bread of charity, and climbing the steep stairs of philanthropic institutions. *Oprikhtn goles* is a heavy and depressing phrase; it need not refer specifically to the act of penance; a man separated from his family and friends, or delivered over to long adversity, especially under oppression, may complain, *ikh rikht op goles*, "I am enduring, undergoing exile."

Oprikhtn khtsos, "to recite the midnight prayers," is

charged with a peculiar melancholy; to those familiar with the Jewish life of half a century ago in eastern Europe it calls up the picture of an old man in a candle-lit room, and the sound of a lament rising faintly above the sleeping village. Throughout the long story of the Jewish exile that voice has been heard weeping in the most various climes for the Destruction, and symbolizing the inability of a people to forget or to abandon hope. Ears attuned to English will find *khtsos* (from the Hebrew and Yiddish *khotsi*, "half") barbarously unpronounceable; on ears attuned to Yiddish and the tradition, it has the effect of a dying bell. There is no way of transferring these charged words from one language and world of discourse into another.

4.

We have seen that the Jews of western Europe brought their language with them into the Slavic countries, and while Yiddish was strongly influenced by Slavic it did not disintegrate. It deepened and ripened, taking in Slavic words and forms and doing with them what it had done with so many of the Germanic words, that is, Judaize them, so that they could not be translated back into the originals. The effect on the religious terminology was, however, altogether minor. The largest, though not the earliest, Slavic channel into Yiddish was Polish; the earliest, and least important, was Czech; with the partitions of Poland, Russian and Ukrainian influences increased, but usually a word of Slavic origin in Yiddish can be identified in most of the Slavic languages.

One indispensable religious term could not, oddly enough, be supplied by Hebrew or Germanic, and was supplied by the Slavic. *Pareve* describes a food that is neither in the meat nor the milk class, and can therefore be eaten with either. Vegetables and fruits are *pareve*; so is fish. But *pareve* has acquired a nonreligious meaning and denotes a person who, one might say, is neither flesh, fish nor fowl nor good red herring, that is, one without character or convictions, a lukewarm, insipid person, in Christian terminology, a "Laodicean."

A parallel to the Germanic verb *oprikhtn* is the Slavic *praven*; *praven a seyder* and *oprikhtn a seyder* are completely synonymous; so are *oprikhtn khtsos* and *praven khtsos*. But there are locutions in which *praven* alone is correct. A *sude* (Heb), "a festive meal," while assumed to be of Jewish character, is not necessarily a religious occasion. However, at a Chassidic *sude* it is expected that *der rebe vet zogn toyre*, "The *rebe* will hold forth on sacred matters." It is taken for granted that a *sude* means kosher food. The proper phrase for such an occasion is *praven a sude*, not *oprikhtn*. For the wholly secular *banket*, "banquet," even if it happens to be kosher on courtesy or prudential grounds, one says neither *praven* nor *oprikhtn*, which are strictly Judaistic terms. One finds a Germanic word, like *gebn*, "give."

5.

We are only at the beginning of our Germanic-Hebraic religious vocabulary.

Leygn tfiln (Heb) "to put on phylacteries," is a technical religious term. Standing alone, *leygn* is "to lay, lay on," as in *leygn a kompres*, "Lay on a compress," "*leygn shlofn dos kind*, "Lay the child to sleep," and has no religious coloration; attached to *tfiln* it changes character.

Geyn oyf keyver oves (the last two words are Hebraic), "to go on (a visit to) the graves of the fathers," was practiced from motives of disinterested piety but also on occasion to obtain intercession in heaven. *Tishebov* (Heb), "the day of the Black Fast," for the Destruction, was the *shtetl* Memorial Day, when one "went on" *keyver oves;* an earnest time for grownups and a jolly open-air occasion for the small fry, celebrated in Yiddish literature as the sweetest of memories: the tombstones, the past generations, the surrounding greenery of late summer, the somber voices of the men, the weeping of the women, the laughter of the children.

Tseyln sfire, "telling (counting) the count," is the practice of adding to the daily prayers the successive numbers of the forty-nine days between Passover and Pentecost.

Faln koyrim, "to fall (in) obeisance," is the act of prostration prescribed for a certain prayer, as a rule carried out symbolically in a deep bow. In the synagogue only a few distinguished individuals are given room enough to proclaim their humility before the congregation when a literal performance of the act is especially meritorious.

Shpringen kodesh, "to leap (in) holiness," again at a prescribed prayer, is to imitate the adoration of the seraphim in the presence of the Divine Glory. (Adoration, the only apt word here, is unfortunately pagan in origin, being rooted in the blowing of kisses from the mouth—*ad ora*—toward an image.) *Shpringen kodesh,* like *faln koyrim,* has been reduced to a symbolic curtailment, a spasmodic rising on one's toes and falling back on one's heels, performed three times. Outside the synagogue both phrases have passed into the folk terminology as descriptions of excessive deference, or of toadying obsequiousness.

6.

Most Germanic words have made their way into Yiddish sanctity in the sponsoring company of a Hebraic term. There are several that have done it on their own, and of these perhaps the most striking is the double Germanic *leygn kneytlekh*. *Kneytlekh*, "(candle) wicks," like *leygn*, has in itself no sacred or folk associations; linked with *leygn* it is lifted into the class of highly specialized folk sanctities; so much so, that it is worth an explanatory digression.

It was a *shtetl* practice among pious Jewesses to gather in a "bee" at which they made candles for the synagogue while listening to improvised prayers and the reading of simple works of piety, all of course, in Yiddish. Mendele Moycher Sforim describes such a session in one of his later novels, *shloyme reb khayems*, "Solomon, Son of Khayem." Writing in the days when the darkness was deepening over Russian Jewry, he abandoned the bitter satire of his earlier works and dwelt without inhibition on the sweeter aspects of Jewish life among the simple folk. To savor the grace that informs the phrase *leygn kneytlekh*, we must summon up the circumstances of the institution, the personalities, the physical and spiritual surroundings. The bewigged Sores and Malkes and Feyges and Gitls and Zisls and Mirls and Beyles sit swaying by lamplight in the living room, which is perhaps also the bedroom, of a primitive cottage. They listen with occasional sighs and interjections to the *firzogern*, "foresayer," as she reads or improvises. About them in the night is a cluster of similar Jewish cottages and beyond, on every side, the Slavic world, vast, brooding, mysterious, ominous. The *firzogern* may be the only one in the room who can read—she may even be able to write—but the only Hebrew words she knows to be such are those that have come over through the *sider* and the *tsenerene*, and even then, a hundred years ago, the Yiddish of these hallowed books was archaic, laden with ancestral memories. The images and ideas the *firzogern* evokes go back still further; they cross the millennia to a far-off place of prophecy and psalmody and palm trees.

As the wax is poured into the wooden mold and the *kneytl* is laid in the right position, the *firzogern* invokes

47

the Patriarchs Abraham and Isaac and Jacob, recalling the special merits and intercessory powers of each. She prays that as Abraham was rescued from the fiery furnace of Nimrod, and as Isaac freely offered himself as sacrifice, and as Jacob triumphed over his enemies, so might they, the wicklayers, find divine mercy in the hour of need. "Help us, so that on the Day of Judgment a good sentence may be pronounced for us, so that we shall not become widows and our little ones orphans. And for the sake of Solomon who built the Temple and called on You to heed the supplications of a stranger, the son of an alien people, when he prayed in it, so, O Judge of the world, keep open the gates of prayer and let us be remembered to the good, we, and our husbands and our children and all good people, Amen."

The lighting of candles in religious ceremonials is very old in Jewish religious practices; the Sabbath lights were an attraction to those numerous Romans, who, hovering about the Jewish faith, were known as the Godfearers. But the lighting of candles as memorials for the dead was not an early Jewish custom; it is therefore not only proper that *yortsayt-likht,* "year-time (anniversary) lights," should have a Germanic name, it is inevitable, for there is no Hebrew equivalent! Yet among acquired customs taken over from Christian practice, this is among the deepest rooted.

Also Germanic in both parts is *neygl-vaser,* "fingernail-water," the pouring of which, three times over each hand, immediately on awakening, is much older than the *yortsayt likht.* The ancient Jews were obsessed by the hygiene of the body, as their religious legislation shows, and their descendants took over the tradition scrupulously. To it they undoubtedly owed their relative immunity from many epidemics, but by the law of compensation, what they thus gained was wiped out by the massacres that their suspicious immunity inspired.

Handwashing was not, of course, confined to the morning act; we have noticed that the mention of God's name was, if only as a figure of speech, supposed to be preceded by a washing of the hands. One could not, one cannot today among pious Jews, sit down to a meal without a ritualistic washing of the hands. An idiomatic way of inviting a Jew to join in a meal was *geyt, vasht zikh*, "Go, wash yourself," which certainly did not imply that a wash was needed. The substantial hygienic difference between the Jew and the peasant was in the weekly bath for the welcoming of the *shabes*. The *mikve*, "ritual bathing pool," with its constantly renewing water, was obligatory for women at least once a month, after menstruation. During the Middle Ages, when public baths were considered in a class with bordellos, the Jewish public bathing system was a religious requirement. There is no Germanic equivalent for *mikve*. The neo-orthodox English *ritualarium* has not yet passed the comical stage.

Kenen (fun) oysnveynik, "to know by heart," was usually, though not necessarily, used in connection with sacred texts. *Er ken shoyn a gantse mesekhte oysnveynik*, "He already knows a whole Tractate by heart," was a proud father's boast about his son, the *mesekhte* being one of the basic divisions of the Talmud. There was sometimes an excessive emphasis on memorizing in Jewish studies, an echo of the time when the Oral Law was really carried forward from generation to generation in the memory only, and when professional memorizers had a special function. Today the term "Oral Law," in Hebrew *toyre shebalpe*, literally, "Torah of the mouth (*i.e.*, oral)," is a quaint survival; it lost its literal meaning nearly twenty centuries ago, when the "Oral Law" began to be written down.

Among the Germanic words that have become "sanctified" without the assistance of a Hebraic companion, a curious one, now passing out of use, is *opshprekhn a beyz oyg*, "to exorcise an evil eye." When I was a *kheyder* boy in England nearly seventy years ago, I often saw this performed by my *rebe*. A child would bring in a handkerchief or an article of clothing to a sick person, and my *rebe* would suspend teaching to mutter an incantation into it and send it back. We thought it the most natural thing in the world.

We find two Germanic words thrust boldly into an area otherwise reserved for Hebrew. They are *kapitl*, "chapter" (originally from the Latin *caput*, "head, summit"), and *blat*, "page, leaf." *Tilim*, "psalms," and *gemore*, "Talmud," are both Hebrew, but for "a chapter of the psalms" one says *a kapitl tilim*, and for "a page of the Talmud," *a blat gemore*.

Daf and *blat* (when the latter means "page," not "leaf") have special meanings in Jewish scholarship. All editions of the Talmud are printed with exactly the same pagination and the same linear contents, originally, no doubt, as an aid to memorization. In quoting the Talmud it is therefore enough to mention Tractate and page. Practice alone teaches the proper uses of *blat* and *daf*. One says *er ken lernen a blat gemore*, "He can learn [*i.e.*, understand and expound] a page of the Talmud," but one cannot say *er ken lernen a daf gemore*. In the Yiddish world *er ken lernen* indicates a man who is not quite a "scholar" but who has more than a smattering of religious learning.

The general Yiddish word for "page" is neither *daf* nor *blat*. It is the Germanic *zayt*, literally, "side." A book has a hundred *zaytn*, not *dafn* or *bleter*, and a *blat* is also a newspaper. The use of *daf* in referring to a secular book would be as outlandish as "verse such-and-such from the *Encyclopaedia Britannica*."

There is no logic that forbids *a parshe tilim* for "a chapter of psalms," or a *kapitl khumesh* for "a chapter of the Pentateuch"; it is simply that the folk has decided against it, and certainly in the matter of language *vox populi vox dei*—at least in the long run.

Two interesting Germanic words are entirely secular except in special contexts. *Mien zikh* (or *bamien*), "to exert oneself, take trouble to," is in ordinary speech without par-

Er hat sich bemüht dem Mädel zu gefallen!

ticular savor. *Er hot zikh gemit* (or *bamit*) *tsu gefeln dem meydl,* "He put himself out to be pleasing to (get himself liked by) the girl," or *a dank, bamit zikh nit,* "Thank you, don't take the trouble," are commonplace phrases (the second can be slightly elevated by substituting the Hebrew *zikh matriekh zayn: a dank, zayt zikh nit matriekh,* which in no way changes the meaning but introduces a touch of dignity). But *mayn mume, mien zol zi zikh,* "My aunt, may she exert herself," goes off literally into another, or rather *the* other world; it tells us that the lady is dead, and, further, that her earthly record was of such merit that the speaker wants her to intercede for him in heaven. But overuse has worn the locution down, so that it means very little about the virtues of the good lady (and "good lady" so used illustrates the point by having no real ethical content); it implies that she is dead and is being asked perfunctorily to busy herself lobbying among the influential residents of heaven, more particularly the Patriarchs and Matriarchs and such members and ancestors of the immediate family as attained some distinction on earth for learning or piety.

Opgesheydt, "separated, set apart," is, like *mien,* an uncharged word as ordinarily used: *er hot gefirt an opgesheydt lebn,* "He lived a life apart from the world," is literal and uncolorful; but *zol er zayn opgesheydt,* "May he be separated (from us)," is a pious reference to one who is dead, and, simultaneously, a courteous and benevolent inclination to the living.

This special use of the Germanic *opgesheydt,* interfused with peculiarly religious Jewish feeling, is an excellent instance of the transference of Hebraic coloration to Germanic or Slavic words.

We have mentioned the *havdole,* the pensive domestic ceremonial of the departing Sabbath, the separating of its holiness from the workaday. The corresponding verb form in Hebrew is *lehavdel,* "to separate," which as a verb is never used

51

in Yiddish, but is familiar from a gracious Hebrew phrase that has passed into Yiddish as a totality, *lehavdl beyn hakhayim vehameysim,* "to separate, make a distinction between, the living and the dead." If you mention a living person in connection with someone recently deceased, you interpose *lehavdl beyn hakhayim vehameysim,* "to distinguish between the living and the dead." So doing, you remove the suggestion of death from the subject of your remarks. The Hebrew locution bespeaks cultural standing, and the Germanic *zol er zayn opgesheydt* is the exact Germanic equivalent of *lehavdl beyn hakhayim vehameysim.*

Lehavdl, as used alone in Yiddish may best be described as a sentence word, and generally means something like "If you'll forgive me for mentioning the two (persons) in the same breath." *Ikh hob gezukht an eytse* (Heb) *fun dem rebn un s'iz mir nit gefeln, bin ikh gegangen, lehavdl, tsum galekh* (Heb), "I went to the rabbi for advice, and didn't like it, so I went, if you'll forgive me, to the priest." Here *lehavdl* indicates the respect due the rabbi as distinguished from the priest. But it can be used satirically to the opposite effect. Simon having spoken of the rabbi and the priest in the same breath without saying *lehavdl,* Reuben reproaches him for lack of manners: *zog khotshe* (Slv·) *lehavdl,* "Say at least *lehavdl*"; to which Simon retorts, *vos far a lehavdl? der galekh iz oykh a shoyte,* "What kind of *lehavdl?* The priest too is a fool." The subtle point is that while Simon wanted the *"lehavdl"* as a mark of regard for the rabbi, Reuben jestingly implies that it was the priest who really deserved the respectful distinction.

CHAPTER FOUR

Hybrids

1.

Much of the charm of Yiddish is lost on those who have not learned some Hebrew in their childhood and have never frequented services that are conducted in Hebrew. For them all Yiddish words have the same coloration, they belong to an undiversified world. It will perhaps be suggested that English, too, has additional values for those who can distinguish between words of Latin and Greek origin and those of Anglo-Saxon origin. I have already observed that it is not at all the same thing; to the Yiddish-speaking Jew who has attended a *kheyder* or *Talmud Torah* and even occasional services, his stock of Hebrew words has a special place in his experience; he will derive a particular pleasure from those phrases that combine a Hebraic with a non-Hebraic word to produce something new and unforeseeable—like oxygen and hydrogen combining to produce water. He will also enjoy, with a smile, the queer hybrids in which familiar Hebrew stems deck themselves out with Germanic or Slavic prefixes and suffixes, to fill ingeniously a blank in the language.

Kashe (Heb), "question" (not to be confused with its Slavic homonym, which means "porridge"), is a very active word in the *kheyder*, the yeshiva and daily life, mirroring the restlessness of the Jewish mind. In the *seyder* ceremony of the first two Passover Eves, the youngest male child present stands up and asks *di fir kashes,* "The Four Questions," the answering of which, in words and ritual, in song and symbol, constitutes the entire lengthy ceremonial. *Fir,* "four," is of course Germanic, and the phrase *di fir kashes* is redolent of childhood and the gaiety of the Passover. There is a folk song that philosophizes on the Question of Questions, the eternal unanswerable Question, in the following cryptic fashion:

The world asks an ancient *kashe*,
Laydi-ridi-ridi-ram,
And one answers:
Laydi-ridi-ram-dam-ray-di-day;
But if one likes, one may also answer:
Laydi-ri,
Laydi-ridi-rayday-ray-didi!
But again the ancient *kashe* remains,
Laydi-ridi-ridi-ram.

Klots, "a wooden beam," as applied to a person, is "heavy, doltish, lumpish," but when this Germanic word is combined with the Hebraic *kashe* in *klots-kashe*, we get something for which there is no English equivalent, and which has to be described at some length. If in the midst of a sophisticated discussion someone simplemindedly harks back to an elementary question to which the answer has long been tacitly assumed, he is offering a *klots-kashe*. We must imagine a high-level conference of Madison Avenue executives, and someone asking earnestly, artlessly, "But gentlemen, is advertising a good thing?" A *klots-kashe* may also be thrown artfully—or artlessly—into a discussion in order to derail it. A lecturer whose subject is "the truth about American intervention in Vietnam" might be asked aggressively, "Sir, what is truth?"

Pust (Slv), "empty, idle," is both literal as in *a puste gas*, "an empty street," or *di puste kretchme* (Slv), "*The Idle Inn*" (the name of a play by Peretz Hirshbein), or figurative, as in *puste reyd*, "empty, idle talk." But if we combine it with *keyle* (Heb), "vessel, instrument," we get, in *a puste keyle*, the idiom for a pretentious empty-headed person, for which the English idiom is "windbag." On the other hand *a tayere*, "precious," *keyle* is a fine, sophisticated idiom for a particularly subtle brain, always, however, in connection with Jewish learning, particularly Talmudic argumentation.

Svore (Heb), "surmise, hypothesis," is a noun that

changes meaning with the time context. Linked to the present it expresses opinion and likelihood: *s'iz a svore az er hot zayn gelt farloyrn*, "It seems, it is surmised, that he has lost his money"; in the conditional it suggests a plausible course of action: *es volt geven a svore az me zol onfregn baym tatn*, "It would be a good idea to make inquiry of his father." *Boykh,** "belly, stomach," combines with *svore* in the plural; *boykh-svores*, literally "belly-surmises," conveys to a shade the flavor and meaning of "scuttlebutt," subtracting only the nautical background.

Mame-loshn, "mother tongue," has an irreproducible sense of separateness, intimacy, tenderness, and uniqueness. The combination has a certain sanctity, in a way like *loshn-koydesh*, "the Holy Tongue," Hebrew. I get an echo of *mame-loshn* when I hear insiders speak of their minority or regional languages, such as Erse or Gaelic. I got it with particular poignancy from Basques in Southern France telling of their Eskualduno. But I do not suggest that the terms in which I analyze *mame-loshn* apply to the other languages.

Zumer, "summer," forms the adjective *zumerdik*, "summery." The Hebraic *sof* ("end") would result in *sof-zumerdik*, "late summer," and *sof-zumerdike teg*, "last days of summer," has a melancholy ring, like "autumnal." The month of *elel* (Elul, all months in Yiddish are Hebrew), coincides with the summer's end, and *eleldike teg* is even more melancholy than *sof-zumerdike teg*, for *elel* heralds the approach of the New Year, the Day of Atonement, and the heavy-hearted Penitential Days.

---

* I shall remind the reader from time to time that all Yiddish words not otherwise attributed are Germanic.

2.

An oddity of Yiddish is the feminine form of a man's profession, trade, or status applied to his wife. The rabbi's wife is the *rebitsn*. It does not mean simply "the wife of the rabbi"; it implies, as it were, a species of woman. To use a word much in favor now, marriage to the rabbi "restructures" a woman. When I was a child in England, I used to think that when a man became Lord So-and-so and his wife Lady So-and-so, a transfiguration took place, making their new and exalted dignity visible at a distance, even projecting it round corners. Some such transfiguration is implied in the word *rebitsn*. Less drastic is the change in a woman who has married a *gabe*, "synagogue trustee, president," and thereby become a *gabete*. But a woman can earn this title for herself, whatever the status of her husband, through communal activity; it is then *honoris causa*, and slightly humorous.

Not humorous at all, in fact very dignified, not to say formidable, is the *negidiste*, the wife of the *nogid* (Heb), "wealthy man." We must pause over the *nogid*, too. In the abstract he merely has money; in *shtetl* life he was something hierarchical. Moyshe Hirsh was the *nogid* of our *shtetl*, Maçin (pronounced Mat*cheen*) in Roumania. I do not remember him personally, he can seldom have condescended to visit us. But I remember the aura surrounding the words *moyshe hirsh der nogid* (we pronounced it *nugid*) when my parents talked about him years later in our Manchester ghetto. Success, influence, and establishment were all comprised in *nogid*. *Negidiste* is not quite as powerful, though it conjures up an impressive picture of a great bundle of keys swinging from the girdle of an ample lady, who is attended by many servants.

In the humbler walks of life the feminine form simply

implied "the wife of" and nothing more. The wife of the *khazn*, "cantor," is the *khaznte*, of the *shoykhet*, "ritual slaughterer," the *shoykhetke*. But not all professions cast their titular mantle on a wife. I have never heard the wife of a *moyel*, "circumciser," called a *moyelte*. On the other hand, I do remember Sore *di blekherke*, the wife of the *blekher*, "the tinsmith," Fanny the *shusterke*, "cobbler," etc. When I took up translation work from Yiddish into English, I found it frustrating not to be able to write "Sarah, the tinsmithess," "Fanny the cobbleress," or "cantoress," or "slaughteress," or "rabbiess," as one writes "poetess" and "administratrix."

A Hebrew syllable will sometimes be introduced into a Germanic setting. *Knipl*, "knot," has come to mean, idiomatically, "a bit of savings" (with a hint of slyness, like "stashed away"), presumably because the coins were kept in a bag, or a stocking, tied with a knot. Usually it is the woman who has a *knipl*, unbeknownst to the husband. But *knipl-be-knipl* (the Hebraic *be* here means something like "within"), slightly humorous, can best be translated as "palsy-walsy."

These are a few anticipations of the many hybrid forms we shall meet, but at this point we should take note of a curious hybridism of grammatical forms—a transfer of biblical Hebrew syntax to Germanic Yiddish. A statement is emphasized in Hebrew by repetition of the verb in a different tense. Joseph, in prison, says to Pharaoh's cup-bearer, *ki gunav gunavti me'erets ha-ivrim*, "For indeed, surely, I was kidnapped from the land of the Hebrews" (literally, "For to be kidnapped I was kidnapped . . ."). Nathan the Prophet, denouncing David for his theft of Bathsheba and his murder of Uriah the Hittite, foretells concerning the child born in adultery, *mot yamut*, "It shall surely die" ("To die it shall die"), and there are many other instances. There has arisen in Yiddish a parallel form, not for emphasis but for clarification. *Esn est er in restoran, nor shlofn shloft er in der heym*, "He does his eating at the restaurant, but sleeps at home" (literally, "To eat, he eats in the restaurant, but to sleep he sleeps at home"). There is even the odd form, *izn iz er fun england, nor voynen voynt er in amerike,* "Actually he's from England, but he lives in America" (literally, "To be, he is from England, but to live, he lives in America").

3.

The Hebraic and Germanic synonyms and near-synonyms in Yiddish deepen its tone, as English is deepened by the presence of similar parallels drawn from Anglo-Saxon and Norman French. But even when we speak of "synonyms" we do not mean that one of the two words can be substituted for the other in every context. (In the following examples the Hebrew is given first, with exceptions noted.)

Milkhome (Heb), "war," and *krig:* in *di rusish-yapaneyzishe milkhome,* "the Russo-Japanese war," *krig,* will do just as well. One may also say *firn krig* or *firn milkhome* (literally, "lead war") for "be at war." But whereas *haltn* (literally, "to hold") *milkhome* expresses the same idea, *haltn krig* rings false.

Kimat (Heb), "almost," and *shier,* although perfect synonyms when they stand by themselves, are used in very different contexts; *shier* must always be accompanied by the negative *nit* or *nisht. Er iz kimat a milyoner,* "He is almost a millionaire," but *er iz shir nisht umgefaln,* "He almost fell," literally, "He almost didn't fall." A folk saying runs: *kimat hot amol dem taytsh fun gornisht,* " 'Almost' sometimes has the meaning of 'nothing,' " *i.e.,* "A miss is as good as a mile."

Terets (Heb), "answer (to a problem), explanation (of a motive), excuse, pretext," coincides with *oysreyd* only in the last meaning. But when the pretext is flimsy, one uses *terets,* preceded by the Germanic *foyler,* literally, "lazy." A *foyler terets* is one that doesn't hold water or cut any ice; an old British idiom is "That all my eye," or, for good measure, "My eye and Betty Martin." If the explanation or excuse is genuine one usually says *a guter* ("a good") *terets*.

"Question" and "answer" usually fall into three pairs of Yiddish couplets. *Frage* and *enfer* (both Germanic) are secular, general terms, as in *zey gleybn az der tsiyonizm iz der enfer oyf der yidisher frage,* "They believe that Zionism is the answer to the Jewish question"; but *shayle* and *tshuve,* like *kashe* and *terets* (all Heb) belong to the religious field. *Shayles utshuves,* "Questions and Answers," is the name given to a vast, still continuing Hebrew literature dealing with problems of ritual and ethics, much of it in manuscript, and in volume probably surpassing all other forms of Hebrew literature combined. It deals with everything, from the blemish on a cow's lung, which casts a doubt on its kosherness, to the terms of a commercial contract, and to the laws of evidence.

Tayve (Heb), "passion, lust," and *laydnshaft* coincide in the first meaning. *Er hot geredt mit laydnshaft,* "He spoke with passion," does not imply sexuality, but *er hot geredt tayvedik* means "He spoke lustfully." In *zi hot a tayve tsu sheyne kleyder,* "She has a passion for beautiful clothes," *laydnshaft* is also correct.

Where we have perfect or near-perfect synonyms the use of the Hebrew word imparts richness to the style, but, as we shall observe later, forcing Hebrew words to do the work of better Germanic words is bad style. It is difficult to distinguish between *leheypekh,* "the opposite (in ideas)," and *farkert;* between *shoykhed,* "bribery," "bribe," and *khabar* (Slv). Sometimes synonyms part company because of context. *Khisorn* (Heb) and *feler* both mean "defect," but the former relates to character, the latter to the body. *Er hot a khisorn, er iz a karger,* "He has a defect, he's stingy," but *er hot a lungen feler,* "He has a defect of the lungs." *Nign* (Heb),

61

"melody, air," and *melodye* mean exactly the same thing, but *nign* is always used for Jewish, particularly Chassidic melodies, while *melodye*, a recent word, applies to all other music.

4.

The interesting linguistic phenomenon known as the *daytshmerizm*, "Germanism," began with the *haskole*, "Enlightenment" (Anglicized as Haskalah), the intellectual modernizing movement set off in the Jewish world by Moses Mendelssohn (1729–86). One of its less fortunate results was the creation of a sort of babu Yiddish, highly Germanized and pretentious, and much affected by certain Yiddish-speaking and Yiddish-writing intellectuals, also by half-educated persons. Germany, consisting then of many states, but dominated by Prussia and its capital, Berlin, was eastern Jewry's door to the Western world. There was a period during the Haskalah when Germanomania took hold of thousands of Jews. Germany meant modernity, education, liberation from superstition, escape from ghetto mentality. To speak German was to rise above the ignorant, obscurantist masses.

So whenever possible, a colorful Hebraic Yiddish word was replaced by a Germanic word alien to the spirit of Yiddish; and thoroughly Yiddishized Germanic words, deeply rooted in the language of the folk, would be dragged back to what was supposed to be their German originals. This strange gobbledegook Yiddish was given the ironical label of *daytshmerish*, from *daytsh*, "German," and a word or phrase belonging to that category was called a *daytshmerizm*.

The fashion gradually died out, but its effects still linger on here and there. Some *daytshmerizms* (to use an Anglicized plural) are easily detected; they stand out like carbuncles; but some are so close to folk Yiddish that a sensitive ear has difficulty in deciding, so that there are frequent and acrimonious disputes about them. The problem is kept alive by the continuous evolution of Yiddish which, in the arbitrary way languages have, makes choices and establishes them without consulting lexicographers. I do not doubt than in some of the examples offered below I shall give offense to many as conversant with the language as I, or more so.

However, some cases are clear-cut. The Germanic *ere*, "honor," once spelled *ehre*, is definitely out, although fifty years ago Sholom Aleichem himself used it. Nowadays we use the Hebraic *koved*, as in *ikh hob dem koved aykh fortsushteln mayn bruder*, "I have the honor to introduce to you my brother." Nevertheless, *mayn ernvort*, "My word of honor," is permissible.

Teykef (Heb), "at once, immediately," had to compete with the Germanic *zofort* and *oygenbliklekh*; these are now indisputably *daytshmerizms*. The same fate has overtaken *niderlage*, "defeat," *apzikht*, "intent, purpose," *oyser*, "except," *bite*, "request," *tsvayfl*, "suspicion." These have been pushed out, respectively, by the Hebraic *mapole*, *kavone*, *akhuts*, *bakoshe*, and *sofek*.

Gesheftsman, "businessman, merchant," is almost completely a *daytshmerizm* by now; the Hebrew *soykher* is both richer and more authentic. Besides, *soykher* yields the fine hybrid adjective *sokhrish*, which is something more than "businesslike," coming nearer to "as becomes a merchant of standing." Nevertheless *gesheft*, "business," is not a *daytshmerizm* and has uses not obtainable from *soykher*: thus, *ikh hob zikh getrofn mit im in zayn gesheft*, "I met him in his place of business." *S'iz nit dayn gesheft*, "It's none of your business," is almost as good as *s'iz nit dayn eysek* (Heb).

Gezikht, "countenance, face," is, I think, drifting toward a *daytshmerizm*: it is in any case nowhere near as rich as the Hebraic *ponem*. Besides, *gezikht* cannot be used in a number of folk locutions where *ponem* is the proper word. Such are, *farshvartsn dos ponem,* "blacken someone's face," meaning to "cover someone with shame, make mud of him, disgrace him"; and *aza ponem hot es,* literally, "such a face it has," meaning, "and it looks it, too," used when something turns out badly, "as might have been expected."

Why did *daytshmerizms* rise and disappear? We can only say they were a fad, that is, passing fancy, a matter of taste at a certain period. But in the long run it is taste that determines the survival of words. Even though I am a lover of the German language I have a distinct preference for the Hebraic word as against the Germanic when both are good Yiddish. I prefer *sakone,* "danger," to *gefar; nispoel,* "deeply impressed, enthusiastic," to *bagaystert; hamtsoe,* "idea, brainstorm, gadget," to *aynfal; nesiye,* "journey," to *rayze.* If a large enough number of people develop my preferences, there will be new *daytshmerizms* and archaisms.

CHAPTER FIVE

Germanic into Yiddish

1.

Germanic words and phrases have slipped into Jewish life and undergone transformations of meaning corresponding to exclusively Jewish experiences. There are countless folk locutions in which every separate word recalls its original Germanic meaning, while the phrase as a whole is unintelligible in German. Thus we have *dreyen mitn grobn finger*, literally, "to turn with the thick finger" (*i.e.*, the thumb). It relates to Talmudic study, and should properly have been Hebraic, but it has not even a Hebraic equivalent. What it describes is the traditional down-and-up semicircular scooping motion made with closed fingers and extended thumb by an excited expositor of a knotty problem; it is as if he were unearthing and scooping up a deeply buried argument. Figuratively, it is "to argue a point speciously," or if I may so put it, "Jesuitically," with excessive subtlety; also "to beat about the bush, argue evasively, dishonestly."

Khlebn, "honestly, take my word for it, really," is a contraction of *ikh zol azoy lebn*, "I should so live," resembling the Hebrew *bekhayay*, "by my life," but not as vehement. It is a slightly *vayberish*, "feminine," or, rather "womanish" colloquialism, quite polite, but not for the pulpit or platform. It is somewhat remonstrative, in a friendly, almost affectionate way; one would not use it to a stranger, or in a quarrel, or a serious discussion. It has the suggestion "We both should live so." *Khlebn, ir volt nisht badarft forn*, "Honestly now, you oughtn't to be taking that trip"; *khlebn, ir kent zikh nit baklogn*, "Really now, you can't complain"; *khlebn, ikh veys nit*, "Honestly, I don't know."

Another word that is deepfolk Yiddish and can never be unscrambled into its Germanic components is *staytsh*, an unusual etymological curiosity. It is presumed to be a contraction of *vi heyst es oyf taytsh*, "How is it called in German Yiddish?" or "What is the meaning of it?" *Staytsh* is an interjection expressing taken-aback incredulousness, remonstrance, supplication, astonishment, derisive but polite skepticism, all according to context. It is an immensely useful word.

A man who has been your regular and apparently satisfied customer time out of mind tells you suddenly, calmly, without explanation, that henceforth he will do his buying elsewhere. You look at him thunderstruck: *staytsh?* A man who is transferring to you the lease of his apartment asks you a thumping price for some sticks of furniture in the last stages of delapidation. You look at him blankly: *staytsh?* A Jew lamenting the fate of his people, and lifting his eyes to heaven in expostulation, wanting to say as briefly as possible, "Lord of the universe, how can You do this to us who have, with all our sins, been faithful to You in a fashion, how can You do this after all we have suffered for Your sake?" will pack it all into a long-drawn out baffled, "*s-t-a-y-t-s-h, reboyne-shel-oylem!*"

But *staytsh*, as we have seen, contains *taytsh*, which also means "translation." Thus the *taytsh-khumesh* is the old Yiddish translation of the Pentateuch. *Fartaytshn* has, however, come to mean "to interpret" (both a text and a situation) rather than "to translate." *Aykh darf ikh nit fartayshn vos dos meynt*, "To you I don't need to explain what this word, text, incident, circumstance means, portends," flatters the person addressed. According to a symbolic anecdote, a Negro trying to register to vote in one of the southern states was asked, as part of the qualifying test, "What is the meaning of the parallax of Aldebaran?" and answered, "The meaning is, you don't want to let me vote"; in Yiddish, *der taytsh derfun iz az ir vilt mikh nit lozn shtimen*.

Epes, "something, somewhat, somehow," cognate with the German *etwas*, is another of those special, elusive words. It can be straightforward: *ikh volt gevolt epes esn*, "I would like to eat something"; but *epes gefelstu (gefelst-du) mir nit haynt*, "You somehow don't please me today," generally refers to signs of ill-health in the person addressed; it can also refer to the person's mood, or behavior. *Epes bistu mir a bisl tsu freylekh*, or *hoferdik*, "You're somehow (to me) a little too cheerful," or "chipper," means "You're hiding something behind that forced cheerfulness of yours." Or let us imagine a buyer for a footwear firm sending back to his employer a list of purchases "so many galoshes, so many shoes, slippers, moccasins, and one fiddle." The startled employer would want to know *vos epes a fidl in mitskederinen*? "What on earth is the fiddle for, in the midst of everything?" (*Mitskederinen* is a sardonic form of *in-mitn-drinen*.)

Fort, "for all that, nevertheless, still," is a little simpler. Speaking of someone of established good character whom poverty has forced into a shady deal, you might say compassionately, *er iz fort an erlekher mentsh*, "He's an honest man for all that"; and of someone who was pointedly not invited to an affair and came nevertheless, *er iz fort gekumen*. About something unbelievable but incontrovertible: *s'iz fort emes* (Heb), "But it's true all the same." *Fort* is always emphasized.

The meaning of *dokh* depends on whether it is enunciated clearly and emphatically, or slipped in unobtrusively, almost elided. In the first case it is synonymous with *fort* as in *er iz fort gekumen*; in the second it is a mixture of "why" and "but" used as reminders. If Reuben remarks with surprise that Simon has taken a whole suite first class on an ocean liner, Levi may answer, *farvos nisht? er izdekh* [*iz dokh*—the *dokh* almost suppressed] *raykh vi koyrekh*, "Why not? he's as rich as Korah" (Korah, the rebel against Moses whom the earth swallowed up, being the Croesus of Jewish folklore.) If Reuben asks Simon how Levi is, and Simon answers that he does not know, Reuben might say in some puzzlement, *hostekh (host dokh) im gezen ersht nekhtn*, "But you saw him only yesterday," or *bistekh (bist dokh) okersht geven bay im*, "But you were with him just a moment ago." And addressing God partly in Yiddish, partly in Hebrew, a Jew might cry out, *helf mir, gotenyu, bistekh an eyl rakhum vekhanun,* "Help me, dear God, for (after all, or don't forget) You are a merciful and gracious God."

2.

Yiddish is rich in expressions of skepticism, warnings against self-delusion and defense against presumptuousness. Most of them are in *heymish* Germanic Yiddish, and the fact that *heymish,* "homey," is itself Germanic bespeaks the total absorption of the Germanic element. But *heymish* has a wider range than "homey" and "homelike." A *heymish shtetl* is best translated as "a cosy townlet" (*heymlekh,* which has a touch of intimacy, could also be used); *a heymisher mentsh* is "one of our kind, just folks," and *heymishe mentshn* is "not stuck-up people or strangers."

Two popular expressions of skepticism and derision are *veys ikh vos,* literally, "know I what," admirably translated by Weinreich as "fiddlesticks," and *a nekhtiker tog,* literally, "a yesterday's day" or "a nightly day." The distinction between these expressions is a very fine one. A *nekhtiker tog* is more appropriate for unfulfilled promises and idle, exaggerated reports. *Me zogt az yankl iz gevorn a gvir,* "They say that Yankel has become a rich man," to which the skeptic replies, *a nekhtiker tog,* "Stuff and nonsense." If the statement is merely untrue but contains no inherent improbability, as, for instance, *ikh hob gehert az ir fort morgn keyn leykvud,* "I heard that you're going to Lakewood tomorrow," the answer might be, *veys ikh vos,* which when uttered emphatically becomes a coughlike *EYsekhvos!* Akin to *a nekhtiker tog* is the popular locution *nisht geshtoygn nisht gefloygn,* "neither arose nor flew," which is said to have originated as a folk **denial** of Christ's resurrection and ascent to heaven, but has wholly lost that connotation (if it ever had it) and become general.

If someone is trying seriously to convince you that just because you had a tiff with your father you have an Oedipus complex, or that you ought to join the Communist party because you believe in the First Amendment, or that you are responsible for an act you did not commit, you may counter impatiently with, *er vil mir aynredn a kind in boykh*, "He wants to talk (persuade) a child into my belly," or "Talk me into a pregnancy," an expression that while not the height of elegance, does not sound quite as earthy in Yiddish as in English. You might also say, *er vil mir onhengen a lung un leber oyf der noz*, "He wants to hang a lung and liver on my nose," an unusually imaginative form of decorative presumptuousness.

On the other hand, if someone is deluding himself that things are better than they are, that black is white, that his creditors will suddenly reveal themselves as philanthropists, that he will pass the difficult examination he has not prepared for, that the young lady who can't stand the sight of him has become besotted about him, it is proper to warn him with *leyg zikh nit keyn feygelekh in buzem*, "Don't lay little birds in your bosom." Though a shade different in meaning, this locution has the exact idiomatic ring of Hamlet's admonition to his mother, "Lay not the flattering unction to your soul."

Context and intonation play a larger part in Yiddish than in German or English. Parallel to the *shoyfer*-trumpet court story there is the one about the Jew accused of stealing a horse and the interpreter whose knowledge of Yiddish was literal, not extending to the inverting effect of certain Yiddish intonations. Asked, *ir hot geganvet dos ferd?* the Jew answered with a pitying smile and a catch in his voice, *IKH hob geganvet dos ferd* "I stole the horse," the tone and manner implying that the denial was an insult to the intelligence of the Court,

who could perceive at a glance that this man was utterly in-
capable of such an act: nothing remained for him but to
repeat the accusation in all its ludicrous implausibility. The
interpreter proceeds to translate by the book: "He says he stole
the horse." The linguistic point of this little anecdote is
usually spoiled by tacking on to it an additional and different
kind of misunderstanding. The judge asks: "What did you
want the horse for?", *tsu vos hot ir gedarft hobn dos ferd?* The
Jew answers, with bitter laughter, *ikh hob es gedarft oyf
kapores*, approximately, "I needed it like a hole in the head,"
but given to the Court by the literal interpreter as "He needed
it for religious purposes."

3.

Germanic words are the basis for large numbers of all-
Germanic idioms and locutions. *Di velt*, "the world" in its
general sense, has no Hebraic equivalent. Only when the
article is emphasized, *DI velt*, meaning *this* life, as opposed to
YENE velt, "*that* life," or "the life to come," do we have
corresponding Hebraic terms, *oylem-haze* and *oylem-habe*.
But there are no Hebraic equivalents for *sheyn vi di velt*, "pretty
as the world," *klug vi di velt*, "clever as the world," and *gut vi
di velt*, "good (in character) as the world"; here the English
colloquialism for "as the world" would be "as all get out."
Popular are: *di velt hot zikh a vertl*, "the world has a word,"
i.e., "There is a universal saying, proverb"; *er ken a velt*, "He
knows a world," *i.e.*, "He is full of knowledge, information,"
but *er ken a velt mit mentshn*, "He knows no end of people";
az di velt zogt meshuge zol men gleybn, "If the (whole) world
says 'crazy' one should believe"; *oyf vos di velt shteyt*, literally,
"on what the world stands," corresponds to "for all he was

worth" and "to beat the band"; *er hot gefresn oyf vos di velt shteyt*, "He was wolfing away to beat the band."

A cluster of idioms has gathered round *vant*, "wall." *Krikhn oyf di glaykhe vent*, "to crawl up smooth (perpendicular) walls," does not imply agony ("clawing the wall"), but desperation and futility; *cf.* "It drove me up the wall." It is a distant relative of *akern mit der noz*, "to plough with one's nose," *i.e.*, "to set about a difficult enterprise without means or equipment." A lonely man comes home *tsu di fir vent*, "to the four walls." *Zikh shlogn kop in vant*, "to beat one's head against the wall," is "to carry on furiously when hope is gone"; while *geyn mitn kop durkh der vant*, "to go with one's head through the wall," is "to knock oneself out trying to do the impossible." *Shlog zikh kop in vant*, approximately, "go beat your brains out," is what you might say to someone who has pestered you beyond reason for advice, and you have given all you can, and he keeps on at it till you see red. However, the phrase belongs properly under the chapter "Malediction and Benediction."

Redn tsu der vant, "to speak to the wall," like *redn tsum lomp*, "to the lamp," is "to waste your breath," though walls, if not lamps, do understand Yiddish, which also has the universal saying, *vent hobn oyrn*, "Walls have ears." On the other hand, walls are in Yiddish the last word in heartlessness, for the equivalent of "move a stone to tears" is *rirn a vant*, "move a wall."

Of one who is ingenious at creating unusual combinations, of harnessing the most incongruous forces, one says *er ken tsuzamenfirn a vant mit a vant*, "He can bring together wall and wall." He is something of what they call in England "a great wangler," and usually not a man to be trusted.

Hoyz, "house," has not the idiomatic range one would expect ("house of cards," "bring down the house," "clean house," etc.), but it has one melancholy idiom of great force, *geyn iber di hayzer,* "to go across the houses," *i.e.,* "from door to door," a beggar. There are two diminutive forms of house, *hayzke* and *hayzl;* the latter, for some unfathomable reason, means "brothel."

Beyn, "bone," like *vant,* has many figurative uses. *Er iz der tate mit di beyner,* "He's his father with (down to) the bones," *i.e.,* "He's the spit and image of his father," does not refer to physical resemblance but to character and habits. *Er shtekt mir vi a beyn in haldz,* "He sticks (in me) like a bone in the throat," changes object and anatomy in English: "He is a thorn in my side." *Oplekhn a beyndl,* "to lick clean a little bone," is a sly and winking expression. It is "to nick in" on some larger transaction between others, "to profit incidentally," though rather modestly, but to one's gleeful satisfaction.

An expression of great love and tenderness, addressed to a small child, is *mir zol zayn for dayn klenstn* or *mindestn beyndele,* "Let it be to me for your tiniest bone," which means something like "Let me take over whatever evil is in store for the tiniest part of you." The expression is sometimes *far dayne eygelekh,* "for your darling little eyes," or *far dayn mindestn negele,* "for your tiniest fingernail."

From the very great number of Yiddish folk words and locutions stemming from the Germanic, I offer here a few more random examples:

Got zol undz hitn fun di kleyne fleshelekh, "God guard us from the little [*i.e.,* medicine] bottles."

Mit yanklen iz gut kugl tsu esn, "Yankl is good to eat pudding with" (*i.e.,* that is all he's good for).

Der biterer tropn, "the bitter drop," *i.e.,* strong liquor, as in *er hot nebekh* (Slv) *lib dem bitern tropn,* "he alas, poor devil, loves, has a weakness for the bottle." "Bitter" refers not to the ruinous effects of whiskey but to its taste, which has never appealed to Jews.

Dos telerl fun himl, "the saucer from heaven," hints at "pie in the sky" but has another shading. *Er hot ir tsugezogt dos telerl fun himl* is rather "He promised her the moon and the stars." Of a man who makes a tremendous show of a little bit of learning one says, *er tseleygt es oyf zibn telerlekh*, "He lays it out on seven saucers" (*i.e.*, He makes a great show of very little).

Gevald (or *gvald*), "violence, row, rumpus, *force majeure*," and its adjective, *gevaldik*, are as often used ironically as literally, where the cognate German *Gewalt* has none of the ironic shadings. *Er hot es genumen mit gevald*, "He took it by force, violence," is straight; so is *makh nit keyn gevald* (or *gevaldn*), "Don't make a row, noise, rumpus," as in the folksong

> *sha! shtil! makh nit keyn gevald,*
> *der rebe geyt shoyn tantsn bald,*
> Hush! Quiet! don't make a row,
> The *rebe* is going to dance soon.

But in a sentence like *ze nor vos fara gevaldn er makht*, "Look at the row he's kicking up," *gevaldn* is ironical, indicating exaggerated protests (which may not be noisy at all). The adjective *gvaldovne*, "terrific," is invariably comic, while *gvaltik* can be used both humorously and seriously; so can the verb *gevaldeven*, "to set up a tremendous noise, protest." The interjection *gevald!* can best be translated by "help!" *Gevald geshrign* (or *geshrien*) is a strong-feeble exclamation expressing helpless incredulity or protest: "How can such a thing be! For God's sake! For the love of God! Has the like ever been heard?"

Honik lekn, "to lick honey, to have it good," is never, as far as I know, used in the affirmative. It is always *bay im hob ikh keyn honik nit gelekt*, "I had no easy time with him." To a German survivor of a concentration camp a Jew once said, commiseratingly, *ir hot dort keyn honik nit gelekt*, "That was a hard life you had there," to which the humorless reply

came, *Mensch! man hat uns sogar kein Saccharin gegeben,*
"Man alive, they didn't even give us saccharin."

Alter hiner-freser, "old chicken-devourer," and *khapt*
(Slv) *im der vatnmakher,* "May the devil [literally,
'wadding-maker'] take him," are two deprecative locutions.
The *hiner-freser* is never anything but *alt,* and he may in
reality be a vegetarian. The nearest in English is "old-timer,"
but with a touch of disrespect; something like "tough old
bird," or better, "rooster," since there is no feminine of *hiner-
freser. An alter hiner-freser* is more likely to be a non-Jew than a
Jew and will certainly not be a man of culture. *Vatnmakher*
seems to have evolved from *tayvlmakher,* "devil-maker," via
the inversion *vatl* for *tayvl.*

Finally, an expression widely current in Yiddish, which
has long puzzled me, as it has thousands of others: *shem zikh
in dayn vaytn haldz,* "Shame on you," "Be thoroughly
ashamed of yourself," literally, "Be ashamed in your far neck."
The explanation, which I owe to Yudl Mark, is very simple,
once you are told: "Blush deep down into your neck."

CHAPTER SIX

Of Marriage, Death, and Burial

The perfect interweave of Germanic with Hebraic in Yiddish is illustrated with particular charm in the three subjects of this chapter. Each source contributes its own flavor to the terminology of these intimate life experiences.

Shraybn tnoyim is the correct term for "entering into a betrothal." The Hebraic *tnoyim*, "terms" or "conditions," is by itself a dry word, and the Germanic *shraybn*, "to write," is by itself equally uninteresting. Paired in *shraybn tnoyim*, they are transformed into a phrase filled with the sap of the folk. Just as "betrothal," rooted in Old English, is at once richer and more restricted than "engagement" (from the Middle French), with its diffused connotations, so *tnoyim*, in the setting of the phrase, strikes deeper than the Germanic *farlobung*, now a *daytshmerizm*, which was a rival as little as fifty years ago.

A synonym for *shraybn tnoyim*, of equal richness, is *farknasn*. *Knas* is the Hebrew for "money fine," but turned with a Germanic prefix into *farknasn*, it loses that connotation as it becomes completely Yiddish. Another colorful combination of Hebraic and Germanic is *knasmol*, "betrothal dinner." *Mol*, "meal" (as distinguished from its meaning as "time"—*eyn mol*, "once," *tsvey mol*, "twice"), never stands alone. One must say *moltsayt* for "meal" (though *tsayt* itself means "time," so that *moltsayt* is literally "timetime," which derives from the periodicity of meals), and *nakhtmol*, for "supper." An unusual Slavic intrusion into this area is *khupevetchere*, where *khupe* (Heb), "canopy," stands for "wedding" and *vetchere* is "supper."

Still another synonym for "betrothal" is the smiling all-Germanic *brekhn teler*, "to break plates," from the folk custom, not strictly obligatory, of smashing a plate at the betrothal as a *zekher le-khurbn* (all Heb), "memorial of the Destruction." At the wedding, too, the eternal shadow on every happy Jewish occasion is symbolized by the crushing of a wineglass under the bridegroom's foot.

When two young people become betrothed they form, it is hoped and proclaimed, a *ziveg* (Heb), "a pairing," in the sense of "a perfect match," with overtones of "elective affinity" and "the predestined." *Mayn ziveg* amounts to "my preordained mate," and—were it not for the deterioration of the English phrase—"my better half." The Germanic *mayn basherter*, "my predestined one," is also sound Yiddish. The tradition has it that God is mightily occupied with the pairing off of souls in heaven for their eventual union on earth, and finds each case as exacting as the miracle of the Red Sea (which for some unknown reason is assumed to have given God more trouble than any other miracle). *Ziveg* is sometimes strengthened by *min hashomayim* (Heb), "from heaven." In English too we say that "marriages are made in heaven," but neither the Yiddish nor the English phrases carry much conviction.

Among orthodox Jews all contracts were confirmed by the ceremony of *kaboles kinyen* (Heb), "acceptance of the purchase," in which the contracting parties each took hold of the end of a handkerchief. In particular the ceremony belonged to the first confirmation of a *shidekh*, "match." A marriage was not less sacred, a *ziveg* not less *min hashomayim*, for being legally confirmed on this earth below.

2.

The Hebraic *khasene* means "wedding" as an act, but not marriage as a state. The Germanic *hayrat* for "marriage" is now a *daytshmerizm*, but the Germanic is imbedded in *khasene hobn*, "to marry," also in a *khasene gehater*, "a married man," literally, "one who has had marriage," and *khasene gehate*, "a married woman." A married man is also known by the Germanic *bavaybter*, "bewived"; but a woman who is a *bamante*, "bemanned," is of uncertain status; she has merely "had a man."

In old-fashioned weddings certain ceremonials are still observed more out of sentiment than as the religious prescriptions they were originally. Immediately before the binding of the knot, the bride is seated in state, like an enthroned queen, and there takes place the *badekns*, "covering" or "veiling." *Badekn*, "to cover," is a quite undistinguished word, without associative values; *badekns*, on the other hand, is heavily freighted with its exclusive function in the wedding ceremony. In the same way, *oysnemen*, "to make a hit with," or "to stipulate," is entirely secular, but *oysnemens* is an exclusively religious term; it denotes the period during which the Torah is read at services, also special periods during the *rosh hashone* and *yom kiper* services. The final *s* in *badekns* and *oysnemens* transforms the personality of the words from the secular to the sacred.

There is only one word for "bride," *kale* (Heb), but there is a compound for a girl of marriageable age, *kale-moyd*. Standing alone, *moyd* is somewhat hoydenish; *kuk nor on a moyd* would be "just look at that strapping creature." Preceded by *kale*, *moyd* is softened and refined. The simple word for "girl" is *meydl*, the diminutive of *moyd* (cf. the French *fille* and *jeune fille*). A diminutive of the diminutive is *meydele*, "little girl."

Some unusually intriguing combinations of Germanic and Hebraic occur in connection with the wedding ceremonies in extremely orthodox circles. There is for instance the use of the *ikhed* (Heb) *shtibl*, "privacy room." Immediately after

the groom recites the climactic words, "Behold thou art consecrated unto me according to the law of Moses and Israel"
(these are the words that constitute the registration of marriage), the bride and groom are led into a private room and
left alone for a brief interval, symbolizing thereby the con-
summation of the marriage. It must be remembered that to
be alone in a room, a man and woman had to be married.
Shtibl is one of the Germanic words that acquired sanctity;
it can be used in its literal sense of "little house," but most
often it denotes a small Chassidic meeting place or prayer
house.

Not less curious is the *mitsve tentsl*, literally, "the good-
deed little dance," which is a *pas seul* performed by one of
the guests in the presence and in honor of the bride. *Mitsve*
(Heb), "commandment, good deed," is an exceptionally
weighty word; *tentsl*, the diminutive of *tants*, is, standing by
itself, a thoroughly absurd word; the combination *mitsve
tentsl*, is tinged with a religious kind of gaiety.

There are other varieties of wedding dances, performed
by individuals or couples, during the festivities and as tributes
to the newlyweds. The *kosher-tants*, performed by a male or
a female, seems to have no particular purpose beyond expressing joy. The *broygez* (Heb) *tants* is a *pas de deux* performed by the fathers of the bride and groom, or their mothers,
and its name indicates its meaning. *Broygez*, "angry, on the
outs," is a very common word; *ich bin broygez oyf im*, "I'm
angry with him, sore at him," *zey zaynen broygez*, "They're
not on talking terms;" but in the *broygez tants* the meaning
is inverted; its purpose is to declare that no ill feeling en-
gendered by the marriage negotiations, or by questions of
precedence at the wedding (and very ticklish these questions
can be), or by any other circumstances connected with the
occasion has survived them. The bride's father may have failed
to "pay over the dowry"—*silekn dem nadan* (Heb) is the
technical term—wholly or in part before the wedding; the

refreshments may not have come up to specifications—all is wiped out by the *broygez tants.*

That a wedding could be attended by other than friendly feelings, could even be the beginning of a vendetta, is attested by the popular phrase *onmakhn a khasene,* "to stir up a holy mess," literally, "to cause a wedding." *Makhn a gantse khasene,* "make a whole wedding (of something)," is "to blow up" a minor incident into a major "production."

Vanishing features of the Jewish marriage are the *droshe* (Heb) "sermon," delivered by the *khosn* (Heb), "bridegroom," before the assembled guests, and the *droshe geshank,* "sermon present," attached to it—something special provided by the father of the bride. Presents to a newly married pair are of course universal, but the *droshe geshank*—the Hebraic and Germanic words fit sweetly into each other—was the expression of a high cultural standard.

Among families with a decent intellectual and religious tradition, a prospective bridegroom meeting for the first time his prospective *shver,* "father-in-law," and *shviger,* "mother-in-law," was given what amounted to a formal examination. He was expected to take part in a scholarly discussion with his elders and to quote Bible and Talmud, commentators, and Midrashim. At the wedding there was the *droshe,* which might be described as a short oral doctoral thesis, adorned with whatever the *khosn* could think up of aptly chosen verses, skilfully woven into each other from various parts of the Bible, together with original interpretations. The *droshe* may seldom have risen above the level of other kinds of doctoral theses, but it bespoke a spiritual aspiration absent from the bumbling banquet oratory of the average Jewish wedding today.

An irreplaceable Hebraic word that carried with it a good deal of the Yiddish world is *mekhutn* (Heb), generally and loosely translated as "in-law." There are, however, some important subtleties. The father of my *eydem,* "son-in-law," or of my *shnur*,* "daughter-in-law," is my *mekhutn*; their mother is my *makhteyneste* (Heb); reciprocally, I am a *mekhutn* or *makhteyneste*, according to whether I am a father or a mother. These are the primary meanings, but *mekhutn* can also mean something like "in-law at large"; *mir zaynen shtiklekh mekhutonim*, "We are little bits of in-laws," meaning "We're slightly related by marriage." If someone presumes on his slender acquaintanceship with you, he should be put in his place with the locution, *vos far a mekhutn bistu (bist du) mir?*, "What kind of *mekhutn* are you to me?"

Mekhutn and its derivatives are Yiddish creations wrought on Hebrew roots; for Yiddish did with a number of Hebrew words what it did with Germanic words, gave them a different coloration and content. Some of these coinages found their way back into Hebrew, so that Hebrew is now tinged with the *goles*.

In its primary sense *mekhutn* is a word of immense respectability, dignity, and status, a grave and substantial word, a rebuke to the young and frivolous, a reproach to the inadequate and incompetent. The word is uttered with becoming self-respect and an equally becoming deference to the peer so addressed; the mutual proclamation of importance and achievement is enriched by the tone of affection. I know of no greater social pleasure than to be present in a small family circle and to hear one father say to another, *zitst mekhutn*, "Take a seat, *mekhutn*." The struggle of a lifetime, the long *tsar gidl bonim* (all Heb), "the griefs of bringing up children," find compensation in this humble trophy, this domestic Nobel Prize; while *zitst, makhteyneste*, as between mothers, lightens the solemnity of the occasion with the sweetness of the womanly touch.

Such is the ideal picture, not always corresponding to the

---

* *Shnur* is one of the oldest traceable Proto-Indo-European forms, no doubt as venerable as *mekhutn* in any form (see *The American Heritage Dictionary of the English Language*, p. 1496).

reality. Marriage is, indeed, among Jews more than among most peoples, a supreme desideratum, combining personal fulfillment with an unusual sense of religious and national obligations discharged. "Old maid" is not quite as sad and withered as its Yiddish equivalent, *alte moyd*, while *alter bokher*, "old bachelor," conveys a degree of disesteem and disparagement not felt in the English. The censure—barely tinged with compassion—directed at the *alter bokher* flowed from every source. A people so set on survival found him derelict in the elementary public duty of a Jew; mothers— and daughters—considered him a parasite as well as a wastrel, the first because he took up room in the community and synagogue that should have gone to a married man, the second because he was an insult to his father, to whose unheeded example he owed his existence. But it cannot be doubted that the most implacable enemy of the *alter bokher* was the *shatkhn* (spelled *shadkhn*), "marriage broker."

I prefer the dignified title of "professional marriage promoter," or "arranger," for the *shatkhn* had an honored place in the social hierarchy, and though he stood firmly on his *shatkhones-gelt*, "match money," since this was his livelihood, his supreme satisfaction was in the bringing together of the right couple, playing here below the role of administrator for the Matchmaker on high. However, we have noted that, life being what it is, the supreme satisfaction was often denied him and he had to be content with second or third best; but so important was his function that a folksaying gives him license to digress "a little" from the strict truth in the promotion of a match. This saying draws its authority from a number of others: *es iz nishto keyn miese kale*, "There is no (such thing as an) ill-favored bride," and *khosn doyme lemelekh* (all Heb), "A bridegroom is likened to a king." The indispensability of marriage is affirmed in *afile* (Heb) *in ganeydn* (Heb) *iz nisht gut tsu zayn aleyn*, "Even in Paradise it is not good to be alone," and its urgency in *fri oyfshteyn und fri khasene hobn shat nisht,* "To be up betimes and to marry early does no harm"; and again, *itlikher shidekh vos me tut iz gut, nokh a yor vert men gevor,* "Every match is a catch, after a year it becomes clear."

Though the accredited *shatkhn* was a professional, it was a *mitsve* for anyone to play the amateur, and matchmaking then, as now, was a favorite activity with busybodies, chiefly among women. To have been the *shatkhnte* in a successful or not so successful marriage gave a woman something to boast about as long as she lived, even unto the second and third generation of the consequences.

Nevertheless, many proverbs counsel extreme caution and deliberation in the search for a mate, and there was widespread skepticism as to the infallibility of the divine *shatkhn* Himself, let alone His earthly representative. The sayings concerning marriage are almost equally divided between dithyramb and denigration. The intervention of God is acknowledged in *got zitst oybn und port untn,* "God sits on high and pairs (them off) below," and disparaged by substituting *porket,* "pokes around blindly," for *port.* Early marriage is sharply discommended in *khasene hobn un shtarbn iz keyn mol nisht tsu shpet,* "It's never too late to marry or die," and the sentiment is supported in various proverbs: *Far vos tantst der ber? vayl er hot keyn vayb nit, gib im a vayb vet er oyfhern tantsn,* "Why does the bear dance? Because he has no wife; give him a wife and he'll stop dancing"; *vayber zaynen gebildet un kenen tsvey shprakhn, eyns far der khasene und eyns nokh der khasene,* "Women are well educated and know two languages, one before the wedding and one after"; *fun a kats a krats und un fun a vayb a klole* (Heb), "From a cat a scratch and from a wife a curse."

3.

Shtarbn is the general term for "to die." Among traditional Jews, however, certain deaths are honored with Hebraic words. It is not proper to say of a notably pious Jew that *er iz geshtorbn*, "He died"; one must say *er iz nifter gevorn*, "He became *nifter*," from a root meaning "to get rid of," or "to dismiss." If the departed one was in a class by himself for learning and piety, he is promoted to *nistalek gevorn*, from a root meaning "to put a distance between." We do not know how this hierarchy came to be established, for all men, of whatever character or condition of grace, when they die are got rid of and put an impassable distance between themselves and the living; and we are the more puzzled when we learn that *nistalek* was at one time used also of the unlettered and impious.

However, a Hebraic verb, *peygern*, "to croak," is at the bottom of the honorific scale, too, and is used of animals and of human beings classed with them. A *hunt shtarbt nit, er peygert*, "A dog does not die, it croaks." The same verb would be used of a Hitler. The Germanic *krepirn*, also "to croak," is not less contemptuous than *peygern*, but its special quality is vindictiveness; *krepirn* is connected with suffering, and unlike *peygern* is never used for animals.

The synonyms for "to die" are numerous and finely shaded:

Oysgeyn, "to go out, pass away," is tactful and reverential. However, it also means "dying" in the trivial, figurative sense: *ikh gey oys nokh a glezl tey*, "I'm dying for a cup (glass) of tea."

In Americanized Yiddish *oysgeyn* has come to include "to go out," as in "I'm going out with a boy." From this incorrect usage has arisen the anecdote of the recent immigrant who wrote to her parents: *mayne tayere eltern, ir megt mir opgebn a mazltov, ikh hob shoyn a feler, a kater, un ikh gey oys mit im,* "My dear parents, you may congratulate me; I already have a fellow (young man), a cutter, and I'm going out with him." But since *feler* in Yiddish is "defect" (here of health), and *kater* is something like "catarrh," and *ikh gey oys mit im* can mean "I'm dying of it," the parents went to the cemetery to pray for her recovery.

The sardonic and derisive attitude toward death is expressed in such phrases as:

Ariberpeklen zikh, "to move over, bag and baggage."

Tsumakhn an oyg, "to shut an eye."

Oystsien di fis, "to stretch out the feet."

Aveksharn zikh, "to shuffle away."

Aynnemen a mise meshune, "to suffer (literally, take in) a strange unusual, unnatural death."

Aynnemen is in many of its usages the same as its German cognate *einnehmen.* In *der dokter hot mir geheysn aynnemen a pil yede sho,* "The doctor told me to take a pill every hour," the German and Yiddish coincide; similarly in *aleksander mukdn hot ayngenumen gants kleyn-azyen,* "Alexander the Great conquered the whole of Asia Minor."

Mise (Heb), "death," seldom stands alone in Yiddish. It is, however, frequently linked to *meshune* (Heb), "different, strange." A *mise-meshune* is a death that does not come naturally from sickness (unless the sickness is "unnatural") or old age. It must be accompanied by horror and repulsiveness, and therefore one does not say *shtarbn (mit) a mise-meshune,* but *aynnemen,* like a loathesome medicine.

Here is a fine illustration of the confusions that arise for those who imagine that a knowledge of German suffices for the understanding of Yiddish. The anecdote is old, it has become part of folklore, but is indispensable in a presentation of the character of Yiddish and of Yiddish humor.

A Prussian sitting opposite a Jew in a railroad carriage kept boasting, as the train passed through various cities: *Sehen Sie mal, diese Stadt haben wir Preussen eingenomen,* "Look you, this city we Prussians took," *auch diese Stadt,* "This city, too," and so on *ad nauseam.* Finally the Jew asked, courteously: *Verzeihung, haben Sie aber a mise-meshune eingenomen?,* "Pardon me, but have you taken *a mise-meshune?" Noch nicht,* answered the Prussian, *aber das werden wir Preussen auch sicher einnehmen,* "not yet, but we Prussians surely will."

4.

Olev hasholem (Heb), "peace be to him," usually pronounced *olevesholem,* has no Germanic-Yiddish counterpart; twisted by mockery into phrases like *olev hasholekhts* (a nonsense phrase—*sholekhts* means "peel"), it connotes disrespect for the dead person mentioned. A deceased person is also referred to in the Hebraic locution *shoykhn-ofer,* "sleeper in the dust." When one mentions in conversation those who have died recently it is good manners to add *aykh tsu lengere yor,* "more years to you."

The melancholy Hebraic *takhrikhim,* "cerements, grave-clothes," is more at home in Yiddish than its equivalent is in English. Pious old Jews and Jewesses sewed their own *takhrikhim* as a *memento mori,* in the fashion of hopeful Jewish girls sewing their trousseaux as a memento marry. It is strange that Jews, whose religion is so fixed on life, should have been so concerned with the proper apparel for the grave, the *takhrikhim* (and for men, in addition, the *tales*), and have contemplated with such anguish the possibility of burial elsewhere than in consecrated Jewish soil, of not resting in *keyver-oves,* "the grave of the fathers."

The longing of the pious to spend their last days in the Holy Land and to be buried there is understandable. They believed that on the Judgment Day they would have to present themselves, together with all other resurrected Jews, in the Valley of Jehoshaphat, and that the farther away they were from it, the longer their corpses would have to roll underground to keep the appointment. They were also deeply concerned that their bodies should receive the proper "purification," or washing, for the grave, and the word for it is Hebraic, *tehare*; but the special phrase for the whole ceremonial of consignment to the grave is Germanic: *tun emetsn zayn rekht*, literally "to do right by someone." But this has an additional connotation: "to punish, to give someone what's coming to him."

Bagrobn, "to bury," is the simplest, least haloed synonym; more elaborate and invested with more pathos are *brengen tsu kvure*, "to bring to burial," and *brengen tsu keyver-yisroel*, "bring to a Jewish grave." *Bagrobn* has a number of figurative uses, such as "to administer a thrashing," "put the kibosh on someone," "do someone in," "mess up an affair," and in the passive, with *lebedikerheyt*, "to lose one's shirt." *Er hot mikh bagrobn lebedikerheyt*, "He buried me alive," like *er hot mikh gekoylet on a meser*, "He slit my throat without a knife," is supposed to mean "He ruined me," but is usually understood to be an exaggeration.

This accumulation of calamitous associations gives more weight to the figurative than the literal use of *bagrobn*; it also makes possible the untranslatable piece of black humor: *shtarbn iz nokh vi es iz, ober dos araynleygn in drerd (der erd), dos bagrobt a mentshn*, "Dying isn't too bad in itself, it's laying the man in the earth that 'buries' him."

In a much-used idiom *bagrobn* takes on the meaning of "concealed." *Do ligt der hunt bagrobn*, "It is here that the dog lies buried," or "This is the nub of the problem, the incalculable, unforeseeable factor." There is somewhere in existence a Yiddish translation of *Hamlet* in which

> To be, or not to be, that is the question,

turns into

> *Zayn oder nit zayn, do ligt der hunt bagrobn.*
> To be or not to be, here the dog lies buried.

To the same rendition belongs a memorable reply by Ophelia to Hamlet's *gey, in a kloyster gey,* "Get thee to a nunnery." Her words are, *mit eytses bin ikh shoyn farzorgt,* "I've got plenty of advice already."

5.

In the vocabulary of the funeral and the cemetery the Germanic and the Hebraic are equally represented both as to numbers and richness of association.

Beys-oylem, "house eternal," is the common Hebraic for cemetery; after it comes *beys-khayim,* "house of life," *beys-hakvores,* "house of burials." Death is also ennobled in the fine Germanic phrases *dos gute ort,* "the good place," and *dos reyne ort,* "the pure place." But there is only one word, and that Hebraic, for the tombstone, *matseyve,* and there is only one word, and that Hebraic too, for the funeral cortege, *levaye.*

On the other hand there is only one unidiomatic word for "death," the Germanic *der toyt. Der malkhamoves,* "angel of death," also, has no current Germanic equivalent. "Angel of death" has a picturesque quality in English; in Yiddish it is, from frequent use, almost emptied of coloration and even of superstition. This is one of the innumerable instances, common in all languages and faiths, of a religious term passing into folklore after losing—perhaps only apparently—its original creedal content. "For God's sake" usually has nothing to do with God. A Jew speaking of the *malkhamoves* is simply referring to death. At the same time the feeling of a presence is quite vivid, and the *malkhamoves* is frequently invoked, especially in imprecations like *khasene hobn zol er mit dem malkhamoves(es)tokhter,* "May he marry the daughter of the *malkhamoves.*"

Gan-eydn, "paradise," has no Germanic synonym, but the life beyond the grave is referred to in the mixed phrase, *di emese* (Heb) *velt,* "the true world," as opposed to this sublunar world of illusion and deceit. *Er iz shoyn oyf der emeser velt,* "He is already in the true world." Quite simply, "He's dead."

It should be mentioned that the funeral oration or eulogy has but one word, *hesped* (Heb), which by itself deserves extended treatment. For the *hesped* was a great form of art, such as Shakespeare makes it in *Julius Caesar,* an occasion not only for eulogy and ululation, but also for a display of sacred learning, pious sentiment, and ingenious moralizing. I say "was" a great art. It was, in times past, as now, part of the duties of a rabbi, and every rabbi had a style of his own. Funeral eulogies are still delivered in Yiddish, but they are just that, and not *hespeydim.* Something of the old-time style will, I hope, be glimpsed in the following classic example of the Yiddish *oraison funèbre.*

The occasion was the death of a Jew known in the community to have been lax in his observance of the ritual commandments, among them the donning of the *tales* every morning for the *shakhris.* To make direct mention of this deplorable blemish in the dead man's record would have been *khilel ha-mes* (Heb), "desecration of the dead"; to ignore it would have impugned the sincerity of the eulogist. The latter chose to convey the tactful rebuke in the form of a parable, which he based on the religious custom directing that a Jew be buried in his *tales*; and we must imagine the parable being recited in the traditional doleful singsong, a controlled keening modified by hortatory fervor.

> *Raboysay*, my friends [literally, "gentlemen"], the other night I was walking down a quiet street at midnight when a sound of weeping reached my ears! A weeping sound at midnight! It seized my heart like *kol-nidre*, and I stopped, asking myself, "What broken heart is this that pours itself out on the midnight air, and no one comes to comfort it? Who is it," I asked, "that cries in the night when all the world sleeps?" Then, approaching the spot whence the weeping proceeded without pause, I came across an open window. *Raboysay!* an open window in the dead of night, and a lonely weeping, a heartbreaking weeping as for the newly dead! "Merciful Father in heaven," I thought, "this is not a natural thing, that such a weeping sound arise and none should have responded." Therefore I knocked on the door, and *raboysay!* there was no answer. Then I said to myself, "I will enter this house, for is it not written thou shalt not stand idly by the blood of thy brother?" And I crawled in through the window, and as my eyes became accustomed to the darkness I wandered from room to room in search of the weeper. I called out, "Unhappy soul, I come to comfort you, where are you? I cannot bear any more the sound of your weeping." Then at last it seemed to me that the weeping came from a sideboard. *Raboysay*, from a sideboard! But how can it be? I therefore opened the top drawer, and there a *talesl*, a little *tales*, lay, weeping as if its heart would break. "*Talesl*," I said, "why do you weep so?" *Raboysay*, I said to the *talesl*, "Why do you weep so?" And the *talesl* answered, "How should I not weep? For my owner has gone on a long journey, and he has taken with him all the household, his wife and his chil-

dren and his servants, and me alone he has left behind. How then should I not weep?" And I answered, "*Talesl*, do not weep, for the day is coming when your *balebos* will go on a very long journey and he will leave behind his wife, and his children and his servants, and you alone he will take with him."

CHAPTER SEVEN

The Blind Side
of Yiddish

1.

The qualities of Yiddish that give it a peculiar relationship to the long national history (a sacred history even when "secular"), and fill it with hints of moral and scholarly preoccupation, were developed at the cost of a relationship to nature such as we find in no other language.

Let us consider two passages out of hundreds like them in English literature:

> And in the warm hedge grew lush eglantine,
> Green cowbind and the moonlight-coloured may,
> And cherry-blossoms, and white cups, whose wine
> Was the bright dew, yet drained not by the day;
> And wild roses, and ivy serpentine,
> With its dark buds and leaves, wandering astray. . . .
> —Shelley, *The Question*

> . . . Call the vales, and bid them hither cast
> Their bells, and flowerets of a thousand hues.
> Ye valleys low where the mild whispers use,
> Of shades and wanton winds, and gushing brooks,
> On whose fresh lap the swart star sparely looks,
> Throw hither all your quaint enameled eyes,
> That on the green turf suck the honeyed showers,
> And purple all the ground with vernal flowers,
> Bring the rathe primrose that forsaken dies,
> The tufted crow-toe, and pale jessamine,
> The white pink and the pansy freaked with jet,
> The glowing violet,
> The musk-rose and the well-attired woodbine,

With cowslips wan that hang the pensive head,
And every flower that sad embroidery wears. . . .

—Milton, *Lycidas*

Despite fairly wide reading in Yiddish poetry I do not
know of a single passage that resembles the two foregoing
pieces in their intimate delight, their fondling of details. I
will go further and submit that these pieces cannot be translated into Yiddish. It is not a question of vocabulary; most
of the names of the flowers and plants can be found in
Yiddish-English dictionaries, and a few of them are common
words: "cherry" is *karsh* or *vaynshl;* "rose" is *royz;* "jessamine"
(*i.e.,* jasmine) is *yasmin.* Some have Yiddish names that are
not widely current: for "primrose" we have *priml;* for "pansy"
khaneles eygele ("little Hannah's eyelet"!), and *shtifmuterl*
("little stepmother"!); for "violet" *fyalke, violet,* and *lila.*
"Ivy" has various names, of which *kleterbleter,* "climber-
leaves," seems the most acceptable.

Then there are the words that either do not appear in
the dictionaries or are defined rather than translated. "Cow-
slip" is simply *a min vilde englishe blum,* "a kind of wild
English flower," while "crow-toe," "cowbind," and "white
cup" are nowhere to be found.

Admittedly these last three English names are known to
few, other than specialists, and while even the most benighted
city dweller can identify on sight a rose and ivy, there will be
large numbers who cannot do so for a primrose or a sprig of
jasmine. But that is not the point. In English all names of
flowers except the most obscure have certain echoes which
they have not in Yiddish. But more particularly, if we look
at the adjectives in the two quoted passages, "lush," "moon-
light-colored," "serpentine," "swart," "quaint enameled,"
"rathe" (blooming early), "tufted," "forsaken," "freaked with
jet," "glowing," "well-attired," "wan," "pensive," we gather
from them, if not pictures, a happiness in individual features,

a discriminating and pleasurable dwelling on them, a thoughtful, smiling scrutiny, a mood that communicates itself irresistibly to the reader.

This anatomizing penetration into nature does not exist in either Yiddish poetry or prose; yet until a hundred years ago the major part of Yiddish-speaking Jewry lived in townlets and villages in close proximity to, though not in, nature. Mendele Moycher Sforim, Sholom Aleichem, and Isaac Leyb Peretz came from *shtetlekh*; so did Chayim Nachman Bialik and Zalmen Shneyer, more famous for their Hebrew than their Yiddish work, but in the latter not inferior to the classic trio. All wrote frequently of nature and their joy in it, but always in general terms and with a restricted vocabulary. Certain trees recur again and again: "pine," *sosne*; "oak," *demb*; "birch," *bereze*; "willow," *verbe*; "palm," *palme*; "cedar," *tsederboym*. Again, the Yiddish speaker will seldom know these objects on sight (and to some extent this is also true of English speakers), and only the words will be familiar to him. But the very words for "poplar," *topolye*; "fir," *yodle*; "aspen," *osine*; "alder," *olkhe*; "juniper," *yalovets* are unknown to the overwhelming majority of Yiddish readers. (The fruit trees are of course in a class apart; though as objects few of them can be identified by either Yiddish or English speakers when the fruit is not on them.)

By comparison with the loving surrender to nature, the scrutinizing contemplation of its details that we find in English and other Western literatures, the attitude of Yiddish literature is almost platonic. That the Jews were, though predominantly rural, more urban than the non-Jews does not explain the startling difference. We must seek its cause first in the life of the Jewish writers, then in that of the Jewish masses. Of the five masters mentioned above, each had received a thorough Jewish—that is, Hebrew—education, and in this way they were typical of almost all Yiddish writers. Of these it may be said even today that they can at least read

Hebrew, know their way about the Talmud and the Midrash, and not infrequently can *davn farn omed* (Heb), "lead the congregation in prayer," literally, "*davn* before the pulpit."

Mendele, Peretz, and others began their writing careers in Hebrew, which, with reservations, might be called the "Latin background of their Yiddish." Of Mendele it can be said he did for both Yiddish and modern Hebrew something of what Chaucer did for English. The analogy between Hebrew as related to Yiddish and Latin as related to English is in some respects overdone, in some inadequate. Milton wrote Latin prose and poetry almost as naturally as he wrote English, but it did not mean to him what Hebrew meant to Bialik; it was not his national and religious past, present and future, his special and incommunicable identity. On the other hand, when Milton wrote in Latin he was addressing the educated world of his time; Bialik in Hebrew was addressing the Jewish elite. But again, the proportion of Yiddish-speaking Jews (themselves two-thirds or more of the entire Jewish people) who read Hebrew with appreciation was far larger than the proportion of Englishmen who read Latin; and the proportion of firstrate English writers—from Shakespeare down—who could not read Latin is far higher than the proportion of firstrate Yiddish writers who could not read Hebrew. Actually this latter group is practically nonexistent; even a work-a-day Yiddish journalist has had a fair education in Hebrew, and can read it if not write it.

Now a sound Jewish education, which absorbed the juvenile and adolescent years of the Yiddish writers, precluded any great intimacy with nature, even at second hand. The nature passages in the Bible, Talmud, and other sacred writings were translated *viva voce* into Yiddish by the students, but the natural surroundings of the ancient Jewish world differed widely from those of the *shtetl*—this apart from the social environment, with its Kings, armies, Priests, and Prophets. The domestic animals were the same, but the "lion,"

leyb; "leopard," *lempert;* "ostrich," *shtroys;* "camel," *keml,*
were never seen in the *shtetl.* They were of course as un-
familiar to the non-Jew as to the Jew, but the *kheyder* boy
was always hearing about them; he lived with them for most
of his formative years and almost got the illusion that he had
frequently seen them, at least in childhood. Yet they were
pure fantasies.

But even such daily realities of nature as thrust themselves on the *kheyder* boy and the yeshiva student were sub-
dued by an ancient discipline. The normal hours of study were
such as would appall a modern pedagogue; for youngsters,
dawn to dusk every day, except Friday afternoon and Satur-
day, and much of the latter spent in the synagogue; for older
and more promising students, sometimes beginning at the age
of eleven or twelve, a daily regimen of fourteen to sixteen
hours. There was simply no time for nature, which was therefore left to untutored folk, who were partially divorced from
nature by other causes. Jewish farmers, huntsmen, trappers,
woodsmen, fishermen were rarities in the *shtetl.* If some of
them became experts in field and forest lore, with private
enthusiasms and enjoyments, their expertise was not held in
esteem. It was not a subject for conversation like the nature
world—a dream world—of the Bible. If anything, it was
regarded as evidence of a spiritually misspent life, the more
so as a Jewish farmer, huntsman, or trapper was usually
illiterate.

In Mendele's novel *shloyme reb khayems,* an adult de-
livers himself thus concerning the propensity of immature
kheyder boys to go larking in the woods:

> All right, nature-shmature—I suppose it's not too bad;
> though if you want to take a good look at it the whole
> thing is just foolishness; it's silly to waste a moment's
> time on it, because what good can you get out of it? Still,
> though a grown man with wife and children, and with a

living to make, has no business piddling around with
nature, you can forgive it in a youngster. Go ahead, go for
your walk in the woods at the back of the house, if you
must; go and commune with nature, as they say; lie down
in the grass if you must, and stare at the insects, the little
ladybugs [*moyshe rabeynu kielekh*, "Moses our Teacher's
little cows"], I think they call them, and look up at the
birds-shmirds. After all, a youngster is only a youngster,
you can't expect him to be serious all the time. But remember, young rascal, don't overdo it; bear in mind, little
rogue, that a boy of your age must be busy with the Talmud. There's the Tractate on Seeds, and the Tractate on
Contracts, and that's what counts.

Here Mendele is writing in his characteristic satirical
vein, but the picture is not a distorted one. Bialik, writing
in passionate protest, confirms the picture in his study of the
masmid, "dedicated Talmud student":

> A prisoner self-guarded, self-condemned
> Self-sacrificed to study of the Torah.

All that the *masmid* knows of nature he has gathered furtively, fearfully, as he hastens through the village before dawn
to his corner in the yeshiva, and retraces his steps homeward
after midnight; and all that it means to him is a poignant
awareness of beauty and sweetness which must be resisted as
the temptation of the Evil One.

Every writer on Jewish childhood in the old Yiddish-
speaking world testifies to the caution with which nature was
treated there, and to the limits set to the enjoyment of her.
She had her uses and her attractions, but she was primarily
for the *goyim*, who were given dominion in this world while
our portion was waiting for us—if we did not forfeit it by
this-worldly indulgence—in the world to come.

2.

The Christian world, theoretically committed to the same system of ultimate values as the Jewish, somehow reconciled it with pagan joys and licenses which were repugnant to the Jews. In A *Midsummer Night's Dream* there is a high-spirited, almost ecstatic exchange between the two lovers, Theseus, Duke of Athens, and Hippolyta, Queen of the Amazons, that will illustrate my point. The passage has nothing to do with the action of the play; it is merely one of those breathtaking outbursts of bravura that abound in Shakespeare:

> HIPPOLYTA: I was with Hercules and Cadmus once,
> When in a wood of Crete they bay'd the bear
> With hounds of Sparta: never did I hear
> Such gallant chiding for, besides the groves,
> The skies, the fountains, every region near
> Seemed all one mutual cry! I never heard
> So musical a discord, such sweet thunder.

> THESEUS: My hounds are bred out of the Spartan kind,
> So flew'd, so sanded; and their heads are hung
> With ears that sweep away the morning dew;
> Crook-kneed and dew-lapp'd like Thessalian bulls;
> Slow in pursuit, but match'd in mouth like bells.
> Each under each. A cry more tuneable
> Was never holla'd to, nor cheer'd with horn,
> In Crete, in Sparta, nor in Thessaly.

On the question of translating into Yiddish, it is again not a matter of vocabulary; even if an equivalent or near-equivalent could be found for every word and idiom, the passage would seem, in Yiddish, to belong to an unintelligible world; huge dogs barking madly and high-born human beings deliriously at one with the "music." That exhilaration, that tingling of the blood, that self-identification of the Duke and Queen with the wildly barking dogs would freeze the Jewish spectator into stupefaction. *Reboyne-shel-oylem, vos tut zikh do!* "Judge of the universe, what's going on here?"

3.

Christian dukes, queens, princes, princesses, and nobles of all degrees were familiar figures in medieval Yiddish literature, so were knights and minstrels, but the conception the Yiddish reader or listener had of the life these figures led was somewhat peculiar. It is quite certain that the first Yiddish writings were religious in character; only later did Jewish counterparts of the non-Jewish *Spielmänner*, "minstrels," arise, and if the attempts to give expression to religious feelings in Yiddish were reluctantly approved as an unavoidable concession, the spread of an idle and alien literature of romances was viewed with abhorrence by the leaders of the communities. So *treyf* (Heb), "unclean, forbidden," was this excursion into gentile worldliness that the very contact between worldly and sacred manuscripts was forbidden by a great religious leader of the thirteenth century: "You shall not cover a prayerbook with sheets on which romances are written." And yet these "goyish" tales, borrowed and adapted from the Arthurian and other cycles, were, in their transition into Yiddish, so denaturized that their authors would have disowned them with indignation.

One sample will suffice to convey the "conversion" undergone by the non-Jewish material before it was considered fit for Jewish ears and eyes. It is the famous *bovo bukh*, "Book of

Bovo," which was a favorite with ten or more generations of Jews, either as read or as passed on orally in the form of the *bovo mayse*, the Bovo story.

Its author, or adaptor, was the scholar Elijah Levitas, also known as *Eliyohu Bokher* (1468–1549), an authority on Hebrew, teacher and protégé of a cardinal, and a believer in harmless Yiddish entertainment for Jewesses—and Jews—unversed in Hebrew. The Bovo story is taken from the Italian version of an English original, *Bevys of Hampton*, which became *Buovo d'Antona*, and Levitas retold it in verse (using the Italian rhyme scheme known as *terza rima*) with sundry alterations which are of great significance in the history of Yiddish.

The English and Italian versions are a typical medieval fantasy of intrigues, adventures, wanderings, fights, coincidences, and deeds of derring-do. The hero is Bovo, a prince whose father was poisoned by his wife; the heroine is Druzana, a Flemish princess, whom Bovo finds, marries, loses, and finds again under circumstances which need not detain us here. The story remains substantially the same in outline, but the atmosphere undergoes a marvelous transformation.

To begin with, the Christian world vanishes into thin air. It is not exactly a Jewish world that takes its place, but it is one that cannot offend Jewish sensibilities. All mention of Jesus or the Virgin or the Christian saints is out. Here and there occur strange interpolations of a Jewish pietistic character. I reproduce the opening lines in exact transliteration, so that readers with a good Yiddish background may compare them with our modern usages:

> *Got den zel man eybig loben*
> *Un zayne vunder zol man kundn*
> *Ven er iz geakhpert un gehoben*
> *In frume layten mundn;*
> *Er iz geveltig unten un oben*

Zayn lob iz nit tsu enden:
Keyn mensh der es kan fulenden
Ven es hot nokh drum nokh enden.
Let God be ever praised
And let His wonders be proclaimed
When He is revered and exalted
In the mouths of pious people.
He is sovereign below and above.
His praise cannot be fathomed
No man can ever complete it
For it has neither beginning nor end.

Reflecting on the wicked queen who poisoned her husband, the Yiddish narrator interpolates a *magidic* (preacher's) lament: *Deriber libe hern, git a kuk vos far an umglik es kumt fun shlekhte freyen.* . . . "Dear men, just take a look at the misfortunes that can come from wicked women; see what King Solomon says, all his life he looked for a good woman and could not find one. . . ."

To be sure, a Christian commentator could have quoted the Old Testament, but he could hardly have composed the words of alarm with which Druzana greets her husband when he returns to her, tattered and disfigured, after a long absence:

Dos beyz gezikht als glaykhn zol
Den eydeln hern dem zaynem?
Oy vol, hamavdl beyn koydesh lekhol
Tsvishn zaynem libn ponim un daynem. . . .
Is this horrid countenance supposed to be the same
As that of my noble lord?
Ah woe, "He that divideth the sacred from the profane,"
(Let Him divide) your face from his. . . .

The quotation from the Sabbath valedictory *havdole* on the lips of a Christian princess does not seem to have disturbed the listeners or readers, and more startling displacements of milieu were to follow. When Druzana brings to her husband the little princes he had begotten on her before the separation, she laments that they have not been circumcised, whereupon her father exclaims

> . . . *nit zorgen*
> A *hipshe bris-mile vel ikh makhn morgen*
> . . . do not worry
> We shall have a fine circumcision ceremony tomorrow.

The last and most bewildering transformation comes with the choral close:

> *Un zol got unz derleyzn fun unzeren payn*
> *Un zol unz di gnad gebn,*
> *Dos mir ale muzn zoykhe zayn*
> *Meshiekhs tsayt tsu derlebn;*
> *Der zol unz firen in Yerushalayim hinayn*
> *Oder irgents in ayn shtetl darneyben,*
> *Un zol unz dos beys-hamikdosh vider boyen*
> *Vekeyn yehi rotsoyn, omeyn troyen.*
> So may God redeem us from our suffering
> And grant us the grace
> That we may all be privileged
> To see the Messiah in our lifetime;
> And he will lead us into Jerusalem
> Or [at least] into a nearby village,
> And will rebuild the Temple for us,
> So be it God's will, amen and in faithfulness.

Standing alone, this closing passage might have been taken by the listening Jews for an apologetic and irrelevant aside, or even an exorcism and repudiation, but after Druzana's excursion into the *havdole,* after her father's happy promise of a *bris-mile,* after the suppression of Christianity and Christian saints and un-kosher banquets, it rings like a deliberate transposition; it is an expression, apparently, of the hopes and dreams of the heroes and heroines themselves. The transformation was purposive, and the listeners knew quite well that this was the Christian world, remote from, hostile to their own world, that was originally portrayed. And a very attractive world, too, it was made to seem, whence, in good part, the scandal of the teachers and rabbis, who saw in this mixture of dishonesty and self-deception a great danger to the people.

CHAPTER EIGHT

The Shtetl and Slavic

1.

Shtetl, "townlet, village," the diminutive of *shtot*, has entered the English language as a sociological term. By association it has come to mean the Jewish townlets of eastern Europe that constituted a special segment of Jewish life until it was wiped out by the twin *malakhey-khabole* (Heb), "angels of destruction," nazism and communism. The instrument of the first was mass murder, the bullet, and the gas chamber; that of the second was and is spiritual and cultural asphyxiation. That the *shtetl* as a form of life was bound to pass away in time is undeniable, but that its positive values could have endured in new forms if it had been permitted to fade out peacefully is equally undeniable. In any case, the Communist line "It was bound to die anyhow" carries as much weight as "He wasn't going to live forever anyhow."

As taken over by English, *shtetl* lacks its Yiddish emotional content. The powerful nostalgic overtone is missing. From the *shtetl* came the grandfathers and grandmothers of some millions of American and British citizens, to mention but two sections of the Diaspora. These grandchildren, if some flavor of Yiddish still clings to them, identify *shtetl* with their own childhood memories of a beloved forebear; and because the grandparent always spoke of the *shtetl* sentimentally—one nearly always does about one's earliest years—the grandchild took over a special feeling for a world he knew only by hearsay. This feeling has been reinforced by a deep reaction to the overwhelming tragedy of "the six million."

If we think of the larger Yiddish-speaking segment of the Jewish civilization, the *shtetl* must be seen as its foundation and most characteristic expression. Paradoxically, it was the

large centers, cities like Warsaw, Odessa, Kiev, that witnessed
first the weakening of Jewish life; the strongest and most
authentic center was the *shtetl,* where for hundreds of years
Jewish, Yiddish-rooted life withstood the pressures of an uncomprehending environment, accommodating itself to physical and economic factors but retaining intact its cultural and
spiritual essence. In America it is the large Jewish centers—
New York, Los Angeles, Philadelphia—that by their very
bulk offer the strongest resistance to assimilation, while the
smallest communities offer the least resistance. Paradoxically
again, *shtetl* evokes the Slavic Jewish world, but the word is
itself Germanic.

The *shtetl* is remembered by the older generation with
affection and tenderness because it represents a marvelous
and vanished time of secure personality, a time when there
was no sickly problem of identity. But we must not romanti-
cize the *shtetl;* we must not conjure up populations of scholarly and saintly tailors, shoemakers, peddlers, butchers,
coopers, tinsmiths, shopkeepers, living an otherworldly life.
There was poverty, snobbery, exploitation, and sharp social
division; there was squalor and injustice; and for the large
majority the cultivation of spiritual enjoyment was limited
and intermittent. But the wonder of it is that such enjoyment did exist, and in a degree unknown to the surrounding
world; and with it existed an awareness seldom encountered
elsewhere that there was a higher life to which even ordinary
folk could aspire.

The richness of *shtetl* life helps to explain why so large
a proportion of gifted writers and thinkers came from places
hard to find on the maps and now remembered only for their
famous sons. I do not know of a study of this subject, but it
is hardly to be doubted that the *shtetl* showed a much larger
per capita yield of creative figures than the Jewish urban
population.

2.

The tug of nature, the lure of the earthy, was felt by the *shtetl* Jew in a limited measure, with corresponding additions to the language. Slavic and German are both represented in the Yiddish nature vocabulary, but the religious terminology was practically set by the time the Jews moved eastward into Slavic territory. Whatever changes were needed came rarely by Slavic additions, nearly always by internal adaptations of Germanic Yiddish. Slavic words did become remarkably homey and intimate; one may even say that of the Slavic words in Yiddish a far larger proportion than of the Germanic became "folk," with a peculiar pungency all their own. This makes all the more noteworthy the resistance to Slavic in the area of religion and ritual.

However, there was some penetration. *Praven* we have already met as the perfect synonym for *oprikhtn,* and used as frequently. In their respective origins these words point back to the same root idea, that of rightness, authenticity (*cf.* the German *richtig,* the Russian *pravda*). *Pareve* has also been noted in its religious and secular senses. *Koyletch,* we have seen, is synonymous with *khale,* but it has not the same aroma of festivity. The *yarmulke,* "skull cap," worn by males in the absence of any other head-covering, may be called a ritualistic object; however, it was not always and everywhere considered a religious obligation never to leave the head uncovered—a fact that will come as a surprise to large numbers of modern pietists for whom the skull cap has become a sort of religious oriflamme. *Spodik,* the high fur hat which the Jews retained long after their Christian neighbors had discarded it, has a vaguely religious—more properly Jewish—connotation; its special value seems to lie in a useful idiom, *dreyen,* "turning," or *duln*, "pestering," *a spodik*, which describes wearisome talk round some particular subject: *er hot mir gedult a spodik mekoyekh* (Heb) *zayn eydems dire* (Heb), "He pestered me [at much length] about his son-in-law's apartment." (We had a lovely word for it in northern England, particularly Lancashire: to "meither"; "stop meithering me.")

Peripheral also to the religious life is the *kantshik*, the three-thong whip, or "cat-o'-three-tails," which was standard equipment for every *rebe* (in the sense of keeper of a *kheyder*). A *rebe* without a *kantshik* was as unthinkable as one without a beard. Any old-world Jew on the analyst's couch would always respond to *"kantshik"* with *"rebe"* or *"kheyder."*

Vaguely religious again, like *spodik*, is *kapote*, "gaberdine," and like it, taken over as article of attire from the surrounding gentiles, long surviving their use of it. In some areas the *kapote* was the standard outer garment of the religious Jew. The association was very powerful, and it may be said with only reasonable exaggeration that such Jews thought of Moses as descending from Sinai in *kapote* and *yarmulke* and of Abraham similarly attired when he greeted the three angels or held the knife above his trussed-up son at the time of the aborted sacrifice. Fifty or a hundred years ago the relinquishment of the *kapote* in favor of a modern, shortened coat was in such circles considered equivalent to apostasy, and the parents of the sartorial insurgent—who would in fact usually be a religious insurgent—would regard him as one dead. A particularly implacable father might even say, *zol im dos lebn farkirtst vern*, "May his life be shortened" (like his coat).

The irreligious certainly despised the *kapote* as the symbol of orthodoxy. An anti-Zionist jingle of half a century ago ran:

> *Ver vet hobn dort di deye?*
> *di kapote un di peye* (Heb)
> *un di shkotsim, di arabes*

114

veln muzn hitn shabes.
Who will have the say there [in the Jewish state]?
The *kapote* and the earlock;
And the gentile boys, the Arabs,
Will have to observe the Sabbath.

Kapote appears in a locution that makes fun of the damage an enemy claims to have inflicted on you: *er hot mir avekgekoylet di kapote,* "He's [just] slaughtered my *kapote.*" Akin to this is the use of *di bobes yerushe* (Heb.), "grandmother's legacy": *vos hostu (host du) tsu derleygn, der bobes yerushe?* "What have you to lose, your grandmother's legacy?" Also, *oy vey, a shif mit zoyermilkh iz mir untergegangen,* "Woe and alas, my shipload of soured milk has gone down," and again: *strashe* (Slv) *nisht di gendz,* "Don't threaten the geese." This last is in response to an "or else!" ultimatum. In Israel the expression has been taken over by literal translation into pure Hebrew, *al tafkhid et ha-avazim,* and sounds as outlandish (except to those who know Yiddish) as it does in the English above.

The penetration of Slavic-Yiddish words into the heart of the language, their at-homeness, as of immemorial adoption, does not depend on any region; the Polish, the Ukrainian, the Russian have all been absorbed with the same transmuting effect, but it must be remembered that nearly all the words have cognate forms in the three languages, as well as in languages like Czech and Bulgarian. That perfection of assimilation that was achieved by Germanic words in the religious field, investing them with an authenticity suggesting an ancient, indigenous origin, has been achieved by Slavic words in the secular vocabulary.

Such words are *kretchme*, "inn"; *kleyt*, "shop"; *ployt*, "fence"; *klyamke*, "latch"; *kolner*, "collar"; *kapelyush*, "derby [man's hat]"; *torbe*, "sack"; *pushke*, "box."

The "in" character of some of the words seems reasonable

enough, *e.g.*, *kretchme* and *kleyt.* Jews were not frequenters of inns, but they were innkeepers and shopkeepers in a much higher ratio than their neighbors. The *kretchme* and the *kleyt* were among the liveliest places in the *shtetl.* They were also, especially the former, the natural meeting ground of the Jew and Christian, and they had much to do with fashioning the relations between them. Except for the traveling, pack-carrying salesmen, the innkeepers and shopkeepers were best placed to learn something of the local non-Yiddish language, and to get to know the good and bad in the characters of their neighbors. On the Jewish side there was a mixture of liking, even affection, fear, and contempt; on the peasant side liking, admiration, even awe, suspicion, and envy. The *kretchme* in particular was the focus of these emotions; few of its frequenters were Jews, and the gap between the frequenters and the owner was often a very wide one, for Jewish innkeepers with a good Jewish education were not a rarity.

One of the remarkable features of the nostalgic feeling of aging Jews for the *shtetl*—I am speaking of those Jews who knew it in their early years—is the warmth with which the peasant is remembered; pogroms notwithstanding, he is seen across the years as a thoroughly likable if often irresponsible child of nature. Hence the ambivalence of the word *goy* (Heb), "gentile" (literally, "nation"). As applied to a Jew it is an insult, denoting illiteracy and/or irreligiosity; applied to a gentile, it is neutral. One can therefore say, *a fayner goy,* meaning more or less "a decent person, non-Jewish," or *a kluger,* " a clever," *goy,* without thereby implying that *goyim* as a whole are the opposite.

The *torbe* usually meant the beggar's sack: it was the symbol of the lowest economic and social level to which a Jew could sink, and that level was never underpopulated. Mendele Moycher Sforim, gives us, in *Fishke the Lame,* an appalling panorama of the beggar-world of east European Jewry a little over a hundred years ago and of its inexhaustible varieties of types: the foot-beggar, the beggar in a cart, the cripple beggar, the scholar beggar, the pious beggar, the singing beggar, the acrobat beggar, the beggar with wife and children, etc. Mendele himself, in his boyhood, was shanghaied by a master-beggar, who exhibited him in synagogues as an *ilui* (Heb), "scholar-prodigy." *Arumgeyn mit der torbe,* "to go around with the *torbe,*" was a phrase often used by Zionist speakers and writers to characterize the petitionary wanderings of the Jewish people in search of lands that would give them shelter.

The *pushke* was related to the *torbe,* for though *pushke* means any kind of small box, it was used predominantly of the charity- or collection-box. Jews have always been making collections, to ransom slaves, marry off orphan girls, feed and clothe widows, provide matzos for the poor on Passover, re-settle refugees, support yeshivas, free imprisoned rabbis, buy off tyrants—the list is endless. To be dunned for contributions in and out of season has become a psychological necessity for the Jewish people; they grumble under pressure in a ritualistic way, to make it harder for the collector, but they would set up a howl if left alone. Chaim Weizmann, first President of the State of Israel, and before that the greatest collector of funds the Jewish people had ever known (his record has since been completely eclipsed), used to say," More than the farmer needs the milk, the cow needs to be milked." This is particularly true of Jewish cows.

Fifty years ago there used to be in nearly every pious Jewish home a *pushke* of *Reb Meir bal-hanes* (Heb), "Reb Meir the miracle-man," for the maintenance of old people who had gone to spend their last days in the Holy Land, there to study the holy books, weep for the Destruction, and pray for the Restoration. There was also an ancient Jewish community, which naturally did not consist entirely of the aged, but was largely dedicated to the same pursuits as the newcomers. Most of them lived on the *khaluke* (Heb),

"charity fund" (literally, "distribution"), which through the
Meir bal-hanes pushkes and wandering solicitors had for centuries been drawing on the Jewish communities throughout
the world. (Something in this is reminiscent of the collections
Paul and others set up for "the saints" in Jerusalem.) In the
youth of the Zionist movement, when dreams were big and
financial operations on a *shtetl* scale, another kind of *pushke*
was introduced into Jewish homes, not necessarily pious ones,
the blue and white coin box of the Jewish National Fund, the
Zionist land-buying agency. Some ultrapious Jews were infuriated, in part by the plagiarism, in part by the desecration
of a symbol, but most of all by the diversion of funds from
a sacred purpose to the godless secularists who were setting
up colonies and speaking Hebrew as if it were an ordinary
language. I remember out of my Manchester days having the
door slammed in my face by a furious, white-bearded patriarch
who, seeing the accursed blue and white box in my hand, did
not wait for the spiel, but hissed, *"meshumed, avek fun mayn
tir!"*, "Apostate, begone from my door!", and spat at my feet.

Since that time many *pushkes* of many colors, representing a huge variety of causes, have become familiar to the Jewish and general public; but sixty years ago the Slavic word
pushke would evoke in the Jewish mind the blessed memory
of Meir, the wonder-working rabbi of second-century Palestine,
or the Assyrian-bearded features of the Zionist leader Theodor Herzl.

3.

The least translatable Yiddish Slavisms are the monosyllables *nu* and *zhe*, both of which are almost as flexible and
multipurposed in Slavic as in Yiddish. *Nu* is so widely known
among those who have a minimum of Yiddish as well as in a

considerable periphery beyond them, that I will dispose of it briefly. Its numerous shadings are partially echoed in the uses of "well," used as interjection: the interrogatory "well?", the exclamatory "well well!", the expostulatory, the placatory, the procrastinatory—each delivered with the appropriate inflection and the appropriate brevity or prolongation. But the throaty, impatient, drawn-out *nu-u-u!*, "for Pete's sake, get moving!", the staccato ironically commiserating *nu-nu*, "Don't ask, that's all he needed," and others cannot be conveyed by "well," however manipulated.

Zhe is neither a word in its own right nor a suffix; it is a sort of floating particle. It cannot stand alone and it cannot begin or end a sentence; it affects not so much the word it is attached to as the spirit of the whole phrase or sentence, and almost everywhere it plays the same role in Yiddish as in Russian and Ukrainian.

Ven vet ir kumen?, "When will you come?", is a simple question; *ven zhe vet ir kumen?* is best rendered in Yiddishized English, "So when already will you come?" The Russians entered the Second World War with the impatient cry *kogda zhe budet vtoroy*, "So when will there be a second [front]?"

Zhe can be tacked on to a word to produce a certain type of locution. *Vos vilstu (vilst du)?*, "What do you want?", is again a simple question; *vozhe (vos zhe) vilstu?*, "So what then, finally, do you want?", presupposes an argument or disagreement, a precedent discussion of terms, a dissatisfied claimant. *Farvozhe (farvos zhe) iz er broygez* (Heb)?, "So why then is he angry, sore?", implies that the subject of the sentence seems to be acting unreasonably.

These are the easier examples. It is more difficult to transmit the difference between *zay gezunt*, "Goodbye, be well," and *zayzhe mir gezunt*. One can only say that the latter presupposes a conversation that is being terminated not discourteously but onesidedly with brevity and decisiveness. It can have the slightly hurried effect of, "Well, be seeing you," or "Is that so? Well, good luck," or "Be that as it may, so long."

When attached to the imperative form of the verb, *zhe* imparts to it an element of cajolery and familiarity, and, as in the above instances, implies a preceding interchange. *Zaytzhe* (pronounced *zaytshe*) *moykhl* (Heb) *un lozt mikh adurkhgeyn* would be approximately "So please be so kind as to let me pass through." The sentence is good-humored and "joshing"; *moykhl*, literally, "pardon, forgiveness," is usually a grave word.

Nu and *zhe* are of the very stuff of Yiddish, especially in conversation. Less frequent, but of considerable importance, is the suffix *nik*, again taken over with practically no change in function. It is a personifying suffix, already known from "sputnik." In Russian *put* is "path, road"; the *s* represents a preposition meaning "with, along of"; thence "sputnik" is something like "along the roader," *i.e.*, "companion, satellite, fellow-traveler" (no necessary Communist connotation).

In Yiddish *nik* is attached to the words for a large and interesting variety of objects and practices.

The Hebrew letters *lamed vov* have the numerical value of thirty-six, the number of the humble and anonymous saints (they are a constantly renewed corps, like the French Academy) in whose virtue (in both senses) the world is suffered to survive. A *lamedvovnik* is one of them. *Kloyz*, "chapel," forms *kloyznik*, a man who passes his days, and perhaps nights, too, in the *kloyz*, the synagogue or study house, to the neglect of his earthly interests; it is a somewhat derogatory term. *Yishev* means, among other things, "settlement"; before the founding of the State of Israel the Jewish community in Palestine was called the *yishev (yishuv)*, from which comes *yishuvnik*, which is worth a separate paragraph.

Round every *shtetl*, at distances varying from twenty to forty miles, lived one, two, or a tiny handful of Jews and their families, often bailiffs to some wealthy landowner, lessees of a mill or an inn. Cut off from their own kind, unassimilated to their primitive neighbors, they lived lonely and frustrated lives, clinging with all their strength to their Jewish heritage. They came into the *shtetl*, their local metropolis, twice a year, for the High Holidays and the Passover, and were received with special consideration by the Jewish villagers, who pitied their condition but could not help looking down on their growing alienation from the Jewish way of life. The particular tragedy of the *yishuvnik* was his children, whose companions were mostly the unlettered children of the peasants. Nearly every *yishuvnik* would have a teacher, usually a yeshiva *bokher*, for his boys, but holding on to one was not easy; for the yeshiva *bokher*, too, no matter how well he was treated, found the environment unbearable, and he had little joy of his charges, who preferred running wild in the woods to sitting over *khumesh* and Rashi. It was a tremendous event in the *yishuvnik* family when a boy, becoming bar mitzvah, was actually able to say the appropriate prayers and read the prophetic passage attached to the week's *sedre*. The occasion was celebrated in the *shtetl*, the whole family attending, of course, and relatives called in from the entire region. If the Jewish upbringing of the boy was a problem, and their future Jewishly bleak, the daughters were in no better situation, and the mother condemned to be a *yishuvnik's* wife would eat her heart out until she could send them to safe lodgment with some relatives or friends in the *shtetl*. Shmarya Levin has rightly protested that the plight of the *yishuvnik* has seldom been sympathetically understood. The word itself was condescending, even offensive: it denoted the "hick"; thus used, it contained much injustice, for the spiritual sufferings of the *yishuvnik* were a mirror of the struggles of his people.

Loshnore (Heb) (written *loshn-hore*), "wicked tongue," becomes *loshnorenik*, one given to indulgence in it. *Oylem-*

haze (Heb), "this world" as contrasted with the better world of the hereafter, becomes *oylem-hazenik,* one who "takes the cash and lets the credit go," and makes the most of the good things here below; usually it means fondness for food and other physical pleasures, like comfortable surroundings and showy appurtenances; but it can also mean the pursuit of egotistical satisfactions. *Oylem-habe* (Heb), "the world to come," the offset to *oylem-haze,* is both the place and the condition of paradise, dedicated to the pursuit of spiritual and blameless happiness consisting of everlasting study of the Torah under the guidance of God as professor and Moses as assistant professor. Oddly enough, there is no corresponding personification, *oylem-habenik,* to set opposite *oylem-hazenik,* as describing one who cultivates the hope of admission to *ganeydn* by anticipating as far as he can its code of conduct.

The outstanding application of *nik* is in *nudnik,* from *nudyen,* "to bore." Usage has given *nudnik* a quality that lifts it above the simple bore; a *nudnik* is a devotee of boredom, often bringing to its practice not only a native talent and commitment, but a considerable body of wearisome information on a very large number of subjects.

Other, less morbid *nik* words are *khabarnik,* "bribe taker," from *khabar* (Slv), the Hebrew *shoykhed,* the perfect synonym for *khabar,* having refused to mate with *nik; lehakhesnik,* "one who does things just to be contrary, or defiant, or spiteful," from the Hebrew *lehakhis,* "to anger"; *rekhilesnik,* "habitual slander-carrier," from *rekhiles* (Heb), "slander, malicious gossip"; and finally, *shvartsmeyenik,* "member of the Black Hundreds," the ill-famed Russian reactionary, pogromist gangs of Czarist days. *Shvartsmeyenik* outdoes the phrase *raboysay lomir bentshn,* which draws on three languages for as many words in perfect Yiddish, by condensing three languages into one word: *shvarts,* Germanic, *meye,* Hebraic, *nik,* Slavic.

Nik could be used to great advantage in English. Thus far

122

we have "beatnik" and "peacenik," but "tomorrownik," or, more colorful, "manyananik," "beernik," companion to "wino," "third-worldnik," indicate some of the possibilities.

4.

Two short, frequently occurring words that Yiddish has thoroughly assimilated with some changes are *ot* and *khotsh*. *Ot* has in one of its chief usages the meaning of *voila!* Of a man who arrives while you are waiting for him, of a thing that turns up somewhat unexpectedly during a search for it, you say *ot iz er, ot iz es*. Sometimes *ot* is equivalent to a sarcastic "right away," meaning "like hell I will," but not quite as rude, in response to a presumptuous request. It again means "right away," but literally and simply, in connection with an impending event. Seeing someone staggering under a heavy load, you might exclaim in alarm, *ot* (or *ot ot*) *falt er um*, "He'll collapse any moment."

Khotsh (or *khotshe*) has two main meanings so wide apart that it is difficult to understand how they came to house in the same word. One is "although," as in *zey hobn khasene gehat khotsh zey hobn zikh faynt gehat*, "They got married though they disliked each other." The other meaning of *khotsh*, "even, at least, if only," is brought out in Peretz's *Song of the Three Seamstresses*, in which one old maid weeps for a husband and is ready to put something in the *pushke* of Reb Meir bal-hanes in the hope that he will move heaven (and earth) to get her someone, *an almen* (Heb) *khotsh, an altn yid, mit kinderlekh a shok*, "if it's only a widower, an old man, with a horde of little children" (literally, "three score").

Abi is another word with a split personality, the use of which is difficult to learn. In one context it stands for "if only, as long as"; in a folksong a girl declares she is ready to

123

follow her loved one into strange lands, to wash laundry and scrub floors, *abi mit dir tsuzamen zayn,* "if only I can be together with you"; and in a popular locution, *abi gezunt,* "if only healthy, as long as one has one's health," meaning, "nothing else matters." But in another context *abi* can only be rendered by a whole explanatory phrase. If someone made a solemn promise to perform a service for you, knowing all the time he could not—for instance, using his nonexistent influence on your behalf—you would exclaim indignantly, after he had failed to deliver, *abi er hot mir tsugezogt,* something like "and here he was, the faker, making those promises."

5.

I have referred to the peculiar pungency of many Yiddish words of Slavic origin. Two of the most powerful are *paskudnyak* and *parekh,* both terms of abuse. In all languages contumelious words are used with a certain degree of carelessness, no doubt because of the attendant emotions, which are not favorable to fine semantic discriminations; "slob" and "son of a bitch," for instance, are often used as if they were closely akin, whereas there is a world of difference between them. In Yiddish the tendency to use *parekh* and *paskudnyak* interchangeably overlooks important distinctions which the language of insult cannot afford to lose.

Paskudnyak is the personalized form of *paskudne,* "nasty," which is only moderately offensive: *a paskudne yid* is not much worse than "an unpleasant fellow"; *dos vaser hot a paskudnem tam* (Heb), "The water has an unpleasant taste"; *es iz mir paskudne oyfn hartsn,*" is not as tragic as "I am sick at heart," nor as colloquial as "I'm feeling lousy," but is somewhere between the two.

A *paskudnik,* too, dismisses a man as "unsavory, displeasing," but when we call a man a *paskudnyak* the quality of nastiness is suddenly enriched into loathsomeness and repulsiveness. "Son-of-a-bitch," though coarser, is much milder than *paskudnyak*; it is not as organic and penetrative; it leaves loopholes of possible redemption not to be found in *paskudnyak*. Above all, "son-of-a-bitch" can be used humorously, even admiringly and affectionately (as with "you old") which *paskudnyak* never can; neither, for that matter, can *parekh*.

Parekh is in a way more offensive than *paskudnyak*, but lacks its reprobacy. It is meaner, but not as malevolent. A *paskudnyak* will go out of his way to do you a bad turn; a *parekh* will, on the whole, confine himself to refusals that are repugnant to elementary decency. A *paskudnyak* is hateful, a *parekh* is disgusting; the *paskudnyak* moves you to rage, the *parekh* to nausea. The difference is partly indicated by the literal meaning of *parekh*, "a purulent kind of mange of the scalp."

A folktale illustrates the special flavor of *parekh*: A young Jew came to a dignified old rabbi and asked him, in a mock respectful tone of voice, "Rabbi, if one eats pork on *yom kiper* is it obligatory to wash the hands first?" The rabbi smiled benevolently and answered, "Bless you my son, with a triple blessing; how thoughtful, how kindly of you to come to me with so complicated and important a ritualistic question. It brings joy into the house to entertain you. Be seated, and I will answer you in the detail your *shayle* merits." Completely taken aback, the young man, who had with inward glee anticipated an exhibition of speechless rage, sat down, and asked what the rabbi could possibly mean.

"Imagine," said the rabbi, "nine Jews waiting at twilight for a tenth to turn up, so that they can *davn betsiber* (Heb) [pray as a congregation]. The minutes pass, the twilight draws on, soon it will be too late to enjoy a fullscale service of the combined *minkhe-mayriv* [afternoon and evening prayer]. Then suddenly at the last moment, a Jew appears as if from nowhere! Joy! The synagogue lights up, the prayers are begun with gusto. Now, isn't that Jew worth a blessing?

"But now imagine a whole congregation of Jews at *nile* [the closing prayer of *yom kiper*], when the gates of heaven are about to close and a last moment of supplication remains, capable, perhaps, of averting a stern decree in heaven. It has been a long, hot day; the synagogue is jammed below, in the men's section, and above in the women's section; bodies are faint, hearts are overflowing with yearning and hope—and just then the curtain of the Ark catches fire from one of the *yom kiper* candles! Help! No one dares put a hand to the fire, no one wants to leave the synagogue at such a fateful moment. And then, the miracle! The *shabes-goy* rushes in and puts out the flames. Should not this goy be blessed from the bottom of the heart?

"Finally, young man, a third incident, as miraculous as the second, but in quite different circumstances. In a poor Jewish home the only breadwinner is the oldest son, and he comes of military age. The father is a sick man, but the authorities are merciless. The czar needs soldiers. And what is the miracle? When the boy presents himself at the *priziv* [(Slv), 'recruitment office'], it is discovered that he has a tremendous *parekh* on his head, and he is sent home. Should not all the blessings of heaven and earth be called down on that *parekh*?

"And now see what has happened to me today. I receive an unexpected call from a young man *vos iz i a yid, i a goy, un a parekh dertsu*, who is both a Jew and a *goy* and a *parekh* on top of it. Can I do less than bless you with a triple blessing?"

6.

Words with a special "bite" are *khapn*, "to snatch," *khaplap*, "helter-skelter," and *trask*, "crash." *Khapn a dreml,*

Träumle
short dream

träumeln

"to snatch a doze," is perfectly echoed in "catch forty winks," and *drimlen*, "to doze," has no Germanic or Hebraic equivalent; *khapn a metsiye* (Heb), "to find (unexpectedly) a bargain" (*metsiye* is related to the Hebrew—not Yiddish—verb for "find"). Things are done *khaplap* when there is systemless haste, whence a proverb, *fun khaplap tsebrekht men dem kop*, "With *khaplap* one breaks one's head." We have seen *tsekhapn* in *me hot es tsekhapt vi matse-vaser*, "It was snapped up like hot cakes."

Trask is literal and figurative. *Er hot gegebn a trask mit der tir*, "He banged the door to," literally, "He gave a crash with the door"; *er lebt mit trask*, "He lives in 'bang-up' style." We also have the verb form *er trasket mitn (mit dem) gelt*, "He flings his money around."

A restful word is *pavole*, "slowly," which implies deliberate leisureliness, with a touch of humor, as well as simple absence of speed: *alts geyt tsu bay im pavole*, "He does everything with deliberation." The opposite of *pavole* is *gikh*, "rapid, hasty," and the sense of hurry is reinforced by repetition, *gikh-gikh*. *Pavole* and *gikh* are pleasantly juxtaposed in a folk jingle about the *shviger*, the "mother-in-law" whom there's no satisfying:

> *Gey ikh gikh, tserays ikh di shikh,*
> *gey ikh pavole, zogt zie ikh krich.*
> If I walk fast, I'm tearing my shoes,
> If I walk slowly, she says I'm crawling.

Pamelekh is a near-synonym for *pavole*, particularly in its suggestion of deliberateness; it is somewhat more self-conscious than *pavole*: *pamelekh vi ir geyt*, "Slowly, how you walk," translates as "Watch your step."

Blondzhen, "to wander blindly, be astray," has somehow caught the fancy of the folk, and is among the words that hang on longest when Yiddish is being forgotten, perhaps because of the musical sound. With its Germanic prefix, *farblondzhen,* "to stray off the track, to lose one's bearings," applies equally to someone taking a walk in the woods, to Dante's "in the middle of the road of our life," and to someone blundering into the wrong bedroom.

Take, "really, honestly," has established itself in a variety of usages. Alone, it is mostly a question mark, implying surprise, and its disparaging extreme, incredulity. When gentle, abused, uncomplaining Bontshe, in Peretz's famous story, is received in heaven with all the *éclat* due a saint despised on earth, and is told that whatever his eye sees of gorgeous jewels and glittering gold is his for the asking, he asks naïvely *take?* "Do you mean it?" As some will remember, he settles, to the embarrassment of the heavenly hosts and the derision of the *advocatus diaboli,* for the luxury of a roll and butter, which he had never tasted before. Occurring in a sentence that contains an unexpected qualification, *take* has the shaded meaning of "it is true that," or "to be sure": *er iz take a groyser lamdn ober nisht keyn ibriker khokhem,* "He is, to be sure, a great scholar, but not an overly intelligent man." *Take* becomes "in fact" in the following: *ikh hob aykh take gezen dort,* "In fact I saw you there."

7.

It is one of the oddities of Yiddish that wherever there are synonyms, or closely related words, of both Germanic and Slavic origin, it is the latter that seem nearer the folk, though the Germanic words must be presumed to be older. *Ferd,* "horse," is a colorless word; figuratively it has an important pejorative use, like "ass" in English, but with its own shading. If a man is a *ferd,* his lack of intelligence inclines toward doltishness and imperceptiveness. Now the Slavic *shkape* and

klyatche, both "mare," and *loshik*, "colt," are colorful of themselves; they are suggestive of the *shtetl*, while *ferd*, incompre-
hensibly, is not. *Shkape* and *loshik* also have their figurative
uses: *alte shkape*, "old mare," as applied to a woman, is vulgar
and offensive (there is no reason why *klyatche* cannot be used
here, but it just isn't): *loshik* as applied to a lively boy is pretty
much the English figurative "colt."

The Germanic *moyl*, "mouth," is colorless, like *ferd*; the
Slavic *pisk*, "jaw," is exactly like the English "jaw," harmless
when used of animals, nasty when used of a person. *Zi hot
geefnt a pisk*, "She opened up her jaw," would be used of a
scold in action; *moyl* is also correct in such a sentence, but
weaker.

The Slavic *khmare*, "cloud," and *tuman*, "mist," are
stronger than the corresponding Germanic *volkn* and *nepl*,
when used meteorologically; but for mistiness of ideas the adjective *nepeldik* alone is correct. The Germanic *regn* is the
only word for "rain," with *shlaksregn* for "downpour" or
"cloudburst"; neither, however, has the force of the Slavic
verb *plyukhen* (used in the impersonal form *es plyukhet*, "it's
pouring"), "to rain cats and dogs." The Germanic *shturm*,
"storm," is, like the English, both literal and figurative, but
the far more powerful Slavic *zaverukhe*, "blizzard" (which
has a only feeble echo in the Germanic *shney-shturm*, "snow
storm"), is exclusively literal.

We should have expected the names of the seasons to be
drawn from the Slavic, but *vinter*, "winter"; *friling*, "spring";
zumer, "summer"; *harbst*, "autumn" are Germanic. Only the
Slavic *osyen* competes with *harbst*, and, more weakly, *vesne*
with *friling*; *harbstik*, *osyendik*, "autumnal," are completely
synonymous in meaning and tonality. They have a melancholy
sound and are much in favor with poets.

The contrast between Germanic words and the Slavic
synonyms is brought out strongly by *zup* and *yoykh*, "soup."
The first is neutral, the second has personality. In its more

specific sense *yoykh* is "broth"; when it takes on the diminutive form *yaykhl*, it suddenly enters the kitchen of our childhood; it becomes tender and solicitous. When a housewife says *ikh vel aykh opkokhn a yaykhl*, "I will cook you a brothlet" (the diminutive is not quantitative), she is, as the formal *aykh* indicates, addressing either a stranger or someone of higher social rank, but the *yaykhl* is cozening and ingratiating; the wheedling diminutive is respectfully transferred to the person addressed.

Di gildene yoykh, "the golden soup," is the technical term for the fat and yellow chicken soup that is the *de rigueur* opening of the wedding dinner. The adjective may apply equally to the grandeur of the occasion and the presumable richness of the soup. It may also have to do with the wished-for prosperity of the newlyweds. Whatever the case, there is something mystical in the phrase; the soup undergoes a chemical transmutation, and one partakes of it as of, *lehavdl*, a sacrament, or at least as of—in non-Jewish circles—the wedding cake. To talk of a *gildene zup* would be simply ridiculous. Slavic are *knish* and *blintse*, which do not need translation. *Kishke* is beginning to make its way into English. In the singular it is a food, "stuffed derma," also "intestine" or "(garden) hose." In the plural it is "guts"; *er krikht mir in die kishkes arayn*, "He crawls into my guts," "He's crawling out of my ears," "I'm fed up to the teeth with him."

Khreyn, "horseradish," indispensable accompaniment to *gefilte fish*, is Slavic, but *knobl*, "garlic," is Germanic, while *tsibele*, "onion," is Slavic but also related to the German *Zwiebel*. *Kashe*, "porridge," is Slavic, and has worked itself into some useful locutions. *Farkokhn a kashe* is "to cook up a stew," "brew up trouble," "get things into a mess." *Zikh lozn shpayen in der kashe*, "to permit one's *kashe* to be spit into," is "to be a milksop," "let oneself be pushed around," "take everything lying down." *Vaser oyf kashe*, "water for *kashe*," is what a man earns when he earns next to nothing.

Indik, "turkey," and *katchke*, "duck," are jolly words, far more redolent of the farmyard that the Germanic *hun*, "hen," and *hon*, "rooster." However, the Germanic *gandz*, "goose," is somewhat warmer, and like the English is used to denote silly human females.

Pupik, "navel," is slightly indelicate, a little like "belly-button." The literal-figurative *er ligt mitn (mit dem) pupik aroyf*, "He lies with his belly-button up," is a cheerful-melancholy reference to death, familiar but not offensive. But *pupik* as "gizzard of a fowl" is quite respectable.

The peculiar likability of the Slavic words that have to do with the home, the kitchen, and the yard may be due to the recentness of the *shtetl* experience. This does not explain why certain domestic words remained consistently Germanic but it might explain why those that were picked up from the Slavic, and constituted points of contact with the simple, likable Slavic neighbors, became nostalgically charged. In the following lists the words of Slavic origin invariably have the greater appeal.

Pokreshke (Slv), "potlid," is used in a folksaying: *a mame iz a pokreshke, zi dekt tsu di kinders khisroynes* (Heb) *un dem mans bizyoynes* (Heb), "A mother is a *pokreshke*: she covers up her children's defects and her husband's humiliations."

Hodeven (Slv), "to rear, feed, breed": *hodeven di gendz* is "to feed the geese"; *hodeven gendz*, without the *di*, is to "breed geese." With children one uses the same verb root with the Germanic prefix *oyf*; *oyfhodeven kinder* is to "rear, bring up children." It is a slightly plaintive phrase, self-pitying, hinting at unappreciated devotion. It would not generally be used by well-to-do parents.

Although *shof*, "sheep," and *rinder*, "cattle," are Germanic, *pashen*, "to graze" (transitive), *pastekh*, "shepherd," and *onpoyen*, "to water" (animals), are Slavic. There were practically no Jewish shepherds and no Jewish-owned flocks of

131

sheep, hence *shof* and *pastekh* had biblical backgrounds. But
Jewish draymen, or "wagoners," were a sizable part of the population (the most famous figure in Yiddish literature, Tevye,
was a drayman before he became a "capitalist"), and *onpoyen
di ferd*, "to water the horses," was immediate and real. *Tsig*,
"goat," and *ku*, "cow," are Germanic; these animals were as
much part of *shtetl* life as the horse, for though the Jews did
not have flocks and herds, a goat or a cow for milk was the
first index of a rise from abject poverty.

Kuh

Zieg

There is probably no accounting for the shifts from Germanic to Slavic in the vocabulary of *shtetl* life. While *ku* and
oks, "ox," are Germanic, *bik*, "bull," is Slavic. *Shof*, "sheep,"
as we have seen, is Germanic, *baran*, "ram," Slavic. *Traybn*,
"to drive" (*e.g.*, a horse), is Germanic, *leytses*, "reins," is Slavic.

The same puzzle confronts us in the names for fruits and
trees. Germanic are *floym*, "plum"; *karsh*, "cherry"; *epl*, "apple"; *bar*, "pear"; while Slavic took over in *fershke*, "peach";
arbuz, "watermelon"; *yagde*, "berry"; *pozemke*, "strawberry";
maline, "raspberry"; *agres*, "gooseberry." But there are certain
berries that Yiddish-speaking Jews will recognize as objects
but seldom be able to put a name to. Such are (all Slavic)
ozhene, "blackberry"; *zhurekhline*, "cranberry"; *tshernitse*
"huckleberry."

Birne

Pfirs

Trees are even more puzzling than fruits, for some of
them have double names, Germanic and Slavic. "Fir" and
"spruce" are not clearly distinguishable, going sometimes by
the Germanic *tenenboym* and *fikhte*, and sometimes by the
Slavic *sosne* and *yodle*. "Willow" has the Germanic *vayde*
and the Slavic *verbe*. But the general relationship of Yiddish
to this and other areas of nature terminology has been treated,
though all too briefly, in the chapter "The Blind Side of Yiddish." We should note that, generally speaking, the Jews were
nearer to nature in the Slavic lands than in the Germanic.
They were dealers in wheat, horses, pig's bristles, and timber,

132

and numbers of Jews became skillful craftsmen, floating logs
up to the Baltic or down to the Black Sea.

8.

Returning to the special "hominess" and "folkishness"
of Slavic-Yiddish words, we find two excellent examples in
hulyen, "to make merry, carouse, carry on joyously and nois-
ily," and *skutshne,* "lonely," with sadness and boredom in the
background. However, the Germanic *benken,* "to long," per-
taining to the irretrievable past, a lost home, distant family
and friends, rivals any Slavic word in its effect.

Slavic and very much of the folk are *khropen,* "to snore";
pamunitse, "household slops"; *pyavke,* "leech"; *bankes,*
"cups" (for drawing blood). The latter two were traditional
shtetl remedies and therefore seem naturally Slavic. A very
popular locution describing a hopeless course of action is
es vet helfn vi a toytn bankes, "It will be as helpful as cupping
a corpse." Of the *shtetl,* again, is *khitre,* "crafty, sly, knowing," which one liked to apply to the Ukrainian peasant who
thought himself, and indeed was, nobody's fool. The word
can of course be applied to a Jew, too, but does not fit him
quite as well.

Optsas, Germanic and Slavic, is "heel," while *pyate,* "foot,
sole," is Slavic. *Pyate* has been chosen for a popular locution,
es ligt im in der linker pyate, or *er hot es in der linker pyate,*
"It lies, or he has it, in his left sole," which translates perfectly
as "He couldn't care less." Sometimes the Hebrew *peye,* "earlock," is substituted for *pyate;* then the phrase is *es ligt im in
der linker peye,* "It lies in his left *peye*"; and the slightly
changed meaning is "He doesn't give it a thought." An allied
expression of indifference is *ikh her im vi yurkes hunt,* "I

listen to him as much as to Yurke's dog" (Yurke is a common Slavic male name). An all-Germanic variant is *ikh her im vi dem farayorikn shney,* "I pay as much attention to him as to last year's snow."

As odd a locution as can be found in any language is *lakhn mit yashtsherkes* (Slv), literally, "to laugh with lizards," as if one were afflicted in some way with lizards, meaning perhaps as if lizards were crawling down one's back; we would say "to laugh out of the wrong side of one's mouth," "to laugh *à la pagliacci.*" It has a wholly Germanic parallel which is rather stronger, more gruesome, also more intelligible, *lakhn mit grine verm,* "to laugh with green worms"; it carries a horrible suggestion of maggots crawling out of a man's mouth. Another form of the phrase is: *es iz im ongekumen mit grine verm,* "He managed it, but it took the guts out of him."

The Slavic *mutshen* and the Germanic *matern,* "to torment," are practically synonymous, with *mutshen* the stronger. They are most effectively used with the Germanic prefix *oys.* *Zi hot mikh oysgemutshet, oysgematert,* may be said by a mother of her daughter, of a woman by her husband, and is tantamount to "She took, tormented the life out of me, left me a wreck." The reflexive, *zikh mutshen, zikh matern,* "to live a toilsome, wretched life," suggests sickness, penury, hopelessness, and can be turned into the form *s'iz a gematert, gemutshet lebn,* "It's a dog's life." *Er hot zikh opgemutshet, opgematert etlekhe yor,* "He dragged a few more years," gives another turn to the verbs. *Got zitst oybn un mir mutshen, matern zikh do untn,* "God sits up there on high and we drag out our miserable existence here below," is a popular way of expressing dissatisfaction with the human lot. And finally, *mit maternish, mit mutshenish,* "with torture, labor, suffering," tells of the thorny, stony path traversed in reaching, at long last, the desired objective.

Again among the strongly or densely Yiddish words are

the Slavic *blote*, "mud"; *bulke*, "(baked) roll"; *shmate*, "rag"; *yatke*, "butcher's shop, stall."

Makhn ash un blot fun emetsn, "to make ash and mud of someone," is to run him down mercilessly, "make mud" of him; *er iz arayn in a blote*, "He landed in a mud," is figurative for "He got himself into a mess, a heap of trouble." *Blote* in the literal sense belongs to the *shtetl* not less than its crooked little streets and wooden buildings; we read again and again in the stories of *shtetl* life of the spring muds ankle deep on the unpaved streets, or rather alleys, after the melting of the snows, turning, with the summer, into carpets and clouds of dust. *Blote* was a primeval fact for Jew and gentile alike in that world, but the Jew took it harder.

A *bulke mit puter*, "a buttered roll," was considered a royal breakfast; we have just recalled how the apotheosized Bontshe considered it literally a heavenly repast. *Bulke* has not passed into English alongside its companion *beygl*, of Germanic origin, because the Western roll is not very different from the east European product.

Shmate, "rag," is used as often in a figurative as a literal sense. A book or play without merit is a *shmate*; a Jewish Caspar Milquetoast is a *shmate*, when he is not a *lemeshke*, "porridge." It need hardly be said that an inferior article of clothing, though new, is also a *shmate*.

If there was one everyday profession that only a Jew could practice among Jews, it was that of a butcher, and it is therefore natural that he should carry the Hebraic names *katsef* and *shoykhet*; but these referred to his function as (ritual) slaughterer, not as purveyor. *Shoykhet* turned into the verb *shekhtn*, "to slaughter," which extended into *oys-shekhtn*, "to slaughter completely, to the last man, etc." In its secular connotation it was synonymous with *oyskoylen*, from *koylen* (Slv). But *koylen* cannot be used for the ritual killing of a kosher animal, for which only *shekhtn* will do, because only a certified *shoykhet* can perform that act, using the prescribed methods and carefully inspected implements, while saying the prescribed prayer. However, the place where the quartered meat was sold had the Slavic name of *yatke*, and its keeper, though invariably a Jew, had no other qualifications unless a traditional coarseness can be called such. The *shoykhet* was a member of the clergy, and was expected to be a scholar. In small villages—and in small, early American communities—he often doubled as cantor; perhaps also as teacher of the young. The keeper of the *yatke* was known by the Germanic name of *fleysher*; he was almost as low in the social scale as the *balegole*, "drayman."

Yatke has entered into the rather obvious piece of folk wisdom, *a hunt shikt men nit in yatke arayn*, "One doesn't send a dog to the butcher's (to bring home the meat)."

9.

The Slavic influence on Yiddish goes far beyond what is suggested in this chapter. Something of the Russian and Ukrainian spirit entered into Yiddish together with the prefixes and suffixes and diminutives. Touches of tenderness and sarcasm, lilts of language, came over from the peasant life, not easily definable, not easily separable from native Yiddish turns of speech and thought. The melancholy of the steppes echoes in Chassidic melodies, and there is kinship between the mystical religious yearnings of certain Russian and Jewish types, as there is between certain Chassidic experiences and Negro revival meetings.

136

CHAPTER NINE

The Flavor of Hebrew

1.

In Chapter Two we mentioned the Hebrew verbs that enter Yiddish unchanged in spelling and are conjugated through the Germanic auxiliary *zayn*, "to be." The particular form of the Hebrew verb so transformed is the third, second, or first person (they are all the same) masculine singular of the present tense. Thus the Hebrew for "he exaggerates" is *hu megazem*, the Yiddish is *er iz megazem*. The Hebrew for "he exaggerated" and "he will exaggerate" calls for changes in the verb; in Yiddish only the auxiliary changes: *er hot megazem geven* and *er vet megazem zayn*.

So the Hebrew *hu goyzer*, "he decrees," becomes in Yiddish *er iz goyzer*; "he decreed," *er iz goyzer geven*; "he will decree," *er vet goyzer zayn*. *Hu mashpia*, "he influences," becomes *er iz mashpie* (spelled *mashpia*); "he influenced," *er iz mashpie geven*; "he will influence," *er vet mashpie zayn*. It should be noted that not all Hebrew verbs can thus be transposed into Yiddish.

2.

The force and beauty of this form of Yiddish verb derives from the rich background provided by forms associated with the Hebrew verb; besides ringing an old, golden bell, the verb conjures up, consciously or not, neighboring areas of meaning that do not exist for the Germanic equivalent, even when the latter is sound, long-naturalized Yiddish.

Thus the Germanic verb "to exaggerate" is *ibertraybn*,

which is thoroughly acceptable; but it has no accompanying effects like those of *megazem zayn*. *Guzme* is Hebrew and Yiddish for "exaggeration," used in two ways: *az er farmogt tsen hayzer iz a guzme*, "That he has ten houses is an exaggeration," and *er hot a guzme hayzer*, "He has a tremendous number of houses." The Germanic equivalent of *guzme*, *ibertraybung* never had the shaded meanings of *guzme*, and is now becoming a *daytshmerizm*.

Goyzer zayn, "to decree," has no real Germanic equivalent (and as already pointed out, the majority of Germanic-Yiddish words have no Hebraic equivalent). Clustered about this verb there are theological and historical associations which it would be difficult to transfer to a Germanic verb. *Goyzer zayn* and *gzeyre*, "decree," are technically neutral words, but their connotations are always ominous or at least stern. I do not remember ever having heard of *a gute gzeyre*, "a good decree." *Der rebe iz goyzer*, "the rabbi decrees," does not awaken pleasant or indifferent anticipations; similarly with *malkhes* (Heb) *hot aroysgelozt a gzeyre*, "The government issued a decree."

Mashpie zayn, "to influence," had until recently an acceptable Germanic equivalent, *baaynflusn*, now gone the way of *ibertraybung*; so with the noun *aynflus*. The proper form now is *di englishe denker hobn shtark mashpie geven oyf akhed haamen*, "The English thinkers greatly influenced Ahad Ha-am"; or *di englishe denker hobn gehat a groyse hashpoe oyf akhad haamen*, "The English thinkers had a great influence on Ahad Ha-am."

Moysef zayn, "to add (as supplement)," is accompanied by the nouns *hoysofe* and *musef*. *Hoysofe* is secular and can mean a raise in pay: *me flegt im batsoln hundert doler a vokh, itst hot er bakumen a hoysofe*, "He used to get a hundred dollars a week, now he got a raise." *Musef* is exclusively religious, and is the name given to the "supplemental" synagogue prayers on the mornings of Sabbaths and festivals.

The Germanic *tsugebn* can sometimes be used for "to add": *az dos vet nit genug zayn vel ikh tsugebn a por funt fleysh*, "If that won't be enough I'll add a couple of pounds of meat"; but *tsugebn* can also mean "to admit, concede"; *moysef zayn* is therefore neater and less ambiguous. Nevertheless *tsugob*, "addition," has its own place as the noun from *tsugebn*: thus *di sforim* (Heb) *zaynen geven a tsugob tsum nadan*, "The books were an addition to the dowry"; and again, there is a wry locution for an "uncalled-for" bit of bad news on top of an already "satisfactory" load: *a tsugob tsu di tsores*, "An addition to one's troubles."

Mayrekh zayn, "to lengthen, draw out," refers to conversation, or a report: *vos zol ikh aykh mayrekh zayn*, "Why should I lengthen it out for you?," *i.e.*, "make a long story of it," is common usage. One also says *vos zol ikh aykh lang brayen*, "Why should I make a long brew of it?" Linked with *mayrekh* is *arikhes*, "length," as in *arikhes yomim*, "length of days," a courtesy phrase of benediction. *Got zol aykh shenken arikhes yomim*, "God grant you length of days," is sometimes made more specific (and wholly Germanic) in *lebn zolt ir biz hundert un tsvantsik*, "May you live to (the age of) one hundred and twenty" (the life span of Moses and of Rabbi Akiba). The recipient of such a benediction will sometimes ask for a *tsugob* of three months, "so that I shouldn't die suddenly."

Mevayesh zayn and *farshemen*, "to shame, put to shame," are, in a prosaic sense, interchangeable, but the Hebraic is much stronger than the Germanic. *Me tor a mentshn nit mevayesh zayn*, "One must not put a man to shame," sounds more authoritative than *me tor a mentshn nit farshemen*, though it means exactly the same thing. The prohibition is sternly worded in the tradition; for putting someone to shame in public, declares the Talmud, a man forfeits the life to come; it is equated with *shfikhes domim*, "the shedding of blood." *Mevayesh zayn* links with the noun *bushe*, which again is stronger than the Germanic *shande*.

Mekane zayn, "to envy," and *kine*, the noun, have no genuine Germanic equivalents. *Banaydn* and *nayd*, both *daytshmerizms*, have sometimes been used but they grated on the ear even to their users. *Zi iz im mekane geven zayn derfolg*, "She envied him his success," can be rephrased using a good Germanic verb: *zi hot im nit fargunen zayn derfolg*. There is no English equivalent for *farginen* (past participle, *fargunen*); it must be paraphrased as "not to begrudge or envy, to accept with pleasure, or at least acquiescence, another's happiness, triumph, etc." We must, however, distinguish between "begrudge" and "envy." What you envy in someone else you usually want for yourself, but you may very well begrudge him that which you already have, *e.g.*, fame, money, social position, beauty. "To begrudge" is meaner and more dog-in-the-mangerish than "to envy." *Er fargint mir nit dos shtikl broyt*, "He begrudges me my piece of bread [*i.e.*, my meager livelihood]," has in fact nothing to do with envy.

I permit myself a little digression here on one instance of the continuous struggle that goes on in Yiddish. *Derfolg*, "success" (above), is an acceptable word, but in my ear it is beginning to sound like a *daytshmerizm*. I much prefer the Hebraic *hatslokhe*, which is connected with the verb *matsliekh zayn*, "to be successful," though a flavor of the Providential clings to both words. In any case, I find myself offended by the Americanism, or Anglicism, *suktses*, perhaps because "success" is associated with the bitch-goddess. But *derfolg* cannot wholly be ignored. "His success with women" comes across perfectly in *zayn derfolg bay froyen*, but rings somewhat improper as *zayn hatslokhe bay froyen*. As a warning to myself and others, I should note that the attempt to force Hebrew into Yiddish where a good Germanic word already exists shows the same poor taste as the *daytshmerizms* of a past generation. I cannot accept *mavtiekh zayn*, "to promise," for *tsuzogn*, or *makkhish zayn*, "to deny," for *leykenen*, or *farleykenen*, unless an old world style happens to demand it.

At the same time the Hebraic *havtokhe*, "promise," and *hakkhoshe*, "denial" (in the sense of giving the lie to), are neater and more graceful even in a wholly modern setting than their corresponding Germanic *tsuzog* and *opleyknung*.

Makrev zayn, "to sacrifice," and its noun, *korbn*, have lost their Germanic synonyms, *opfern* and *opfer*. These last, even before becoming *daytshmerizms*, had no religious-ritualistic echoes. *Korbn* is one of the words a *kheyder* boy absorbs early into his vocabulary. In Hebrew it competes with other words, but these have not come over into Yiddish, which therefore exploits it on a wider range. *Korbn* retains its strong *khumesh* flavor, but extends into general use in such a phrase as *milkhome* (Heb) *korbones*, "war victims," or *er iz a korbn fun zayn eigener akshones* (Heb), "He is the victim of his own obstinacy." Although the form of sacrifice in which Abraham was to offer up Isaac uses another Hebrew verb, in Yiddish it is proper to say *avrohom ovinu* (Heb) *iz greyt geven makrev tsu zayn zayn zun yitskhokn*, "Abraham our father was prepared to sacrifice his son Isaac." *Er hot zikh makrev geven far zayne kinder*, "He sacrificed himself for his children," is wholly secular.

Goyver zayn, "to overcome, surmount," is linked with several nouns: *gvure*, "might, power, heroism," a word of noble sound, retaining an echo of its Hebrew use as an attribute of God ("Thine is the greatness and the *gvure*"); *giber*, "hero, man of great physical strength, doer of great deeds," linked with Samson in the Hebrew *shimshon hagiber*; *gavres*, "virility"; *gvar*, "a strong, manly person," the last two having no religious associations.

We have already encountered *gvir*, "wealthy man," an odd variation on the root of *giber*. *Gvir* is an extremely respectful word, especially when it is fortified by the Hebraic adjective (never used in Yiddish except in this connection) *adir*, "mighty." One uses a special tone of awe in saying *gvir adir* (as in Hebrew, and not *adir gvir*), for something more is implied than in the specific measurement of "millionaire." But this curious deflection of meaning is not so curious after all, for wealth has always meant power and status (one of the most revealing words in the English language is "sovereign," as meaning the gold coin, lordly and supreme). When Boaz, husband-to-be of Ruth, is called *ish giber khayil*, "a mighty man of valor" (Ruth 2:1), the meaning is simply "man of great wealth."

Khayil, "army," is both Hebrew and Yiddish, and in a deflection similar to the above, we have the Hebraic Yiddish phrase, *eyshes khayil*, "woman of valor" (Proverbs 31). The *eyshes khayil* is not an Amazon with bow and arrow; she is a formidable and resourceful housewife with spindle and loom who runs her house like a factory: "She considereth a field and buyeth it . . . she maketh linen garments and selleth them, and delivereth girdles to the merchant," while "Her husband is known in the gates when he sitteth among the elders of the land." This commendable division of functions was not unknown in the *shtetl* world, where scholarly husbands were sometimes supported by their wives, though seldom in the grand biblical manner. The *eyshes khayil* usually kept a store, or a stall in the marketplace, and the nearest she came to buying a field was owning a goat for milk.

Goyver zayn is often used in a moral sense, as in *goyver zayn dem yetser hore*, "to conquer one's evil impulses"; and a Talmudic aphorism so often quoted that it has become almost Yiddish is *eyze hu giber? hakoyveysh es yitsroy*, "Who is a hero? He that overcomes his (evil) inclination."

Mefarnes zayn, "to provide with a livelihood, subsistence." We can say of the *eyshes khayil* above that *zi iz mefarnes ir man*, "she earns the living for her husband." (More about this word in Chapter Eleven.)

Megadl zayn, "to bring up (children)," is connected with a variety of forms. *Godoyl*, "big, great," is the Hebrew adjective, which has not passed into Yiddish; but the noun *godl*

144

(spelled *godoyl*) is good Yiddish, and is well covered by "VIP"; *a godl beyisroel*, "a great man in Israel," will generally mean scholarship, but can imply public service, the role of the *shtatlen*, a negotiator for the Jews in high gentile places. A *godl* is liable to be infected with *gadles*, "pride, arrogance"; but the root takes a dive with *gdule*, literally, "grandeur, exultation," by usage often a word of mockery. A *groyse gdule*, "a great (cause for) rejoicing," is used sarcastically for a picayune success or triumph; also a *gdule oyf zayn boben*, "much joy to his grandmother." Of a man in a high cheerful mood for no reason at all one may say *a gdule vos zayn mame hot im gehat*, "He rejoices that his mother (and not a strange woman) bore him."

Menadev zayn, "to donate," is linked with a whining word, *nedove*, a charitable gift," which is mostly used for a trifling handout. The beggar on the street or at the door will say, *git a nedove*, or *shenkt a nedove*, "Give, donate a handout," but the related word *nadven*, "philanthropist," belongs to another world.

Menatseakh zayn, "to triumph, conquer, be victorious," is related to *nitsokhn*, "victory," "triumph." A *bal nitsokhn*, literally "man of victory," is one who can't bear to be worsted in any kind of encounter, deal, argument, contest, dispute; he must come out on top. Thence the noun *nitskhoynes*, "truculence, contentiousness," and the corresponding adjective, *natskhonesh*.

Khoyshed zayn, "to suspect," and *khshad*, "suspicion," have no real Germanic equivalents. When used to refer to a person, the proper form is *ikh bin khoyshed az er iz a ligner*, "I suspect that he is a liar," or *ikh hob a khshad az er iz a ligner*, "I have a suspicion that he is a liar." One of the intramural self-denigrations Jews are fond of is *a yidn darf men keyn mol nisht khoyshed zayn, er iz zikher a ganef*, "One should never harbor suspicions against a Jew—he's definitely a *ganef*." I do not translate *ganef* here literally as "thief"; it is nearer to "rascal" in the less pejorative sense. Sayings of this kind, not meant seriously, must remain intramural because the psychological context cannot be conveyed in another language. This must not be taken to mean that the Yiddish-speaking Jew was not seriously or even savagely self-critical; in that respect he inherited the pitilessness of the Prophets. But such self-criticism must not be confused with merely jocular digs.

Mekhabed zayn, "to honor," bifurcates into *koved,* "honor, respect" (already considered with its *daytshmerish* equivalent, *ere*), and *kibed,* "tribute, honor, refreshments," offered to a visitor. *Mekhabed zayn* is often used with a smile, friendly but not deprecatory: *men iz im mekhabed geven mit shlishi,* "He was allotted the honor of reading the third (the most coveted) section (of the week's division of the Torah)," is straight; but *ikh bin im mekhabed geven mit a shmek tabeke,* "I offered him the courtesy of a pinch of snuff" (the offer being literal), is jocular. However, *men iz im mekhabed geven mit aza portsye az er iz shir nisht ayngezunken in der erd,* "He got such a reception (abuse, criticism), that he all but sank into the earth," is ironic. *Kibed* is the obligatory offering of hospitality to a visitor, which may be token, a glass of lemonade, a piece of candy, or elaborate, including tea, sweetmeats, and fruit. A much more serious content fills the phrases *kibed av, kibed eym,* "honor due one's father," "honor due one's mother." These fixed phrases have been taken straight from the Hebrew into Yiddish; otherwise the Yiddish words for "father" and "mother" are, as noted, *foter, tate, muter, mame. Kibudim,* the plural of *kibed,* never carries the meaning of hospitality; it is used exclusively in the sense of "honors due to" or "honors distributed."

Mekhalel zayn, "to desecrate," is linked with *khilel,* "desecration, profanation": *er iz mekhalel shabes,* "He desecrates the Sabbath," is an extremely wide term, since it applies to anything forbidden on that day, from doing business, lighting a fire (including the striking of a match), smoking a cigarette (particularly odious), writing something down, and tearing a piece of paper. *Mekhalel shem zayn*, "to desecrate the Name (of God), blaspheme," also has a very wide range, from the profoundly serious to the nationally questionable. Obviously a man is *mekhalel shem* (or *es hashem*) if he publicly affronts the Jewish religion; he is also *mekhalel shem* if he behaves publicly in a way likely to bring discredit on the Jews. *Khilel hames*, "desecration of the dead," has already been noted.

Opposite *khilel hashem* is the solemn term *kidesh hashem*, "sanctification of the Name," equivalent to "martyrdom." The Jews who have died throughout the ages because they refused to repudiate their religion all died *al kidesh hashem*, "for the sanctification of the Name." Sometimes, in a generous extension, this supreme designation is conferred on such Jews as died simply because they were Jews and were not given the chance to repudiate whatever loyalty they harbored for the Jewish religion or the Jewish people. Thus it is common to speak of the six million exterminated by the Nazis as having died *al kidesh hashem*. The justification is grounded in a feeling that having been singled out for death simply because they were Jews, however remotely so in their consciousness, they have been gathered into the fold of the martyrs; they too have testified even if reluctantly or uncomprehendingly, with their lives. They were at least the witnesses to the fidelity of their fathers, who imposed their Jewish identity on them.

3.

We have also considered briefly in Chapters Two and Four the type of hybrid Hebraic verb that consists of a Hebrew stem unchanged as to spelling, but ending in the Germanic *n* on *en* for the infinitive and conjugated like a wholly Germanic verb. But these too retain a strong flavor of Hebrew because, as we have seen, the Hebrew stem is separated (or was till recently) from its Germanic accretions, and because the Hebraic background and associations are not less rich than in the case of wholly unchanged Hebrew verbs with *zayn*.

Khezhbenen "to reckon, calculate," does not derive from a verb; its anchor is the noun *khezhbn*, which has passed from Hebrew into Yiddish. *Khezhbenen* and *khezhbn* apply equally to financial transactions and spiritual accounting: *er hot gemakht a khezhbn az es kumt im dray hundert doler*, "He drew up an accounting according to which he had three hundred dollars coming to him"; but *khezhbn hanefesh* (Heb), "accounting of the soul, a review of one's moral condition," is something that every Jew is called upon to make periodically, and especially during the ten penitential days between the New Year and the Day of Atonement. *Zikh opgebn* ("to render to oneself") *a khezhbn hanefesh* is the proper form, but it can also mean a stocktaking of one's general human condition in other than religious terms, to find out where one stands, to strip away false assumptions, etc.

Khanfenen, "to flatter," is accompanied by *khnife*, "flattery, cajolery, bootlicking." They are unpleasant words. One may say, in English, "You flatter me" without imputing insincerity or toadying, but the apparent equivalent, *ir khanfet mir*, is highly offensive. To avoid that, one would have to resort to the Germanic *ir makht mir a kompliment*, "You pay me a compliment." A *khoynef* is a toady, and *khnife* (the very sound of which suggests a Uriah Heepish hypocrisy) is a constant crooking of "the pregnant hinges of the knee where thrift may follow fawning." The Hebraic roots are biblical and Talmudic.

Ganvenen, "to steal," is generally more literal than its noun, *ganef*, "thief," which, as we have seen, can also denote a not unattractive "rascal." Only *ganeyve*, "theft," is wholly and everywhere the blunt "theft." *Ganvenen* has spread out, by means of Germanic prefixes and the reflexive into areas wholly foreign to the original Hebrew. *Araynganvenen zikh,* "to sneak in," and *unterganvenen zikh,* "to sneak up on," and their like are not perjorative. *Tsuganvenen,* a reinforced form, implies a definite act: *dos dinstmeydel hot tsugeganvet a zilbernem lefl,* "The servant girl stole a silver spoon." *Baganvenen,* "to rob systematically," usually contains the element of time: *di meshorsim* (Heb) *hobn dem balebos baganvet,* "The shop assistants constantly pilfered from, robbed the owner."

Though *ganeyve* cannot be softened in any context, the adjective *gneyvish,* like *ganef,* is by no means so rigid. *Gneyvish,* "rascally," can be used admiringly, with humorous disapproval, to describe a beguiling trickster, or admiringly, without disapproval of any kind, to describe a startling piece of ingenuity. Had Autolycus, the "snapper-up of unconsidered trifles," been a Jew, he might be described as *a yid a ganef.*

The use of *ganef* in the manner just adduced is illustrated by a story I have heard attributed to Sholom Aleichem, though I cannot remember having come across it in his works. A Jewish merchant came into a large silk emporium owned by a Jew and ordered a large quantity of goods. The *balebos* had never seen this customer before and was delighted when he received cash payment on the spot. Just before leaving, the customer bethought himself and exclaimed with some embarrassment, *oy veyz (vey iz) mir, khob (ikh hob) fargesn tsu davnen minkhe; zayt azoy gut un lozt mikh arayngeyn in a tsimer opdavnen minkhe,* "Goodness me, I've forgotten to say the afternoon prayers; please let me go into a room to say them." *Mitn (mit dem) grestn koved,* "With the greatest honor (pleasure)," said the *balebos,* conducted the customer into a room, and left him there. A little while later the *balebos* chanced to pass that way, and looking through a crack in the door, saw the new customer stuffing the capacious pockets of his *kaftn,* "gaberdine," with silk handkerchiefs, silk scarves, and silk stockings. He let it pass and wrote off the loss to public relations. A year or so later the *soykher*, "merchant," was delighted to see his *koyne*, "customer," again. The latter again made handsome purchases, again paid cash on the spot, and again broke out suddenly with, *oy veyz mir, khob fargesn tsu davnen minkhe*, and the rest of it. Again the *balebos* replied *mitn grestn koved*—and conducted the customer to an empty room. Thereupon the latter turned on him with a reproachful but admiring look: *ay zayt ir a ganef!* "What a *ganef* you turned out to be!"

4.

Some of the Hebrew-plus-*zayn* verbs are double-barreled; the verb has a Hebrew noun fixed to it, the whole sometimes forming an indivisible Yiddish phrase.

Thus *mevaker*, "(he) visits," is not a Yiddish word, it is exclusively Hebrew; *khoyle*, "sick person, patient," is Yiddish when standing alone; *mevaker khoyle zayn*, "to visit the sick," is as a phrase thoroughly Yiddish. The practice itself is of course held in high esteem. Again the noun *biker*, "visit," is Hebrew not Yiddish; but *biker khoylim* is good Yiddish for a kind of hospital.

Similar in structure and composition are:

Poyser kholem zayn, "to interpret a dream": only *kholem*, "dream," is detachable as Yiddish, and has the hybrid verb, *kholemen*, "to dream."

Makhnes oyrekh zayn, "to extend hospitality [generally including lodgment]": Only *oyrekh* is Yiddish, and is a "loaded" word; it means not only one who is given lodgment, but a visitor, one who is welcomed.

An oyrekh oyf shabes, "a guest for the Sabbath," usually meaning a stranger picked up at the Friday evening services and brought home for at least the ensuing twenty-four hours, was what we might call a great ethical delicacy, enjoyed by poor and rich alike. It was a stroke of good luck if the stranger turned out to be something of a scholar, and the table talk was enlivened with quotations and interpretations or tales of rabbis and their followers. One was not supposed to pick and choose, so the *oyrekh* might be a bore, or a professional *shnorer*, "mendicant"; then one had to make the best of it. On the other hand, appearing to be a *shnorer*, he might be Elijah the prophet in one of his innumerable disguises, or a *lamed-vovnik*. From many points of view, then, the practice of *hakhnoses orkhim*, "the bringing in of guests," was an intelligent gamble as well as a high *mitsve*, "commandment, good deed."

Menakhem ovl zayn, "to comfort the mourner, pay a condolence call," ranks next to *mevaker khoyle zayn*. Again, *ovl*, "mourner," is a good current Yiddish, while *menakhem* standing alone is unknown to Yiddish except as a male name.

Melamed zkhus zayn, "to see the actions of others in a favorable light" (literal translation is impossible), is the moral obligation, strongly enjoined in Jewish ethics, to give a man the benefit of the doubt. *Zkhus* in current Yiddish is "privilege, right, merit," and there is a strong phrase, *zkhus oves* (Heb), "the merits of the Fathers," conveying a plea for the descendants of the righteous; one might translate it as "for the sake of the Fathers." It was for "the sake of the Fathers," and not for their own merits, that the Israelites (as Moses sternly reminded them) were privileged to inherit the Holy Land. A popular quotation from the "Ethics of the Fathers," a section of the Talmud, runs, in the accepted translation: "Judge your neighbor in the scale of merit," which is almost meaningless. I suggest, "When you judge your neighbor, weight the scale in his favor." In *melamed zkhus zayn*, each Hebrew word stands up separately in Yiddish, but *melamed* standing alone, is, as we have seen, "teacher."

5.

A type of Hebraic verb that adds intimacy to gravity and courtliness is the *zayn* construction in reflexive form but with active meaning (*cf.* the French *se rappeler*, Italian *ricordarsi*, German *sich erinnern*, "to remember"). The type of Hebrew verb here discussed may be "single" or "double-barreled."

Zikh noyeg zayn, "to be in the habit of, to have made a custom of," is close to the Germanic reflexive, *zikh oyffirn*. *Zikh noyeg zayn* is used mostly in a religious and ceremonial setting. One may say: *reb zorekh iz zikh noyeg geven az ven zayn zun der rov iz gekumen tsu im oyf shabes hot er im opgegebn zayn ort bay der mizrekh vant*, "Reb Zorekh had made it a custom when his son, the rabbi, came to visit him over the Sabbath, he would yield to him his seat by the eastern wall (of the synagogue)." It will not do to substitute in this sentence *fleg zikh oyffirn* for *iz zikh noyeg geven*. But there is not a good Hebraic noun for "conduct"; the Germanic *oyffir* is used.

Zikh koyne shem zayn, "to win oneself a name," is the double-barreled reflexive in which both Hebrew words are, separately, good Yiddish. We have just met *koyne* as "purchaser"; *shem*, "reputation," as a Hebrew word is also "name" in the ordinary sense ("and the name of his mother was . . ."), but not so in Yiddish, which for this purpose uses the Germanic *nomen*. For *zikh koyne shem zayn*, one can say, correctly, *zikh makhn a shem*, "make oneself a name." Of a man who has become famous it is correct to say *er iz gevorn a shem dover*, literally, "He became a thing of renown."

Zikh mesasek zayn, "to occupy oneself with," has a religious coloration because of the accompanying noun, *mesaskim*, "those that occupy themselves with preparing a corpse for burial"; but an *askn* is a man active in public life generally. For me, at least, *askn* has a touch of cant, self-importance, pretentiousness. There is a slightly better, mixed expression, *klal tuer*, of which the first half is Hebraic, meaning, in this context, "public doer," hence, "doer of public things." *Klal* is here almost synonymous with another Hebraic term, *kool* (pronounced *koel*), "community." One may use here the Germanic verb, *basheftikn: er basheftikt zikh mit kolishe inyonim* (Heb), or *er farnemt zikh . . .* "He occupies himself with communal affairs."

In the life of the *shtetl*, public service of any kind was touched with the odor of sanctity. It was inconceivable that a man who did not attend synagogue services regularly should be permitted to occupy a prominent place in secular affairs—but there were after all no secular affairs: Charity was distributed through the synagogue, the building of a public bath was a religious enterprise, the entertainment of visitors and the care of wanderers was under synagogue supervision, the slaughter-house or at any rate the proper carrying-out of animal slaughter again was a strictly religious matter. Sometimes, if a *nogid* had the ear of *natshalstve* (Slv), "official-dom," he would act as the lay representative of the community; but a *nogid* who was not a pietist, at least in appearance, would very rarely be accepted by the community as a leader. Hence every aspect of public activity in the *shtetl* stood under the sign of an accepted theocracy.

Zikh meshadekh zayn, "to enter into matrimonial relations," is a very dignified, even slightly pompous expression. It may apply to an individual, when it is simply, "to marry," or a family, when it suggests an alliance. *Er iz zikh meshadekh geven mit a tokhter fun der gumbiner mishpokhe,* "He married a daughter of the Gumbiner family"—that is the substance of it—but the phraseology suggests negotiations, considerations of status, almost of state, and families of repute. Similarly with *zey zaynen zikh tomid meshadekh geven mit gerer khasidim,* "They always married into families that were followers of the Chassidic rabbis of the Ger dynasty." Connected with *meshadekh* are *shatkhn* and *shidekh.*

Zikh mekhaye zayn, "to enjoy with relish, be delighted, refreshed, revived": *ven es blozt a kiler vint iz men zikh poshet* (Heb) *mekhaye,* "When a cool wind blows one is simply delighted, refreshed, etc."; *ikh bin zikh mekhaye mit zayne briv,* "I enjoy his letters deep down." There is also the noun *mekhaye,* with the impersonal form: *es iz a mekhaye,* "It's a joy, pleasure, refreshing delight."

Zikh meyashev zayn, "To take under advisement, to deliberate, ponder, confer," has a number of Germanic near-synonyms of inferior force: *batrakhtn, iberklern, barekhenen, zikh iberleygn. Zikh meyashev zayn* has more thoughtfulness in it; it is related to *yishev hadas,* "reflection, consultation," which itself relies for its gravity on *yishev* (Heb), "sitting," suggesting a session or conference, and *das* (Heb), "opinion, reason." *Ikh bin zikh lang meyashev geven eyder ikh hob geshribn dem briv,* "I turned the matter over carefully before I wrote the letter," might also mean "I took counsel with others." The noun form would be used thus: *ikh hob geshribn dem briv nokh a langn yishev hadas.* In both uses there is to the sensitive ear a reinforcement from the echo of *yeshive,* the place where one sits and learns and meditates.

Zikh toye zayn, "to err, make a mistake, be in error": *ikh bin zikh toye geven un gemeynt ir zayt an anderer,* "I made a mistake and thought you were someone else (another)"; *ikh bin zikh toye geven un bin arayngegangen in a fremd hoyz,* "I erred and went into a strange (wrong) house." In this last instance *toye* touches on one of its Hebrew meanings, "to wander," just as "err" connects with "errant." *Toes,* "error," is as frequently used as the verb: *oyb ikh makh nit keyn toes,* "If I am not making a mistake," is the equivalent of *oyb ikh bin zikh nit toye.*

The verb form I have just been discussing must not be

154

confused with the ordinary reflexive, applicable to many transitive verbs. *Er hot oyfgehangen dos bild,* "He hung up the picture," and *er hot zikh oyfgehangen,* "He hanged himself," are Germanic examples; *er iz goyver geven zayn yetser hore,* "He overcame his evil impulse (lower self)," and *er iz zikh goyver geven,* "He mastered himself," are Hebraic examples.

CHAPTER TEN

Idioms and Yiddish Grundyisms

1.

In the chapter, "Germanic into Yiddish," I included the little folk story of the Jew accused of stealing a horse and of his indignant statement to the court that he had needed the horse *oyf kapores*—meaning that he had needed it "like a hole in the head"—only to have the helpless interpreter tell the judge: "He needed it for a religious ceremony." The time has now come to explain the "joke," which, like all "interior" Yiddish jokes, needs a considerable background of information.

To begin with, *kapore* "atonement," is one of those Hebrew words which in their transference to Yiddish has taken on new meaning and is used in ways as alien to Hebrew as to English. We meet another form of the word in *yom kiper*, "Day of Atonement"; but whereas *yom kiper* evokes humility and awe, *kapore* often evokes a smile, or even a grin. It would in fact be impossible to invent a more ludicrous contrast than that between the exalted concept of *yom kiper* and the voodoolike ceremony of the *kapore*, known as *shlogn kapores*, literally "beating the (animal of) atonement," though both of them have to do with sin and cleansing from sin.

On the Day of Atonement in ancient times, the High Priest, tested and purified, made his one annual entry into the Holy of Holies, there to implore, in the presence of the Ark and the Winged Cherubim, the clemency of God toward His sinful people. In the later Middle Ages there had grown up—probably beginning in Babylonia—the ritual of the home, performed on the day before *yom kiper*, which acquired the mixed Germanic-Hebraic name of *shlogn kapores*.

A rooster was taken for the males of the family, a hen

for the females. Certain psalms having been read, the rooster was waved three times over the head of each male, the hen over the head for each female, while the following Hebrew prayer was recited: "This shall be my substitute, my vicarious offering, my atonement, '*kapore*.' This rooster (hen) shall go to death, while I shall live a long and pleasant life of peace." The rooster and hen, having absorbed the combined sins of all the males and females, were slaughtered by the *shoykhet* and sent as gifts to the poor. This is not to be interpreted in terms of class exploitation, the poor being forced or bribed to act as the ultimate repository of the sins of the rich, for it was just as meritorious to consume the fowl *en famille* and distribute the money equivalent to the poor.

It is now more than sixty years since I last saw the *kapore* ceremony performed. As far as I remember, none of the branches of my family honored it, but my *rebe* did, though great scholars and pietists of old had denounced it as heathen and therefore utterly un-Jewish. (I do not know if it has ever actually been forbidden.) What remains strongly in my memory is the frightful heartrending squawking that accompanied the ceremony, and my speculations—and those of my fellow *kheyder* pupils—as to whether the wretched fowl forefelt their approaching death or were maddened by the load of human sins being infused into them. This queer piece of magic was never taken very seriously except among the ultra-orthodox, and even there it was (and is) performed with nothing like the emotion proper to so dark and weighty a moment of salvation; in fact, the whole business is, if anything, rather jolly. However, it has brought some felicitous idioms into Yiddish.

A *sheyne reyne kapore*, literally, "a lovely, pure *kapore*," may be called a frozen idiom. All three words must be there and in that order; one may not say *a sheyne kapore*, or *a reyne kapore*, or *a reyne sheyne kapore*, but only *a sheyne reyne kapore*. The meaning is "Good riddance," or even "To hell with him (her)." If a fiancé breaks off a betrothal, the flouted maiden will express her contempt, relief, indifference, etc., real or affected, with *a sheyne reyne kapore!* A prospective partner withdrawing from a business deal will be dismissed with the same formula. On hearing of the death of a beloved or respected person, one utters the all-Hebrew formula of resignation, *borekh dayen emes*, "Blessed be the True Judge"; for the death of one hated or despised, one says, *a sheyne reyne kapore!*

The slighted young lady above may have been wildly in love with her faithless fiancé, in which case it was said of her *zi vert di kapore far im*, "She becomes the *kapore* for him, she's mad about him, besotted, ready to do anything for him." Hiding her chagrin, she could also say, instead of *a sheyne reyne kapore, ikh darf im oyf kapores*, "I need him for *kapores*," that is, "for nothing at all." She could multiply the emphasis with *tish-un-nayntsik kapores*, "nine and ninety *kapores*," making the defaulter a multiple zero. (*Tish*, the Yiddishized form of the Hebrew *tesha*, "nine," occurs nowhere else in Yiddish usage; and one never uses the regular *nayn-un-nayntsik* in this idiom.)

A *kapore gelt, abi koved iz groys*, "To hell with money as long as the honor is great," is a tongue-in-cheek folk saying. If a man was made to assume the guilt of another, and to pay for it, one said of him *er iz gevorn di kapore* or *dos kapore hindl*, "the *kapore* chicken"; he became the scapegoat, the fall guy; he took the rap.

In Bialik's outcry against life's inequities, meanness, and humiliations, called sardonically (in his own Yiddish translation from the Hebrew) *a freylekhs*, "A Merry One," there are two lines that convey powerfully one of the meanings of *kapore*:

Hefker, hefker, alts iz hefker,
hefker vayb un hefker kind;

a kapore hundert veltn
far eyn sho fun mut und zind.
Hefker, hefker, all is worthless,
Worthless children, worthless wife;
Let a hundred worlds be damned
For one hour of sin and life [literally, "daring and sin"].

If a person is no good on the job, if an object is useless for the purpose it is supposed to serve, one says, *er, es toyg oyf kapores,* "He, it, is good for (nothing but) the *kapore* ceremony." There is a proverb, *az di ershte shure* (Heb) *iz krum toyg der gantser briv oyf kapores,* "If the first line is crooked (misses the mark), the whole letter is good for nothing," or "Ill begun, all undone."

I must pause for a moment over *hefker* (Heb). It has no equivalent word in English; it is fairly near the German *vogelfrei,* "outside the protection of the law, any man's game or property." There is a story concerning a saintly rabbi who was seated early one morning at his window, deep in study. Suddenly he heard a noise in the yard, and saw a thief making off with some of the firewood. Thereupon he threw open the window and called out, *"hefker!",* thereby declaring the wood to be no one's and everyone's property. His concern was that the thief should not be committing a sin for the sake of his, the rabbi's, property. The common phrase *a velt iz nit hefker* is an outcry against a particularly odious act of injustice: "There's still some law in the world." Balancing it, there is the humorous phrase, applied when someone is trying to put over an unusually impudent trick, *hefker tsibeles,* "onions," or *hefker petreshke,* "parsley," well translated by Weinreich as "everything goes!"

162

2.

With *yikhes*, "lineage, status," we are in the very heart of the Yiddish Mrs. Grundy country. Like *kapore, yikhes* is far richer in Yiddish than in the Hebrew original, though the deviations are not as striking.

The Midrash uses the word, relating that in Egypt only the three tribes of Reuben, Simeon, and Levi "guarded their *yikhes*," that is, "kept the records of their lineage." There, *yikhes* is used in its simplest sense. Yiddish has made of it a gold mine of snobbery, discrimination, and contention. When a man had *yikhes*, and was therefore a *miyukhes* or *yakhsn*, it meant primarily that his ancestry was distinguished —presumably for learning. Thence *yikhes* spread out to include distinction for wealth. Going still further it ceased to refer to anything in particular: *er iz a groyser miyukhes baym (bay dem) Birgermayster*, "He's a big-shot with the mayor," does not indicate wealth, learning, or any other quality; it is importance as such. Of someone pushing his way to the front for no other reason than that he has the gall, of someone claiming any unwarranted privilege, one says indignantly, *vos far a miyukhes iz er?*, "What kind of *miyukhes* is he?"—a milder form of "Who the hell does he think he is?"

People with *yikhes* are touchy. This or that, acceptable to ordinary people, *shteyt zey nisht on*, "is not becoming to them, is beneath their dignity." "This" or "that" may be a *shidekh* with a less distinguished family, a second-class seat in the synagogue, a run-down residential district, taking in a boarder to help with the rent, polishing their own shoes, doing their own washing, accepting an inferior role in the community. They sniff and say *es past nisht*, "It is unfitting, unbecoming"; *s'iz nisht far mayn zgal*, "It's not for my kind";

and the same word is used for the denigration of a third person, *s'iz nisht far zayn zgal*, "It's not for the likes of him."

What was the greatest humiliation that could befall a *yakhsn?* It was to be compelled by poverty to accept the one negative honor connected with an *aliye*, a calling up to a Torah reading; that is, on the two Sabbaths of the year when the *toykhekhes* are read. The *toykhekhe* is the blood-curdling list of afflictions and calamities with which the Israelites were threatened in the wilderness if, on entering the Holy Land, they fell away from the Law. No one wanted his name to be publicly associated with the hideously detailed punishments listed in the *toykhekhe*, and Jews fought to be spared the humiliating distinction. But someone *had* to be found. When the Torah is read by the *bal koyre*, "reader," every section of the week's *sedre*, "portion," must be preceded by the announcement of a name of some member of the congregation. Such was the horror attached to the *toykhekhe*, that the community often had to resort to bribery, loading this particular *oyfrufns* (the Germanic equivalent of *aliye*), on the village beggar, who was never honored with a "real" *aliye*, or upon a wandering stranger. But sometimes a scapegoat simply could not be found and then as a last extremity the *bal koyre* would intone the passages without an *oyfrufns*.

When a man has *yikhes* his son is known as *a tatns a kind*, "a father's child," in contrast to the status-less children who were begotten by nobodies. Somehow *a tatns a kind* referred only to boys, and no girl, however distinguished her parents, was ever called by that name, or, for the mother's sake, *a mames a kind*, "a mother's child." Yet women were on the whole more *yikhes*-conscious than men. A *yakhsnte*, the female of the species, could also of course be a *negidiste*. It was often said of her that *zi goydert zikh*, literally, "double-chins herself": if she hadn't a double or a triple chin she carried herself as if she did, that is, she held her head proudly, her chin, if she had only one, drawn back at least to suggest

164

the possibility of another; and when she walked, a little quiver ran through her real or symbolic *goyder*.

Being a *yakhsnte*, either by marriage or in her own right, or both, she was the Yiddish Mrs. Grundy *in excelsis*, and she was forever giving out with worldly wise sayings, maxims of prudence to the right-minded, such as: *vos tsu got iz tsu got un vos tsu layt iz tsu layt*, "What's God's is God's and what's due to (respectable) people is due to (respectable) people," in other words, "render unto Caesar. . . ." She trembled lest she or her children or anyone connected with her might through some indiscretion, hasty word, foolish act, or the like, be *oysgeshtelt tsu laytish gelekhter*, "exposed to the laughter, ridicule, scorn, of (the right) people." She would also say, with much complacency, *à propos* of evil company that corrupted good manners, *az me leygt zikh shlofn mit hint shteyt men oyf mit fley*, "If you lie down to sleep with dogs you get up with fleas." I knew one such woman in my boyhood in Manchester (there, as in Roumania, my family had little contact with *negidistes* and *yakhsntes*); she was the wife of an insurance agent who was reputed to earn a pound (five dollars at that time) a day, and her father had been a rabbi in Braila. I can still hear her using such locutions; I can see the round pious face, the pursed lips, and the imperious "goydering" when she handed my father a pair of shoes to be mended.

I suppose the father of all Grundyisms is the verse in Psalms 37:25: "I have been young, and I am old, and I have not seen the righteous forsaken or their seed begging for bread." It is part of the grace after meals, and it has always sent me into spasms of fury. It should be recorded that when a poor man is at table with the family, *an oyrekh* (Heb) *oyf shabes*, it is the custom to sing that verse in an undertone, and as it were furtively—the unfortunate effect being, of course, to emphasize it.

Of the *yakhsn* and *yakhsnte* it is said, figuratively, that they *blozn fun zikh*, "blow from themselves," that is, "breathe importantly, portentously," and this characteristic has passed into an Israeli-Yiddish joke. "Why is it cool in Jerusalem, while it is hot in Tel Aviv?" "Because in Jerusalem you have 200,000 Jews *vos blozn fun zikh*, while in Tel Aviv you have 500,000 Jews *vos kokhen zikh.*" *Kokhn zikh*, literally, "cook, boil oneself," is "to be hotly busy, excitedly protesting, or asserting." *Di shtot hot zikh gekokht* would be "the whole town was seething."

The *yakhsn* riding high was *ex officio* a *takif*, "a man of influence," laying down the law, brooking no contradiction. Of course there were those who jeered at times; his hunger for *koved*, "honors," was matter for mirth even when they catered to it. The saying was, *me shtarbt nisht fun hunger, me shtarbt fun koved*, "People don't die of hunger, they die of (frustrated) honors." The *yakhsn* was often suspected of being far less well-to-do than he pretended to be; his learning might be of the thinnest kind. Behind his back he might be called *shuster ben shuster*, "shoemaker-son-of-a-shoemaker" (the shoemaker was near the bottom of the scale for learning), parodying the noble titles of *novi ben novi*, "prophet, son of a prophet," and *koyen ben koyen*, "priest, son of a priest" (but a priest was perforce the son of a priest). If the *yikhes* was founded only on ancestry, the *yakhsn* himself being notoriously both a *kaptsn*, "pauper," and an *amoretz*, "ignoramus," they would say concerning him, *yikhes oyfn beys hakvores un in der heym iz tsores*, "nobility in the cemetery and misery in the house."

Such talk was wholly lacking in *derkherets*, "respectfulness." In the original Hebrew *derekh-erets*, literally, "the way of the land," meant "correct behavior, social know-how," but in Yiddish it has become predominantly a Grundy word, denoting the proper comportment of a Jew toward his betters. It can however be employed with dignity. The formal signature on a letter to an important person is *mit derkherets*,

"respectfully," or even *mit groys derkherets,* "very respectfully." One may also say *er hot groys derkherets far zayn
lerer,* "He greatly respects his teacher," implying only a proper
deference. But in general the word belongs to the Establishment. Anyone without respect for his betters is a *sheygets*
(Heb), literally, "gentile boy." While retaining that meaning
for one purpose, the word has developed another meaning,
"an impudent, 'fresh' Jewish youngster" (it can be extended
to an older person, too), one without *derkherets* for his betters. From *sheygets* has evolved a hybrid verb, in which the
Hebraic is enclosed by the Germanic at each end: *oysshey-
getsn,* "to rebuke sternly, bawl out, administer a dressing
down," for behaving like a *sheygets.*

3.

Amorets, a most important word, is intimately connected
by opposites with *yikhes* and *yakhsn.* In the Bible the *am-ha-
arets,* "man of the earth, soil," is simply the peasant or land-
worker, without pejorative connotation; the word is also used
to indicate the people of the land, generally. In Talmud literature the *am-ha-arets* is the common designation for a thick-
witted, illiterate man, whether of the town or the countryside,
who spoke only the vernacular Aramaic, knew no Hebrew, and
was ignorant of the Torah and the minutiae of the Oral Law
and its vast legalistic literature. Between the *am-ha-arets* and
the *khaver,* "the fellow" of the learned brotherhood (not to
be confused with *khaver* as used in Yiddish), lay an abyss.
The *amaratsim* (I use the Yiddishized plural) glared at the
khaveyrim with rancor and envy. The *khaveyrim* repaid with
denunciation and contempt. That is the impression we gather
from passages in Talmudic and Midrashic literature. Often
the mutual hostility was softened by awe on one side and

167

compassion on the other. But until this day the Jews—insofar as the old spirit lives in them—are more fervid than any other people in their pursuit of learning, more disdainful of those who lack it and make no effort to acquire it.

Of course it is all mixed up not only with status but with economic advantage. The Talmud warns against the practice of making the Torah a crown to glory in or a spade to dig with; and of course there are instances among the Sages of high-minded men pursuing learning and wisdom on the borderline of starvation; but then as now the ideal shone the more brightly as it stood out against the real. This much must, however, be said of our times: there is far less likelihood of respect being paid to learning when it is linked with poverty than there was in the far-off past; the reason is that it is so much easier to cash in on an education today than it was then. The consequence is that if a man is learned and poor his learning is suspect.

"Ignoramus" is not a complimentary term in any language, but in the Yiddish *amorets* something more is conveyed than passive ignorance; it is, rather, the embodiment of a principle. According to the proverb, *amaratses* (the abstract noun from *amorets*) was worse than the abandonment of the faith; further, *an amorets ken keyn epikoyres nit zayn*, "an *amorets* cannot (even) be an unbeliever," lacking the training and intelligence for it. "Talking sense to an *amorets* is like describing music to a deaf man, a rainbow to a blind man, and the pleasures of sex to a eunuch," says the Talmud.

Grober yung, literally, "coarse youth," that is, "lout, boor," is often used interchangeably with *amorets*, thereby blurring the fine semantic differences between terms of abuse and diminishing their effectiveness. It is not incorrect to say *er iz a grober yung, er ken zikh afile nit untershraybn*, "He is a *grober yung*, he can't even sign his name," but one can also say, *emes, er iz nit in gantsn an amorets, ober er iz fort a grober*

168

yung, "To be sure, he is not entirely an ignoramus, but he's a lout for all that."

Amorets is so offensive a term that even an ignorant Jew would prefer to be called a *dover akher*, literally, "other thing," meaning "pig." But *dover akher*, too, must be used perceptively. The pig is so unclean an animal that the Talmud refers to it elliptically; the straightforward name, *khazir*, Yiddishized in pronunciation as *khazer*, is offensive. But *dover akher* and *khazer*, once synonymous, have drifted apart. *Dover akher* in Yiddish denotes predominantly, piggishness of the moral kind (*cf*. "swine"), while *khazer* is both literal and figurative, and in the latter use refers to the physical as well as the moral.

Thus, "the peasant slaughtered a pig" can only be translated as *der poyer hot gekoylet a khazer*, but if a man refuses to give to charity you may call him *khazer* or *dover akher* with equal propriety. The proverb says, *a kargn ruft men a khazer, a shlekhtn a kelev* (Heb), "A stingy man is called a *khazer*, a bad man a *kelev* (dog)." But the distinction does not always stand up; one who will not do you a service at no cost to himself is equally entitled to any of the three designations, *khazer*, *kelev*, or *dover akher*.

Dover akher is rarely used to describe physical filth. A filthy house will be called a *khazershtal*, "pigsty," or *khazermark*, "pig market." The people in it *lebn vi khazeyrim*, "live like pigs." A gross, intemperate eater, for which the Germanic word is *Fresser*, will be called a *khazer* rather than a *dover akher*; "hog" is then the correct translation. *Eyner vos est dos vos kvitshet*, "one who eats that which squeals," is himself a *khazer*, in which case "pig," connoting filthiness, is the correct translation. A *khazer* is also a greedy man; in the saying, *vil men zayn a gvir darf men zikh farshraybn oyf tsvantsik yor a khazer*, "If one wants to become a rich man one must sign up for twenty years as a *khazer*," the correct translation would be "swine."

169

Fun a khazer a hor iz oykh gut, "A hair (bristle) from a pig is good, too," can mean that a donation is not tainted by its source, or *pecunia non olet*. The saying has particular point because there were orthodox Jews who traded in pig's bristles —which Jewish law did not forbid. Another popular saying runs, *az men est khazer zol rinen iber dem moyl*, "If you're eating pig, let it run over your mouth," which is idiomatically akin to "going the whole hog," "in for a penny in for a pound," "as well be hanged for a sheep as a lamb." *Lebn a khazerishn tog*, "live a hoggish life," a popular locution, is not as bad as it sounds; the connotation is usually humorous, and the corresponding idiom is "living it up." It can be used in connection with a very modest splurge or binge.

Why *khazer* should have become for Jews the last word in offensiveness, with no rival, is not easily explained. According to the law, all animals that neither chew the cud nor have cloven hooves are *treyf*, "tabu, unclean," and unfit for consumption. Now the hare disqualifies on both counts, while the pig does qualify on one, for though it does not chew the cud it has a cloven hoof; yet the *hoz*, "hare," is quite inoffensive in Yiddish, though the flesh is not less strictly forbidden as food. It might of course be asked why the pig is universally despised, at least in our Western civilization. The usual answer, that it lives a filthy life and will eat practically anything, does not hold water. In any case it will not account for the almost convulsive repulsion it inspires among Jews. Does it date from the time when the Seleucid tyrant defiled the altar of Jehovah by sacrificing a pig on it? But perhaps he chose a pig, rather than an ox because that was the most offensive form his insult could take, and we are back at the original *kashe*. Perhaps it is the very fact that the pig half-qualifies by having a cloven hoof that accounts for the Jewish antipig syndrome, just as a half-truth is so much more dishonest than a downright lie. *Der khazer shtelt aroys dos koshere fisl,* "The pig thrusts out its kosher little leg," runs the saying; or, more briefly, *kosher khazer fisl,* describing the attempt to put over a fraud by presenting a *kosher, i.e.,* "honest," feature of it, the come-on, as it were. The use of *kosher* in that sense is good Yiddish and has passed into English.

I will close this brief note on *khazer* with a Yiddish pun, and as with all Yiddish puns and jokes we must make some explanation. As we have seen, the word describes, among other unappetizing types, the stingy man, the nongiver, who is sometimes referred to ironically as a *tsadik,* "saint," instead of as a *khazer.* A saint is one who behaves *betsedek,* "with righteousness," but in the case of the human *khazer* his real character is betrayed by the four Hebrew letters *b,ts,d,k* which spell out the name. They are an acronym for the Yiddish *biz tsu der keshene,* "as far as the pocket."

4.

Among the more pungent words is *kadokhes,* literally, "fever," usually malarial, but used figuratively in a number of hearty and homey expressions, none of them friendly. A *naynyerik kadokhes,* "a nine-year fever," is a commonplace curse, competing with *a kholerye oyf im,* "a cholera upon him," both vulgar. *Ikh vel im gebn a kadokhes,* "I'll give him a kadokhes," is an angry and emphatic way of saying "I'll give him nothing!" (in England, somewhat more vulgar, "I'll give him bugger-all!") and is somewhat stronger than *ikh vel im gebn a krenk,* "I'll give him a sickness." For additional emphasis the sentence is inverted: *a kadokhes vel ikh im gebn, a krenk vel ikh im gebn.* To make it more offensive, *mit koshere fodem,* "with kosher thread" (a reference to the pious measurement of graves) may be added (in England "with knobs on").

171

There is also the nasty and mincing phrase, *a kadokhes in a kleyn tepele*, "a kadokhes in a small pot." These belong properly under "Benedictions and Maledictions."

Gilgl, "reincarnation," sounds a philosophically sophisticated note in English, but is in Yiddish a folk concept, freely used. One can hear very simple people say *oyf an andern gilgl*, "in another incarnation." I find something Yiddish in the exchange between the clown and Malvolio in *Twelfth Night*:

> CLOWN: What is the opinion of Pythagoras concerning wild-fowl?
> MALVOLIO: That the soul of our grandam might haply inhabit a bird.

Malvolio's answer translates neatly into Yiddish: *az di bobe ken megulgl vern in a foygl*.

Dayge, "care, worry," is biblical, and, like *kapore*, richer in Yiddish than in Hebrew. The verb is *daygen* and *a yid dayget*, "A Jew worries," or *a yid iz fardayget*, is a description of his nature: The Jew is a worrier. One could use, with milder effect, the Germanic *der yid iz farzorgt*, but *farzorgn*, as a verb, also means "to provide." The most customary form of *dayge* is the wholly Hebraic *dayges parnose*, "worry for one's livelihood." Another Germanic word in the same category, but this time very powerful, is *kopdarenish*, literally "withering of the head," from worry. *Di verm esn toyterheyt un dayges lebedikerheyt*, "Worms gnaw the dead, worries the living," says one proverb, and another, sardonic, *fremde dayges ken men aribertrogn*, "The other man's worries can (easily) be borne." These melancholy sayings are balanced by the stout-hearted admonition *nisht gedayget!*, "chin up!" To express indifference to another's *dayges*, or toward an unfortunate event, one says, with a shrug, *mayn bobes dayge*, "My grandmother's worry," *i.e.*, "I should worry."

5.

Some thousands of Hebrew and Hebraic words are indispensable for a knowledge of Yiddish. A number will be found scattered throughout the text; some of the most popular, chosen more or less at random, follow here:

Boser-vedom, "flesh and blood," reminds a man what he essentially is. A *proster* (Slv) *boser vedom,* "a plain, ordinary man," any Tom, Dick, or Harry, is also called *a proster khay vekayem,* "an ordinary living, existing thing." In the Jewish prayers we are admonished that when we must give an accounting of ourselves on the Judgment Day, it will be before the King of kings, who is not that hollow thing, *a melekh boser vedom,* "a king of flesh and blood."

Gey shray khay vekayem, "Go cry (God) the living and existing," reflects a hopeless situation, when nothing can be done, and appealing to God is the last useless resort. The feeling is reflected in the anecdote of the old lady who, told by the captain of the ship at the height of a storm, "Madame, we are in the hands of Providence," replied, "Is it as bad as all that?" From overuse *gey shray khay vekayem,* has dwindled into nothing more than a petulance. The Hebrew letters for *khay,* "living" (often misused to mean "life"), add up to eighteen, whence donors to charitable causes frequently offer *khay* dollars, etc., or multiples of *khay,* for good luck.

Mamesh, "actually, literally," is a self-canceling word, which is partly true of the English; it has become a sort of filling noise, and in the cliché, "The table was literally groaning under the weight of the good things" we are speaking figuratively, and "literally" has literally become its own opposite. So with *mamesh: er hot im mamesh tserisn vi a hering,"* "He literally tore him apart like a herring," said, for instance,

173

of a merciless review of a book, and never under any circumstances implying physical violence.

Roshe, "the wicked man," the antonym of *tsadik,* "saint," so often appears opposite him in the Bible, that the two go in a pair both in Hebrew and in Yiddish. The word is attached with especial vehemence to certain historical figures. Haman, who sought to destroy the Jews of the Persian Empire, is naturally referred to as *homen haroshe,* "Haman, the wicked one"; so with Titus, who destroyed the Temple, *titus haroshe.* Oddly enough, Pharaoh, one of the most wicked of men, is never referred to as *paroy haroshe;* he is merely *paroy melekh mitsrayim,* "Pharaoh, King of Egypt." An emphatic form of "wicked man" is the repeat form, *roshe merushe,* "irreclaimably wicked."

Yemakh shemoy, "Let his name be wiped out," to which may be added for good measure, *vezikhroy,* "and his memory," is Hebrew that has passed without change into Yiddish, and is not so much a curse as an expletive of hatred. The expression began, in not quite the same grammatical form, with the story of Amalek, who remained one of the bitterest memories in the earliest history of Israel. We read in Deuteronomy 25:17-19: "Remember what Amalek did to you on your journey, after you left Egypt—how . . . when you were famished and weary . . . cut down all the stragglers in your rear. Therefore when the Lord your God grants you safety from all your enemies around you . . . you shall blot out the memory of Amalek from under the heavens." The name of Hitler has in a sense replaced that of Amalek for Yiddish Israel, and one says almost automatically, "Hitler, *yemakh shemoy.*" The expression has been turned into a noun, *yemakh-shemoynik,* which, while pejorative, has not the original rage of *yemakh shemoy.*

Haklal, aklal, "Be that as it may," like *nu,* is a filler-word without intrinsic meaning. It can also be rendered by "so, well, to sum up, to make a long story short, what's the use of talking," and perhaps by the repulsive "like," "like one day I was going down the street."

Makhteyse, "Okay as far as I'm concerned, good by me, makes no difference." "Shall I cook you some noodles today?" "*Makhteyse!*" It is the mildest possible form of approval.

Nishkoshe, nishkoshedik, "so-so, all the same, considerably"; *er vet nishkoshe nit untergeyn,* "All the same, he won't go under"; *dos iz a nishkoshediker nar,* "That man is no inconsiderable fool"; *vi geyt es mit ayere eyniklekh? a dank, gants nishkoshe,* "How are your grandchildren getting along? Not badly, thank you."

Akhtsn un draytsn, literally, "eighteen and thirteen," etymologically not Hebraic but Germanic, belongs among Hebraisms by way of content. The numbers eighteen and thirteen add up to thirty-one, for which the Hebrew notation in letters is *lamed alef,* which make up the word *loy,* "no." But the negative content of the phrase *akhtsn un draytsn* is indirect; it indicates a subject of discussion that is not to be mentioned directly. It is always humorous in effect. *Ikh vil mit aykh redn mekoyekh akhtsn un draytsn* seems to have different meanings in different localities: (1) as an introduction to a negation, (2) as compelling someone to return to a subject he wishes to evade, (3) as introducing a discussion of money matters: *ober vos hert zikh mekoyekh akhtsn un draytsn,* "But what about that matter we were discussing?" or "What about the money side of the question?"

Hekdesh, "flophouse," maintained by the community for wandering beggars and even entire families; thence any rundown, neglected, orderless, filthy place. Originally the word, related to *koydesh,* "holy," meant anything sanctified to the Temple, but it has suffered the same fate as the English "imprecation," which, rooted in the Latin for "prayer," has wound up as a curse: *bay mir in hoyz iz a hekdesh,* "In my house there's (physical) chaos."

Makhsheyfe, "witch," feminine of *mekhashef,* "wizard,

magician," but with a twist of its own. *Mekhashef* is a simple word, without shadings; *maksheyfe* is quite complicated. Formally it can denote a female practitioner of magic, but as a rule it is an opprobrious description of a woman rather than a sorceress. *Makhsheyfe* impugns either character or appearance or both; in English we can speak of "an attractive witch," but no such locution can be used of a *makhsheyfe*. Often one speaks of *an alte makhsheyfe*, "a mean, unpleasant old woman," in a general way. Most of the offensive words for a woman are formed from the Hebraic: *klafte*, "bitch," the feminine of *kelev*, "dog," denotes nastiness, and goes deeper than the English equivalent; *klipe*, "evil spirit," describes a corrosive persistence; *marshas* (connected with *roshe*), "wicked one," suggests ill temper, cruelty, brutality. All are topped by *arure*, "accursed one," the homicidally shrewish, nagging, pitilessly faultfinding woman.

Kholile, khas-vekholile, khas-vesholem are synonyms: "God forbid, *absit omen*." The phrases are used as a kind of warding-off incantation, like the Italian thumb-and-little-finger gesture: *er iz kholile nit in shpitol?* "He is not, God forbid, in the hospital?" The expression is both negative adjuration and disclaimer: *er iz nit ibrik opgehit, ober er vet zikh khas-vekholile nit tsurirn tsu khazer-fleysh*, "He is not particularly observant, but he will not, God forbid, touch pork."

Avade, "assuredly, undoubtedly, it goes without saying, obviously": *avade iz er der raykhster in der shtot*, "Beyond contradiction he is the richest man in the town," but *er iz avade der raykhster man in der shtot*, "He is undoubtedly the richest man in the town," which is not quite as strong. *Kumt er morgn? Avade!* "Is he coming tomorrow? Certainly!" But *er vet avade kumen morgn*, "He will undoubtedly come tomorrow," has a shade of doubt.

Sgule, "specific, remedy," quite different from the Hebrew original: *di dozike kraytekhtser hob ikh a sgule nokh fun mayn zeydn,* "These herbs I have still as a specific (cure) from my grandfather"; *me zogt az a trunk bronfn iz a sgule tsu a tsonveytik,* "They say that a drink of whiskey is a specific against toothache." When Leo Pinsker published his *Auto-Emancipation,* famous in Zionist history as one of the first calls to self-liberation by the Jewish people, Mendele Moycher Sforim called it, half-ironically, *a sgule tsu yidishe tsores,* "A cure to the woes of the Jews."

6.

There is a large class of words, practically all Hebraic, that personalizes qualities by placing the Hebrew word (not used by itself in Yiddish) *bal,* "owner of, characterized by," in front of another noun. *Baal,* "lord," was the generic title for a "god" as distinguished from the God of the Jewish people. To worship a *baal* was a mortal sin. Specifically, Baal was the Canaanite god whom we know in English from one of his attributes, Beelzebub, "Lord of the Flies," whom Milton finds particularly repugnant. When followed by another noun, as in the following examples, *bal* can be regarded as a prefix. The whole is completely and warmly Yiddish (the attached word is translated first):

Bal-deye, "opinion," a man whose opinions are respected, whose advice has weight, who has a say in communal affairs.

Bal-mum, "defect," a man with a physical defect, hence a cripple of some kind.

Balebos, a popularization of *bal habayis,* meaning in Yiddish (but not in Hebrew), "householder."

Bal-gayve, "pride," a proud, boastful, pretentious, arrogant man, is sometimes oddly reinforced with the Slavic personalizing suffix *nik* and becomes *bal-gayvenik.*

Bal-kaas, "anger," a choleric man, one who flies easily

177

off the handle, is also known, by another development of the same word, as a *kaysn*.

Bal-aveyre, "sin," and *bal-tayve*, "lust, desire," hence "sinful man," or "sinner," and "lustful man, lecher," like *bal-gayve*, have additional identities as *bal-aveyrenik* and *bal-tayvenik*. The Slavic suffix adds very little—perhaps a suggestion of "habitual," but that only in the case of *bal-aveyre*, for this word can be used of a person who happens to have committed a sin. But *bal-tayve*, "lecher," already implies habit, and the addition of *nik* does not make him more inveterate. *Bal-tayvenik* enjoys the privilege of a feminine form, *bal-tayvenitse*, not extended, as far as I know, to *bal-aveyrenik*. A *bal-tayvenitse* is a peculiarly unnatural creature. How dare she encroach on male territory?

Bal-melokhe, "craft, work, occupation," is at once a proud and a humble word. The "working man" is the salt of the earth, the mainstay of a people. He was regarded with respect as the antithesis of the *luftmentsh*, literally, "man of air," who has no visible means of support, and grabs his livelihood out of the atmosphere; the *bal-melokhe* was the honest craftsman, with two creative arms and ten creative fingers. On the other hand, the *bal-melokhe* was the pitiful laborer, who relied on hands and fingers because he hadn't the brains or training or status to dispense with them. Those born into the class of *bal-melokhes* accepted their fate as self-understood, but for the son of a scholar, or rabbi, or even *shoykhet* (though Lord knows the last was dependent on hands and fingers), to be apprenticed to a *shuster*, "shoemaker," or *shnayder*, "tailor," or *bodner*, "cooper," was the last word in disgrace; not less so for the son of a merchant. The keeper of a miserable hole-in-the-wall store, stocked with a barrel of herrings and half a barrel of flour, was a *soykher*, "merchant"; he was not a wage-slave, trembling before a boss. He was secure in his self-esteem, though his humiliations might exceed a hundred-fold those of the *meshores*, "clerk, assistant." Linked with the savage social snobbery of the attitude toward the *bal-melokhe* was the original notion that the worker with his hands had neither the capacity nor the inclination to devote a portion of the day to study.

But, again, the *bal-melokhe* in his own way, and especially in the circle of his peers, was a fortress of respectability, and even of pride. A *melokhe iz a melukhe* (Heb), they punned, "A craft is a kingdom." There were, as separate institutions, the *balmelokhishe shuln*, "the workingmen's synagogues," *die shnayderishe shul, die shusterishe shul*, and so on. The standards of learning there were lower, but the workman could aspire to honorable office on his own level. We have already seen that *shuster* was a synonym for lack of learning; it must be added that for some reason this honorable craft—exalted in the Talmud as that of one of the great scholars, Rabbi Yokhanan—was regarded with extreme and unwarranted disdain. *Di shustergas*, "the street of the shoemakers," was the figure of speech for coarseness, ignorance, and uncouthness. To call a man a *shuster* when he isn't one is even more offensive than to remind one who is that he is.

Bal-tsdoke, "charity," a charitable man, in the sense of almsgiver, not of kindliness in thought. Writers on Jewish ethics correctly insist that the original meaning of *tsdokoh* in Hebrew was "righteousness," hence it followed that the giver of *tsdokoh* was simply obeying the moral law and not dispensing favors. But just as the *kadish*, which was originally a paean to the greatness of God repeated in connection with the memory of the dead, declined in popular usage into a redemptive incantation, so *tsdoke* has declined into something like a cant word. It is also a snivel word; to accept *tsdoke* has about it the unpleasant flavor of "going to the charities." It further resembles the deterioration of *kadish* in its redemptive association, but then in most religions the distribution of part of one's earthly possessions is supposed to represent an investment in the life to come. (I once heard a speaker at a

United Jewish Appeal dinner say, "You can't take it with you, but you can send it ahead.") It was also a *sgule* on this side of the grave. At Jewish funerals, collectors for various institutions would circulate among the mourners rattling their *tsdoke pushkes* and intoning ominously the well-known Hebrew admonition, *tsdoke tatsl mimoves*, "Charity saves from death," a rather tactless reflection, one would think, on the man just being buried.

Bal-khoyv, "debt, obligation," a man liable in some respect, a man burdened by debts—a richly environmented designation. *Khayev*, with the meaning "guilty, responsible, being liable to," is a frequent word in Talmudic legal discussion, taken over into Yiddish; *oyb der vogn iz arayngeforn in a blote iz der balegole khayev*, "If the wagon drove into a mudhole, the wagoner is guilty, responsible." The reflexive *zikh mekhayev zayn*, "make oneself responsible for, to undertake responsibility," is sound, homey Yiddish: *ikh bin zikh mekhayev oystsuhaltn tsvey yesoymim*, "I undertake to support two orphans."

Bal-makhloykes, "quarrel, dispute," denotes a litigious, disputatious, quarrelsome man, one who "cavils on the ninth part of a hair," who is forever at odds with his fellowmen on some point of honor or property. He should be compared with the *bal-nitsokhn*.

Bal-tshuve, "penitence, turning from sin," one of the very important words in Yiddish ethical and religious discourse, is treated more fully further on.

Bal-nes, bal-hanes, "miracle," a wonder-worker. We have met Reb Meir *bal-hanes*, the wonder-worker, whose *pushke* stood in so many orthodox Jewish homes half a century ago. Though there have been many wonder-working rabbis with records of staggering performances, I cannot recall that in the popular usage the title *bal-hanes* was ever applied to anyone other than Reb Meir. His purported tomb is a place of great sanctity in Israel, and a visit to it is a meritorious act.

180

But there are other purported tombs in the Holy Land, like that of Simeon ben Yokhai, that compete with it.

Bal-shem, "name," literally, "master of the name," has two senses. One has to do with the name of God, and therefore designates a miracle worker; standing by itself, the *bal-shem* is understood to refer to Israel ben Eliezer (1700–60), the founder of Chassidism, though the title has been conferred on a number of the thaumaturges of east European Jewry from the Middle Ages on. To Israel ben Eliezer was reserved the name of *bal-shem-tov,* "master of the good name," but here it does not seem to mean the man who wrought miracles by his command of the Name, but merely "the man of good name."

Bal-khay, "life" (plural, *baley-khayim*), literally, "possessor of life," refers to any living thing, and is part of a moving phrase that has passed straight from the Talmud into Yiddish, *tsar baley-khayim,* "sorrow of, for living things." It has the compassionate touch of *lachrymae rerum,* "the tears of things." In ordinary usage *tsar baley-khayim* stands for "kindness to animals," and pity is expressed for a suffering animal in the phrase *s'iz a tsar baley-khayim.*

CHAPTER ELEVEN

Hebraic But Not Hebrew

1.

If the Jews had continued to speak Hebrew throughout all their vicissitudes—the Babylonian exile, the Return, the Diaspora—it would, to use an Irishism, have ceased to be Hebrew; it would have become, under the name of Hebrew, as different from its early self as Anglo-Saxon is from modern English. Or there would have been many varieties of "Hebrew" developed throughout the Diaspora, unintelligible to one another. The survival of Hebrew, and its restitution to the status of a vernacular, has in fact been due to its long preservation in warm storage. It was not used often enough, between the expulsion from Judaea and the reestablishment of the Jewish State, to undergo the changes that attend daily handling. The Hebrew of the Mishnah is understood without difficulty by anyone familiar with the Hebrew of the Bible; so is the Hebrew of Rashi and the other medieval commentators. The modern Hebrew writers of prose and poetry—let us say Ahad Ha-am and Bialik—call for a little adjustment in grammatical uses and vocabulary. But the Hebrew of an Israeli newspaper is another story; as for the Hebrew of the army, the street and the factory, one must learn it almost like a new language.

On the whole it is astonishing that the Hebrew which has been preserved in Yiddish is so close to the original, and that the adaptations that need complete reinterpretation are so few. Nevertheless there are many examples of Hebrew words taken into Yiddish and given totally new meanings. An outstanding instance is *mesles*, which denotes a period of twenty-four hours, just as "fortnight" denotes one of fourteen days. The etymology of *mesles* is simple: *me-eys le-eys*, literally "from the time (of day) to the time (of day)." But *mesles* is not Hebrew, modern or ancient; it is Yiddish and only Yiddish.

Among the examples that follow, some are far richer in Yiddish than in the original Hebrew; they have absorbed wonderful colorations from Diaspora history and illustrate the creative ingenuity of the folk.*

2.

Mayse, "deed, fact, story," is a word of enormously greater versatility in Yiddish than in Hebrew. The usages overlap and one is not always sure when the sense is Hebrew or has a new and Yiddishized meaning. However, all the words and phrases listed in this chapter are sound Yiddish.

Mayse shehoye (Heb), "a story that was, that actually happened," is the antonym of *mayse sheloy hoye veloy nivre* (all Heb), "that never was and never came to pass." *Mayse shehoye* is also "a thing of the past":

> *Itster iz zi rak* (Heb) *an alte goye,*
> *Un ir sheynkeyt iz a mayse shehoye.*
> Now she is only an old gentile woman,
> And her beauty is a thing of the past.
> —Jacob Glatstein

Mayse bereyshis, "the story, the fact, of the beginning," refers to the Creation; *bereyshis*, "in the beginning," is the first word in the Hebrew Bible. But *onfangen* (or *onheybn*) *fun bereyshis*, "to begin with the beginning, to start all over again," does not have a biblical connotation.

* Unless otherwise indicated all the non-Hebrew words in this chapter are of German origin; the few exceptions are Slavic (Slv).

Mayse sotn (Heb), "act of Satan," is a semihumorous colloquialism with little of the satanic about it. The nearest English equivalent, "as ill luck would have it," is a trifle too prissy: *dafke* (Heb) *ven ikh bin gegangen shpatsirn in mayn shabesdik* (Heb) *kleydl hot mayse sotn oysgebrokhn a shlaksregn*, "Just when I went out for a stroll in my holiday dress there came on, devil take it, a downpour"; but "devil take it" is too strong.

Mayse is widely used in the sense of *à la*, "in the manner of." *Er hot mikh oyfgenumen breytlech, mayse gvir* (Heb). "He received me in great style, as becomes a man of wealth"; *borgn bay an oremer almone* (Heb) *un nit opgebn heyst bay mir mayse parekh* (Slv), "To borrow from a poor widow and not pay back is what I call the act of a stinker"; *kharote* (Heb) *iz nit mayse soykher* (Heb), "Regretting, changing one's mind, going back on a deal, is not the way of a businessman."

Gor a mayse!, literally, "Altogether a story"; idiomatically, "What kind of story is that?" It is a two-edged skeptical expletive: It either decries the story as implausible, the teller himself not believing it, or it derides the teller if he claims to believe it.

Gekhapt (Slv) *in der mayse*, literally, "caught in the act," but quite different in meaning, nearer to "ideologically tainted," though not so formal. A man reputed to hold unorthodox beliefs will be described as *a bisl gekhapt in der mayse*, which does not mean that he has "been (a little) caught at it," but rather "caught in it." "Caught in the act," meaning *in flagrante delicto*, is *gekhapt be-eys* (Heb) *mayse*, "at the moment of the deed," or *beshas* (Heb) *mayse*, literally "the hour of the deed."

Mayse sdom, "act of Sodom," is, technically, "homosexuality," but has broadened to cover all of forms of evil. Many readers will remember that on a wall of Pompeii, excavated eighteen hundred years after its burial by the eruption of Vesuvius in the year 79, someone had scribbled, ap-

parently in the last hour, *Sodoma!* Whether it was a Jewish
or a Christian hand that wrote the frantic word we do not
know, but that *Sodoma* stood for wickedness in general and
not for a particular perversion is quite clear. So it is in Hebrew
and in Yiddish, too. The Jewish legends tell that the Sodom-
ites were the inventors of the Procrustean bed for the entertainment of trapped wayfarers; a favorite Hebraic term, which
has passed into Yiddish, is *sdom-betl* (diminutive of *bet*),
"bed of Sodom."

Maysim toyvim (Heb), "good, pious deeds," a collective
phrase without a singular; "a good deed" would have to be
translated as *mitsve*. The prayer of God-fearing parents for
their sons was that they might grow up to *toyre, khupe, un
maysim toyvim*, "to Torah, the wedding canopy, and good
deeds."

Maysim tatuim (Heb), literally, "wild, irregular deeds,"
i.e., wickedness, is the opposite of *maysim toyvim*, including
anything from parricide and incest to eating pork on *yom
kiper*.

Dos iz keyn mayse nit, literally, "This is no story," meaning "This won't do at all," "I can't accept that."

A *mayse on a sof* (Heb), "a story without an end," does
not relate to a narrative but to an affair dragging out inter-
minably: "There's going to be no end to this business." Similarly, *heybt zikh on a mayse*, literally, "a story begins," is an
exclamation of protest, "Once you begin this business, there'll
be no end to it."

Vos iz di mayse, literally, "What's the story?", is the
same as *vos iz der mer*, "What's the matter? What's wrong?"

Bobe (Slv) *mayse*, "grandmother story," is either a story
for children or the equivalent of "rubbish, baloney, etc." In
the former it is supposed to be a corruption of *bovo mayse*,
or "Bovo Story," the medieval romance described in Chapter
Seven. The origin of the phrase was forgotten and *bobe mayse*
no doubt owes its survival (perhaps it is a case of parallel

birth) to the accidental resemblance of *bovo* to *bobe*. But *bobe* does not, here, mean grandmother; it is nearer to "old crone." *Bobitse*, diminutive of *bobe*, never, in fact, refers to a "grandmother." Similarly, *bobske refues* (Heb) is "old wives' remedies." A man offering clumsy excuses or explanations will be told *dertseyl mir nit keyn bobe mayses*, "Don't give me any cock-and-bull stories."

A *mayse noyre* (Heb), "a tale of dread," describes an unusual calamity or tragedy, involving death, murder, demons, and all "moving accidents by flood and field."

Mayse nes (Heb), "miraculous event," *per contra*, tells of providential intervention at the last desperate moment and, generally, hairbreadth escapes in the imminent deadly breach —except that the last must not be taken militarily, as described by Othello, and would often involve the universal benefactor, the Prophet Elijah.

A *miese* (Heb) *mayse*, "an ugly story," refers to a piece of villainy or meanness, and is more or less the same as *maysim sheloy yaasu* (Heb), "deeds that are not, ought not to be done."

A very popular locution is *oyf a mayse fregt men nisht keyn kashe*, "regarding a story you don't ask questions," *i.e.*, since it is all a matter of the imagination, it is foolish to look for rhyme or reason. The saying has been contracted into *a kashe oyf a mayse!*, a phrase with which one shrugs off an irrelevant challenge to probability, as if to say: "God knows! In these circumstances, from what you tell me, or with that person, anything could be true."

Mayse bikhl, "story book," is a somewhat derogatory phrase. A serious person had no time or taste for *mayse bikhlekh*, which were for women (and men) who were able to read Yiddish but not Hebrew. There were enough of these, however, to support a regular trade, and the *pakntreyger*, "pack-carrier," who made the rounds of the villages derived a goodly portion of his income from *mayse bikhlekh*. These, wretchedly printed on coarse paper, were very often edifying accounts of rabbis and wonder-workers. The learned and pious Jew would not touch them with a barge pole; but then, for him the *Iliad* and the *Odyssey* too were *mayse bikhlekh*.

Arbetn maysim, "to work deeds," is "to carry on vigorously, make a great to-do, move heaven and earth," much like *kern veltn*, "turn worlds upside down" in order to get what one wants. Both phrases are on the light side.

Opton a mayse, literally, "finish off a deed," is "to play someone a dirty trick" or "to pull off a neat [usually shady] piece of work": *er hot mir opgeton a mayse*, "He put one over on me."

Herst a mayse!, literally, "You hear that story!", is an exclamation of astonishment, not so much at the content of the story as at the credulity, unreasonableness, etc., of the man who relates it. It may be rendered as "What did you expect?"

Zikh onton a mayse, literally, "to do a deed upon oneself," is "to commit suicide." It is most often used as a threat, *ikh vel zikh onton a mayse*, "I'll do something to myself"; however, frequent use has taken the terror out of it. Therein it resembles the threat with which a pious young Jew terrified his equally pious father: "If you don't give me what I want, I will do a deed which no Jew or *goy* has ever done in the history of the world." After long pleading the father prevailed on the son to reveal the nature of the awful act. *Ikh vel onton tfiln* (Heb) *shabes*, "I'll don my phylacteries for the Sabbath prayers." (This is forbidden by the religious code, the phylacteries being reserved for the weekdays.)

Emese (Heb) *mayse*, "true story," is on the one hand literal, "a thing that really happened." There is a humorous saying, *dos iz nit a fakt, dos iz an emese mayse*, "This isn't merely a fact, it's a true story." On the other hand, *di emese mayse* can be very ominous, hinting at what is too painful to mention: *ikh hob gehert az ruvn iz krank, vos iz der mer*

190

mit im?, "I've heard that Reuben is sick, what's the matter with him?" *Ikh hob moyre* (Heb) *az s'iz di emese mayse,* "I'm afraid it's the real thing," meaning a fatal disease, usually cancer.

3.

We have noted that *balebos* is the Yiddishized form of *bal-habayis* (so written in Yiddish, too), meaning in the original "lord, owner of the house," also that *balebos* has come to mean "boss," *tout court.* The word has, however, the weight of a class, the solid middle class, usually the man of substance, but not excluding the respectably established working man, head of a family. The *balebos* is the backbone of society, the mass counterpoise to the wealthy *gvir.* One does not become a *balebos* merely by having a trade and marrying. At first, one is only a *balebesl,* a miniature *balebos;* as status is confirmed over the years, also as one accumulates possessions and progeny, one becomes a *gantser balebos.* But this last phrase is also used ironically of one who assumes authority without warrant: *ze nor, ikh bet dikh, er iz mir gevorn a gantser balebos,* "Look at him, will you, he acts as if he owned the town."

A man's household and its contents were his *balebatishkeyt,* the little realm that made him a *balebos;* but sometimes the word referred only to the physical possessions: *ikh hob ayngepakt mayn bisl balebatishkeyt un zikh aribergepeklt keyn varshe,* "I packed up my few belongings and moved to Warsaw." In that sense a man needed little indeed to speak of *balebatishkeyt* or *balebos: yeder hunt iz a balebos oyf zayn shvel,* "Every dog is a *balebos* on his own threshold," as every cock is lord on his own dunghill. But the real *balebos* was something else again: *eyder vos, eyder ven, a balebos blaybt a balebos,* "Come what may, *balebos* remains *balebos*"; and *di gzeyre* (Heb) *iz farbay der balebos blaybt balebos,* "The evil decree has passed away, the *balebos* is still *balebos,*" which can be loosely interpreted as "Tyrants come and go, laws are passed and abrogated, a *balebos* is always a *balebos.*"

The female of the species is the *baleboste,* who lacks the pretentiousness of the male. The *baleboste,* without qualification, is simply the housewife. She can, however, rise to the rank of a *berye* (Heb), by her diligence, resourcefulness, spotless cleanliness, ability as a cook, etc., and can also decline to a *shlumperke,* "slattern," or a shade lower, to a *shtinkern,* literally, "stinker." *Berye* also means a woman (and sometimes man) of great general ability, a doer of things, a go-getter; the housewife of Proverbs 31, "the woman of valor," is of course the *berye* of *beryes.* To go back to the other extreme, *az di baleboste iz a shtinkern iz di kats a nashern,* "If the *baleboste* is a slattern, the cat has a sweet tooth (snatches tidbits)"; or *zibn yor iz di baleboste in shtub und veyst nit az di kats iz on an ek,* "Seven years the *baleboste* is in the house and doesn't know that the cat is without a tail."

The *balegole,* "drayman, wagoner, coachman," the role in which we find the immortal Tevye before he became *oyfgerikht,* "lifted up," by the near-miracle, was with a possible single exception, at the bottom of the social and cultural scale—and therefore we must be careful to remember that Tevye did not belong to the species *balegole;* he was far too thoughtful, too sensitive to ideas. Certainly of all *bal-melokhes* (Heb), "working men" (but one hardly thought of a *balegole* as a *bal-melokhe,* it was no kind of profession), the *balegole,* ranking below the *shuster,* was least likely to develop a spiritual life. He was so often on the road, and led such an unnaturally healthy and outdoor life, that he was identified with the illiterate Slav peasant. His occupation was supposed to need no skill; its monotony and its physical demands reduced the mind to a coarse hebetude. *Der balegole fort azoy lang mitn ponem*

(Heb) *tsu di ferd, biz er vert aleyn a ferd,* "The *balegole* travels
so long with his face toward the horses that he becomes a horse
himself." (We must remember that the horse, which has not in
Yiddish its nobler aspect as "steed, courser, charger," etc.,
was the symbol of stupidity.) *Leyz undz oys, got, fun goles
un fun di balegoles,* "Deliver us, O Lord, from exile (*goles*)
and the *balegoles,*" was no doubt partly inspired by the pun,
but *balegoles,* meaning here "coarse, illiterate, ignorant people," is another illustration of the low esteem in which the
unhappy drayman was held (*cf.* the taxi-driver, the mech-
anized *balegole,* of a generation ago).

Lower even than the *balegole* was the *bodyung,* "bath
attendant," whose duty it was to stoke the fire and douse the
heated stones with water, sending bursts of steam up through
the wooden tiers of the bathhouse for the delight of the naked
Jews smiting each other with willow-withes. This was not a
penitential exercise, but a thorough body cleansing generally
preceding the Sabbath. *Bodyung* became detached from the
occupation and turned into an insult at large, coarser and
with more moral opprobrium than *balegole.*

The *balmelokhes,* the little shopkeepers, the masses, made
up *amkho* (Heb), the common people, the plebs. In the Hebrew, *amkho,* literally, "Thy people," covered all, rich, poor,
scholar, *amorets* (Heb), sinner, saint; but in the Yiddish it
excluded the wealthy, the distinguished, and the learned. However, *amkho* is not an offensive term like "the great un-
washed"; it is affectionate, if condescending. *Amkho* reads
the yellow press, sobs over *shmaltsy* plays, and loves (or
loved) hideously sentimental songs like *a brivele der mamen,*
"A Letter to Your Mother," and *eyli, eyli,* "My God, My
God, Why has Thou Forsaken Me?"

Botl (Heb), "void, of no effect," a prominent key word,
can best be explained by referring it to a Hebrew-Yiddish
phrase *botl beshishim* (Heb), "voided, made of no effect in
sixty (parts)." As almost everyone knows, Jewish religious

193

regulations forbid the mixing of meat and dairy foods. Meat dishes cannot be cooked in a pot used for dairy dishes, and vice versa; plates and utensils for meat dishes and for dairy dishes must be kept apart. If something from a dairy dish falls into a meat dish the contents of the meat dish must be thrown out, and the dish itself must be purified in a special way before it can be used again. There is, however, a limitation on this stringent ruling. If the contents of the meat dish thus contaminated exceed by sixty times the quantity of dairy food that fell into it accidentally, the contamination is ignored; it has become *botl beshishim*, "void in sixty." The phrase has passed into secular use. It may be said of German Jewry, which once ruled the roost in America, that it has become *botl beshishim* in east European Jewry; it may be said that anti-Zionist American Jews have become *botl beshishim* in the tide of pro-Israel American Jewry.

Associated with *botl* is the noun *batlen*, which has also drifted some distance from its original Hebrew usage. A *batlen* meant a man without a fixed occupation and therefore free at all times to help constitute a quorum of ten for prayers. A great city, according to the Talmud, should have at least ten *batlonim*, a constant ready-made *minyen* (Heb), "prayer quorum." In Yiddish, *batlen* is a term of high derision. It is almost a "void" person, or "non-person." If you want to demolish a man (there is no feminine form of the word) who has pretensions to being an executive, a leader, a public figure, you call him a *batlen*. He is, you aver, infected with *batlones*, congenital incapacity, fecklessness, shiftlessness, aimlessness, a sort of city beachcomber. From the verb, *batlen*, you say of such a man that *er batlt op di teg*, "he fiddles, lazes, dribbles the days away."

The *yeytser hore*, "the evil inclination," is the nearest in Jewish thinking to the doctrine of original sin, which it avoids by attributing to man the compensating *yeytser toyv*, "the good inclination." Unfortunately the *yeytser toyv* is in popular usage a rather sickly thing beside the *yeytser hore*; but, then again, the latter is often used in a fairly inoffensive sense. To be sure, Yiddish folklore represents the *yeytser hore* as insatiable. *Der yeytser hore hot an ayzernem pisk*, "The evil inclination has an iron jaw [consumes everything]." Primarily, however, the *yeytser hore* is associated with the sexual impulse, with *tayve* (Heb), "lust." Secondarily, and quite extensively, it is used to denote a powerful inclination which may be harmless in itself, sometimes even attractive, and reprehensible—if at all—only as denoting something uncontrollable. A man confessing to an inordinate addiction to stamp collecting may say, somewhat sheepishly: *ikh ken zikh nit helfn, ikh hob aza min yeytser hore tsu markes*, "I can't help myself, I have a kind of evil inclination to postage stamps."

4.

Dales, "poverty," has become hypostasized in the Yiddish folk mind, and is a living presence. The poet Mani-Leyb sings:

> *In dem oremland fun lite*
> *Zingt a foygl in a shmite,*
> *Un derfar oyf yeden rog*
> *Zingt der dales yedn tog;*
> *Zingt der dales un der oylem*
> *Zingt mit im oyf ale keylim.*
> In the poverty-land of Lithuania
> A bird sings once in seven years,
> But to make up for it, on every corner,
> Poverty sings every day.
> Poverty sings, and all and sundry
> Sing along with all their organs.

195

Of a poverty-stricken home one hears it said, *der dales fayft fun ale vinkelekh,* "Poverty whistles from every corner"; *der dales tantst in mitn shtub;* "Poverty dances in the middle of the room"; or, in the early stages, *der dales hot zikh arayngeganvet in hoyz,* "Poverty stole into the house."

But I should like to establish *dales* in English with some of its Yiddish status; I shall capitalize it henceforth, and I shall not translate it, but speak of it as one does of the Muses, Clio for history, Melpomene for tragedy, and Dales, the tenth, for poverty, a masculine Muse unknown to Parnassus, the dominant voice in the life of the Yiddish-speaking masses of eastern Europe.

Some may argue that *parnose* (Heb), "livelihood," was not less a presence in the Jewish mind than Dales, and is entitled to equal honors. Certainly the word was as familiar and as often on the lips of city and *shtetl* Jew alike, and it is not easy for American Jews of today to think themselves into the desperation with which their grandfathers prayed on the High Holy Days, and especially on Yom Kippur, for *parnose* in the new year. *Vos tut nit a yid tsulib parnose?* "What won't a Jew do to provide for his family?" reflects the humiliations of the oppressed Jew. Sometimes *khayune* (Heb) stands for *parnose;* in Poland and Hungary they also called it *pinosi,* which Jews elsewhere parodied.

God is the *mefarnes* (Heb), "He that provides," but God was occasionally forgetful, as Berel the tailor protested in Peretz's story. Since the *parnose* of so many Jews was, or came from, a tiny, wretchedly stocked shop, or a stand in the market place, or a basketful of produce (usually tended by a woman), a word closely related was *leyzn,* "to take in money (on a sale);" and *git mir tsu leyzn,* "Buy something from me," was the pitiable refrain from thousands of throats.

But if I give Dales precedence over *parnose,* it is because he was so much more present as a reality; he haunted the Jewish mind. In the opinion of Professor Dov Sadan, perhaps the

foremost authority on Yiddish, Dales was once actually a
demon, a malevolent spirit with an independent existence
which was acknowledged in countless sayings.

*Vu der dales klept zikh on ken men fun im nit azoy laykht
poter* (Heb) *vern,* "Where Dales has once fastened on, it's
no light matter to get rid of him, shake him off"; and a similar
sentiment runs to rhyme, *der dokter ken ales ober nit aroys-
traybn dem dales,* "The doctor can do everything except drive
out Dales." For Dales is the ever-present threat; *farn (far dem)
toyt un farn dales ken men zikh nit bavorenen,* "There's no
insurance against death and Dales." Moreover, *der dales hot
a grobn kop,* "Dales has a thick head," *i.e.,* where Dales reigns
one sees not the brains, which is confirmed by another saying,
der dales farshtelt di khokhme (Heb), "Dales conceals (a
man's) wisdom."

Farvos fayft der dales? "Why does Dales whistle?", that
is, why does he make his presence so manifest? The answer is,
vayl er hot nor a dude, "Because a whistle is all he has." Again,
in the same spirit, *farvos klapt der dales?* "Why does Dales
make such a racket?", *vayl er geyt in klumpes,* "Because he
wears clogs."

Dales has grades and degrees—*a dales vi a kurfirst,* "a
Dales like an Imperial Elector," or a *kuflshmoynediker* (Heb)
dales, "a Dales of eightfold amplitude," or a *draygorndiker
dales,* "a Dales three stories high," when two-story buildings
were a rarity—and Dales is hard to disguise, for *az me makht
dem dales a kaftn vert der kaftn klener,* "If you clothe Dales
in a cloak, the cloak shrinks."

Dales iz nit pasles (Heb), "Dales is not dishonesty," says
one proverb, and is contradicted by another, *dales makht
pasles,* "Dales occasions dishonesty"; however that might be,
the Grundy sector of the Yiddish world was as ashamed of
Dales as of a crime. There was another side that accepted
poverty with resignation, even with cheerfulness and gaiety;
there were some who considered it the proper condition of

the Jew, according to the Talmudic saying, "As a red ribbon becomes a white horse, so does poverty become the Daughter of Judea."

This was the view to be found among the workers rather than among the lower middle classes. Most Jews were poor, pious, and prolific, but the workers seldom dreamed of wealth, while the middle classes seldom dreamed of anything else. Among the privations of poverty none was harder to bear than its humiliations, and the desire to dissimulate it was as passionate as the desire to rise out of it.

Mit a barsht un mit a nodl bahalt men dem dales, "With a brush and a needle you hide Dales," says one proverb, and another, *mit a groshn leym makht men dem dales reyn*, "With a pennyworth of clay you clean up Dales." *Farshteln dem dales*, "concealing (the presence of) Dales," was a social imperative, failure to do so a moral disgrace. But how difficult was concealment! *Der dales leygt zikh tsu ersht oyfn ponem* (Heb), "Dales settles first on your face." Of what use then were needle and brush and a pennyworth of clay?

5.

Round the central personification, Dales, are grouped various figures and concepts. The chief of these, second only to Dales, is the *kaptsn* (Heb), "the poor man." Alas, to translate *kaptsn* as "a poor man" is to depersonalize the word, reduce it to the status of the simple Germanic *oreman*, which seems to say the same thing but by comparison says nothing at all. There are "poor men" among all peoples, but the *kaptsn* was to be found only among the Jews. He was an affirmation, an institution, in a sense the chief representative of the Jewish people. He was everywhere: *vu me geyt un vu me shteyt dreyt zikh der kaptsn in mitn*, "Whichever way

198

you turn, the *kaptsn* is there in the midst of everything." And
he was everywhere as of right, even when the well-to-do rebuked him contemptuously with *kaptsn vu krikhstu (krikhst-
du)?*", "*kaptsn*, look where you're going," or "*kaptsn*, know
your place!"

The *kaptsn* was of course haunted by Dales, but he was
not the embodiment of it, for Dales conveys indigence of
spirit as well as material want, whereas the *kaptsn* could also
be a *kasril* (Heb), an irrepressibly cheerful pauper, *orem ober
freylekh*, "poor but merry."

He would acknowledge that *der shverster ol* (Heb) *iz a
leydike keshene* (Slv), "The heaviest yoke is an empty
pocket," but he carried it with *panache*. He jested about it; he
brought to bear upon it, in high mockery, the scraps of learning left over from *kheyder* years and collected from religious
ceremonies and the visits of wandering *magidim* (Heb),
"preachers." He created an intellectual culture of poverty
whose like I have not met elsewhere, and which it is all but
impossible to convey in a language other than Yiddish.

Let me nevertheless make an attempt. I offer here an example of the wit of the *kaptsn*, with a bleak explanation (the
best I can work out) for those without Yiddish or Hebrew.
It was sung with an imitation of the *kheyder* melody of childhood.

> *Vayiten lekho* (Hebrew)
> *Keyn gelt iz nishto* (Yiddish)
> *Mital hashomayim* (Hebrew)
> *Nishto vu tsu layen* (Yiddish)
> *Mishmaney ho-orets* (Hebrew)
> *Dos gelt iz baym porets* (Yiddish)

Every Yiddish line rhymes with the Hebrew line preceding it, but instead of being a translation it is a completely
irrelevant statement, which, however, makes sense in itself

and in connection with the other Yiddish lines. The Hebrew lines contain, almost word for word, part of the blessing bestowed by Isaac upon Jacob (Genesis 27:28) under the impression that he was Esau.

Now to repeat the lines with complete translation:

Vayiten lekho (Hebrew), "He will give unto thee"
Keyn gelt iz nishto (Yiddish), "money there's none"
Mital hashomayim (Hebrew), "of the dew of the heavens"
Nishto vu tsu layen (Yiddish), "there's nowhere to borrow"
Mishmaney ho-orets (Hebrew), "of the fat of the earth"
Dos gelt iz baym porets (Yiddish), "the landowner has the money"

In this laborious elucidation nothing remains of the black gleefulness pervading the original. Here was not only a delicious piece of verbal ingenuity bringing a grin to the faces of the hungry; it was also an exercise in pious mockery, respectful irreverence, and bantering blasphemy. For the Hebrew text is from the Torah, and what could be more submissive? The translation (!) is from life, what could be more relevant? And of course the pleasure of it rose from "insideness," from that familiarity with the sacred texts in the original which was the mark, and the exclusive privilege, of the Jew still faithful to the God of the Fathers.

Still faithful, and still rebellious in faithfulness. The ambivalence extended to God's people not less than to God Himself, for no one is more bitterly critical of the Jewish people than the Jew lovingly committed to its perpetuation. Not that there is in Yiddish anything like the blood-curdling denunciations of the Prophets of old. The Yiddish form of Jewish self-denigration is in low key, sibilant, sardonic, and subtle, occasionally blasphemous, *a kleyn folk, ober paskudne* (Slv), "A small people, but a loathsome one"; *a got hobn mir, aza yor oyf undz, un a folk hot er aza yor oyf im,* "A God we have, such a year on us, and a people He has, such a

200

year on Him." Concerning piety there is a folk saying: *tsu vos darf a yid hobn fis? az in kheyder muz men im traybn, tsu der khupe* (Heb) *firt men im, tsu kvure* (Heb) *brengt men im, in shul arayn geyt er nit, tsu shikses* (Heb) *krikht er, haynt tsu vos darf er hobn fis?*, "What does a Jew need legs for? To *kheyder* he has to be driven (forced to go), to the *khupe* he is conducted, to burial he is brought, to *shul* he does not go, and he crawls after gentile girls; so what does he need legs for?"

CHAPTER TWELVE

The At-Homeness of Tevye

1.

It is Sholom Aleichem who has given to the world, for its everlasting edification, the prototype of the Yiddish-speaking east European Jew whose natural habitat was Dalesland and whose natural condition was that of the loving, sardonic, conforming, and contumacious child of God and His people. It is true that by the grace of that same God, Tevye the dairyman escaped from semidestitution into semi-demi-affluence, acquiring, *mayse nes*, a cow, a goat, and thirty-seven rubles of working capital, and leading thenceforth a life of labor free from actual want. But all his days he remained the original Tevye, whose inquiring mind and challenging spirit mirrored the physical neediness and spiritual indestructibility of the Yiddish masses. Come what might, Tevye would hold on to his identity as thinking man, believing Jew, and protester against God's mistreatment of the Jewish people.

He expressed this harmonious triune personality by his avenging mistreatment of sacred texts, sardonic mistranslations conceived not in the callow manner of the apostate but, more subtly, in the expostulatory spirit of the submissive devotee. He believed that God had a Jewish sense of humor, and far from being displeased by a display of mutiny, would smile understandingly as long as all was couched in the wit of the Torah. It was for Teyve a basic tenet that God hates an ignoramus, or more exactly, an *amorets*, a devotee and pillar of ignorance.

And here lies the painful tragedy of the attempt to portray Tevye in English without his fundamental instrument of self-expression, namely, his manhandling of sacred Hebrew texts in ingeniously blasphemous Yiddish. It was a form of folk humor, and we have seen a specimen of it in the parody of Jacob's blessing. In Sholom Aleichem it became a personal style. But when Tevye is remodeled on the English stage for audiences innocent not only of Yiddish and Hebrew, but even of the Bible—not to mention the *sider*, the Mishnah, and the Talmud—he is denaturized into a kindly imitation of a Shakespearean clown without the wit we expect, but steeped in a low sentimentality made to order for *amkho*, Jewish and non-Jewish. Thus transformed, he has been received round the world with loving lachrymosity and complete misunderstanding. For the clearest and most refreshing characteristic of Tevye is the mocking brightness of his mind, without which as background his sentimentality is simply mawkishness; it is as though we were to judge Heine by *Du bist wie eine Blume* without knowing that he was also the author of *Atta Troll*.

Some of the background needed to appreciate Tevye's wit, such as a knowledge of the Jewish Bible, should be but is not universal; some acquaintance with the Prayer Book, Talmud, and Midrash might be expected among a majority of Jews but is found only among a self-respecting minority. Even so, the curriculum is not complete; without enough Yiddish (and therefore Hebrew) to follow him in the original, even the sharpest and most perceptive mind, relying on translation, must guess at the inner Tevye. To be sure, what can thus be glimpsed is impressive enough, and since miracles do happen, a genius may yet find a way of reproducing Tevye's monologues in English without loss of their essence. God speed the day!

To clarify the nature of Tevye's gnomic mutilations, we must imagine an American college graduate addressing an audience of his intellectual peers. We must further imagine that all of them once took a course in Latin, and have preserved in their memories the familiar tags with which "cultivated" essays were peppered a century or two ago. The speaker throws them in from time to time accompanying them with English paraphrases and explications which are sometimes utterly nonsensical, sometimes ingeniously tangential, sometimes both, and always with a vague suggestion of authenticity and relevance.

Here are some imperfect examples (the game can be played by any number):

Sic transit gloria mundi, "Here today and gone tomorrow."
Reductio ad absurdum, "A fool and his money are soon parted."
Caveat emptor, "A pig in a poke."
De mortuis nisi nil bonum, "Once you're dead it's for good."
Ars longa vita brevis, "That's the long and the short of it."
Semper fidelis, "The more the merrier."
Delenda est Cartago, "Neither a borrower nor a lender be."
Carpe diem, "Shoot the works."
Non compos mentis, "Look who's talking."
Aere perennius, "Airy nothings."
Alea est jacta, "Throw the bum out."

Another condition must be added: the texts thus deliberately deformed in translation must be, without exception, sacred, belonging to prayers that have been an immemorial consolation, an everlasting shelter from the storms of history. What, then, is the meaning of this indecorous frivolity, this burlesquing of ultimate values? Strange as it may sound, it is an antipodal declaration of loyalty, an assertion of independence in submissiveness.

Among the most beloved of the biblical "scrolls" is the Song of Songs, and among the (now trite) similes used by the king concerning his shepherdess is *keshoyshane beyn hakhoykhim,* "like a lily among thorns." Sholom Aleichem "translates" it as *vi a finfter rod tsum vogn,* "like a fifth wheel to a cart."

In the valedictory Prayer to the Sabbath, when the visiting Queen is ushered out, there occurs the phrase: *hamavdl beyn koydesh lekhoyl*, "He that maketh division between the sacred and the profane." Sholom Aleichem accompanies this with the translation: *ver es hot di klingers dem iz voyl*, "If you've got the ringers (coin), bully for you" (the Shakespearean phrase is "happy man be his dole").

In the daily *shimenesre*, also called the *amidah* ("standing prayer"), occurs the supplication *refueynu venerape*, "Heal us and we will be healed." This emerges as *shik undz di refue, di make hobn mir shoyn aleyn*, "Send us the healing, we've managed to get the affliction without Your help."

And a final example: In the *pirke oves*, "Ethics of the Fathers," a Mishnaic book familiar to many of the simple folk, there is a famous admonition: *shloyshe sheokhlu al shulkhn ekhod*, etc., "Three that have eaten at one table and have not exchanged words of the Torah, it is as if they have eaten of sacrifices to idols." *Shloyshe sheokhlu* became the key phrase to the entire passage, "Three that have eaten." Sholom Aleichem, once seeing a Jew gormandizing at table exclaimed, *shloyshe sheokhlu, er hot gegesn far dray*, "He was eating like three."

2.

The Sholom Aleichem spirit played about the concept of poverty, explored all its possibilities, and created a multitude of denominations. We are not yet done with the *kaptsn*, "pauper," of whom there were many subspecies: a *kaptsn vi der shabes hagodl*, that is, having the grandeur of the Great Sabbath that preceded the Exodus from Egypt; not the *kaptsn* in person, of course, but his *kaptsones*, his *kaptsnhood*, one might say, awesome in its sweep, its venerability and its inde-

structible grandeur; and then a *kaptsn mit ale kheyngribelekh,*
"a *kaptsn* with all his dimples," meaning, of course, again his
kaptsones, and not his doubtless unprepossessing self. Very
homey, too, is a *kaptsn in zibn poles,* "a *kaptsn* in seven
garment-skirts," that is, a bedraggled and ragged *kaptsn,*
swathed, figuratively, in sevenfold castoffs.

Oni and *evyen* are likewise synonyms for "poor man,"
but they have not the status of *kaptsn.* Oni is connected with
anives, "humility," and *evyen* with the name given to a dis-
sident Jewish sect of the first century, the Ebionim, "the poor
(of understanding)." Conscious of their separate weakness,
the two words joined forces in the phrase *oni ve-evyen,* an
emphasis by addition, "A poor man, poor man," while the
evyen-shebe-evyoynim was emphasis by intensification; he was
"the poor man's poor man," as one speaks of the poet's poet.
Then, in a sudden turn of modernity, the folk created *oni-ve-
evyon et kompani,* which may be freely translated as "Poverty,
Inc.," itself confronted by the rival firm, *kaptsnson un hungerman,* "Pauperson and Hungerman."

One way of grinning at poverty was in tender love names:
A *kaptsn* became *kaptsenyuk,* an *evyen* an *evyok;* or in bittersweet diminutives set to rhyme:

> *In eyvele keyn fendele*
> *In shtaygele keyn hendele*
> *In baytele keyn rendele.*
> In the little stove no little pot,
> In the little coop no little chicken
> In the little purse no little coin.

Nor must we forget the *dalfn* (by coincidence the second
son of Haman). Etymologically he stands close to Dales, for
dal is Hebrew for poor, and *dalfn* has a special ring because
of its similarity to *khalfn,* a money changer. A *khalfn* is one
whose business is to change money, a *dalfn,* one whose

business it is not to have any. He is sometimes called *a dalfn vi in posek shteyt,* "a *dalfn* such as is written into the biblical verse," that is, fulfilling all his functions and obligations as a *dalfn. Vi in posek shteyt* does not mean that there is a biblical verse on the subject; it is an idiom in wide use meaning "the real thing plus," or "in spades."

Kaptsn, oni, evyon, dalfn are all of Hebraic origin; the Germanic equivalents are not nearly as colorful. *Oreman* is unemotionally descriptive; *betler,* "beggar," when not actually indicating a mendicant, has some sting; so has *shleper,* "low person, vagabond, hobo." Both are offensive words, and have never been touched with the sardonic pathos of the Hebraic. *Shnorer* has accumulated some color; literally it means "beggar," but *betler* is more commonly used of one who goes from door to door, or stands cup in hand on the street. A *shnorer,* more generalized, is a sponger, a deadbeat, even a parasite; but the verb *shnorn* is also used semihumorously for fundraising in good causes. Chaim Weizmann was wont to call himself the greatest *shnorer* in Jewish history, and beside being a statesman of the first rank, he was indeed the most remarkable fundraiser of his time, praised as such by Lloyd George.

I may seem in these observations on privation and humiliation to be indulging in the sin I have just denounced, sentimentalization. There was nothing jolly and hilarious about the destitution that lay like a curse on millions of Jews in the Yiddish-speaking world; and it would be grotesque to speak of Sholom Aleichem's and Mendele's *kaptsonim* and *evyonim* as "poor and happy." They were miserable, and knew it; but the question that haunts us historically is, why did they not disintegrate intellectually and morally? How were they able, under hideous oppression and corroding privation, under continuous starvation—the tail of a herring was a dish—to keep alive against a better day the spirit originally breathed into man? The answer lies in the self-mockery by which they rose above their condition to see afar off the hope of the future.

3.

Oyker horim zayn, literally, "to uproot mountains," has a highly restricted meaning in no way connected with the feats of a Paul Bunyan or an Og, King of Bashan, or any other fabled prototype of physical *gvure*, "might." The reference is to something so far removed from the muscularly gigantic that the contrast provokes a smile. In this Hebraic-Yiddish phrase the uprooters and hurlers of mountains are frail, wispy scholars whom a moderate wind would carry off, beard, *peyes*, *yarmulke*, and all. Their prodigious feats, purely intellectual, may not even disturb a folio of the Talmud, for they are apt to work from memory; at most something will be written in the quiet of a study—and this is called "the uprooting of mountains." It is also called *maresh oylomes zayn*, "the storming of worlds." But *az me vil tsurik-shmuesn*, "If one wants to reconsider the matter," Einstein uprooted Newton's universe of celestial mechanics—and much else—in the quiet of his study, and the only occasional physical disturbance accompanying the feat was the movement of pencil over paper.

If we set down side by side the apparently fruitless ingenuities of a classical Talmudist and the cosmic mysteries of a theoretical physicist, we shall find more resemblance than difference, and more than one Jewish Nobel Laureate first learned the gymnastics of the mind in a yeshiva. A question worth some study is whether the current respect for science does as much for the intellectual standards of the masses at large as respect for the Talmud once did for that of the Jews at large. Has the untrained general public as much grasp of the intellectual process as Jews brought up with the minimal standards of a Jewish education? I am speaking of *amkho*, the folk, and its vocabulary of intellectual modes and types in common currency, in which the following distinctions were clearly established.

A *gelernter*, "a learned man," *a kener*, "one who knows," and *an intelligent*, "an intellectual type," all referred to general knowledge, and the designations are Germanic. Against the *gelernter* for worldly reading there was the *yedeya seyfer*, "book knower," for one widely read in Jewish literature. In the same way, opposite *kener* stood *lamdn*, "knower (sacred books)." One could, however, use the partly Germanic designation *kener in di kleyne oysyes* (Heb), "knower in the little letters" (*i.e.*, fine print), to indicate Jewish scholarship. In certain scholarly Hebrew books the nub of text in the middle of the page is usually imbedded in successive quadrangles of commentary and commentary upon commentary in diminishing type, the outside circumvallation so tiny and crowded together as to be legible only with a reading glass. *Lamdn* and *yedeya seyfer* are Hebraic, as we might expect; so is *melumed* from the same root as *lamdn*, but designating worldly knowledge.

The *talmid khokhem*, or sage, is a very old and honorable designation, already current at the beginning of the Common Era, and *talmidey khakhomim* are divided into types: the *boki*, "the deeply versed one," the *kharif*, "the sharp-minded one," the *oymek*, "the deep one," the *yadn* (from *yodea*, "to know"), "the man of wide-ranging information, the encyclopedic one," also called, but by no means ironically, the *yedeya hakl*, "the know-it-all," the *khakren*, "the speculative thinker." Then, in mixed Germanic and Hebraic, there was the man with *a sharfe tfise*, "a quick grasp," while one with a good head was called *a tayere keyle*, "a precious vessel, instrument."

The supreme title was *goen*, "Excellency, Eminence." It once was the official designation of the heads of the Bab-

ylonian Academies in the days when the law went forth
from Sura and Pumbeditha and Nahardea. These have been
closed for nearly a thousand years, and since then only one
scholar has by common consent been accorded the title,
Elijah of Vilna (1720–99). It cannot be doubted that—to
take two outstanding instances—Rashi and Maimonides were
held in as high esteem, but Elijah of Vilna alone is unchal-
lengeably *der goen*, or *der vilner goen*. However, the word is
sometimes used unofficially and loosely for scholars of ex-
ceptional brilliance, and sometimes it rises to a shrill climax in
a goen oylem, "a world genius," or even *a vilder goen* (sometimes ironical), "a wild genius." Nearly every such scholar
was at one time an *ilui*, "child prodigy," often an expert in
Talmudic subtleties by the age of ten, but before he became
a *"goen"* he had to pass through the stage of the *masmid*,
described by Bialik.

4.

We have already taken note of the key words, *mitsve*,
"good deed," *aveyre*, "sin, transgression," *tsdoke*, "charity."
One of the noblest words, *khesed*, "kindness, loving-kindness,"
has a grave, reflective beauty, especially in the phrase *khesed
shel emes*, "grace of the truth, true grace," which has been
turned into an idiom for decent burial of the forsaken dead.
But *gmiles khesed*, literally, "fulfillment of grace," is a very
homey term, meaning "a free interest loan." It whines a little
when it turns into the diminutive *gmiles khesedl*. A *khevre
gmiles-khasodim*, which translates magniloquently into "Association of Fulfillment of Grace," is merely a Free Loan
Association.

A good, homey, unpretentious word for kindness is *toyve*,
from the Hebraic adjective for "good." *Tut mir a toyve*, "Do

me the kindness, do me a favor," covers every variety of friendly action, from a generous deed to a common courtesy: *tut mir a toyve un farmakht dos fenster*, "Be so kind as to close the window," is sound idiom.

A Jew of perfect piety and unblemished moral behavior was described as observing the *taryag mitsves*, "the six hundred and thirteen commandments," listed in the Talmud and codified by Maimonides. (*Taryag* is made up of the letters *tov resh yud giml*, which as numbers add up to 613.) There are 248 affirmative commandments; 365 are negative. However, since the time of the destruction of the Temple, it is impossible to observe the *taryag mitsves*, for they include, among others that have been long theoretical, the bringing of sacrifices. But the phrase remains.

Most of the words relating to ritual and to moral values are Hebraic, but the Germanic element is well entrenched. One of the most important terms, *a frumer yid*, "a pious Jew," is Germanic, but if he overdoes his piety he is given a Slavic suffix and is called *a frumak*, "a fanatical superpietist." Germanic, too, are the warm *anshtendik*, *orentlekh*, and *erlekh*, all approximating to "decent." *Erlekh* puts the stress on honesty and adds a flavor of religious fidelity. *Eydl*, "gentle, refined, delicate," is somewhat more sophisticated, with a hint of nobility, while *a zaydener kharakter*, "a character of silk," almost implies a superfluity of moral qualities, and *a zaydener yungerman*, "a silken youth," already invites the shadow of a smile.

5.

Perhaps the heaviest and deadliest Yiddish word is *shmad*, deriving from the Hebrew for "destruction, wiping out," and having the single meaning of "apostasy, conversion from Judaism to another religion." *Zikh shmadn* is "to apostatize," and a man who has done that is a *meshumed*, which etymologically would be a "destroyed one," but as used in living Yiddish implies something much more hateful than "self-destruction." The emotional charge in the word did not spring solely from religious intolerance. Mixed with it was the rage of an embattled minority made more of a minority with every defection; but there was an even stronger motivation. One of the characteristics of the *meshumed* has frequently been the zeal with which he becomes the assistant, or even the renewed inspiration, of the oppressors of his repudiated people.

There is a long list of such worthies. It is headed by the primitive Christians who invented the slander of the Jews as God-killers; it reaches with undiminished density into our times. Of course the religion to which *meshumodim* have turned has not always been the same. In the early days of the Common Era it was mostly Christianity; later Mohammedanism took over a sector, today communism of one kind or another is in the lead. The rancor of extreme Jewish leftists toward Judaism, the Jewish State, and the will to survive of the Jewish people, cannot be adequately described without bringing in the concept of religious fanaticism; hence *meshumed* is the appropriate term.

The majority of *meshumodim*, ancient, medieval, and modern, were undoubtedly men (and women) who only wanted to get out from under a burden that they found both intolerable and meaningless. Countless thousands accepted baptism under duress, ranging from harsh discrimination to the immediate threat of expulsion or death. Hence, for all the odium attaching to the word, *shmad* was not considered an inexpiable sin. The road back was open; any sinner could become a *bal tshuve*, "penitent returner," which is the Hebrew meaning of the word, although strictly speaking, a *meshumed*

215

returning to the fold was not a *bal tshuve* because he was not a penitent Jew; he was a convert beginning all over again though with a difference.

There is a curious, quite unacrimonious idiom for the act of *shmad*, namely *baytn dos rendl*, "change (or exchange) one's ducat." A ducat was a gold coin, and *baytn dos rendl* therefore was, literally, "to change a gold coin into small currency." Another, more pointed idiom, and current in many languages, is *iberkern dem shmoys*, "turning one's sheepskin"; curiously, a parallel idiom, *iberkern dem pelts*, refers not to apostasy but to any transfer of loyalties, exactly like "turning one's coat."

These milder synonyms for *shmad* and *meshumed* reflected a distinction between types. While the bitterest feelings were directed against those whose new religion made them persecutors of the old, there was a kind of smiling contempt for those who merely transferred to the church the religious indifference they had felt toward the synagogue; that feeling was extended to the church which cynically "received" them, gaining nothing more in the idle transaction than the satisfaction of recording it.

There were instances of "conversion" so palpably spurious as to border on farce. In the Russia of the Czars it was not unknown for duly baptized and registered converts to Orthodox Catholic or Protestant Christianity to continue attending services at synagogues that tolerated their presence. The most famous Russian Jewish apostate was the great Orientalist Daniel Khvolson who, though he did not attend synagogue services after his baptism into the Greek Orthodox Church, devoted himself no less to the defense of Jews against the Blood Libel than to the training of Christians at the leading seminary in St. Petersburg. His case is so curious as to warrant a digression.

Superficially, he was said to be a cynic. When he was asked why he, who had promised to be a great light in Israel, had suddenly and hideously turned apostate, he answered, "Out of conviction." Pressed to explain, he went on, "Out of conviction that it is better to be a professor in the St. Petersburg Academy than a *melamed* in Shklov." But it is also told that in his old age his conscience troubled him, as it had reason to, for the graduates of the St. Petersburg Academy were almost invariably anti-Semites. He made a great career, and he could not bring himself to renounce his apostasy, but he is said to have longed for burial in consecrated Jewish ground. Zalman Shazar, President of Israel, still remembers attending the classes that Khvolson, then on the brink of the grave, used to conduct discreetly for Jewish students. There were long, earnest, even passionate discussions on the subject of Khvolson's conflicting loyalties, and thereby hangs a pathetic and comical story, attributed to a famous rabbi.

In a pious Jewish family a daughter fell sick with a strange disease which the doctors were for a long time unable to diagnose. Finally a great specialist identified it, and declared that there existed only one cure, a special extract of hog liver. Now Jewish law in general declares that any purely ritualistic law except the prohibition against idol-worship may be broken in the case of *pikuakh nefesh*, "danger to life." But the piety of this particular Jewish daughter was of such unbending stuff that she preferred death to such contamination. She was overruled by a rabbinical board which declared that her pietistic obstinacy was itself an impiety. Thereupon she yielded, but made one condition: she would drink the horrible draught if the rabbis could find a way of slaughtering the pig with all the ritual prescribed for a *kosher* animal.

How the matter turned out the story does not tell, but the converted Khvolson was not buried in consecrated Jewish ground.

Untroubled by scruples or a split personality was the *meshumed lehakhes* or *mumer lehakhes*, "one who apostatizes

217

(in order) to vex" his parents, his friends, his *rebe*, the Jewish people, or some other focus of his resentment. The Hebrew *lehakhis*, "to anger," has been extended to *tselokhesnik*, "one who does something nasty merely to spite someone"; and when the someone cannot be identified, and the action seems to spring from general contrariety, it is performed *oyftselokhes der boben*, "to spite his grandmother."

6.

We must distinguish between the *meshumed* and the *apikoyres*. The latter, whose name is a form of *Epicurus*, is one who has ceased to believe in Judaism, or most of its principles, but has not passed over to another religion. He is "epicurean" not in self-indulgence, but philosophically; he might even be an ascetic.

A sharper form of *apikoyres* is *koyfer-beiker*, "denyer of the basic principle," that is, of the existence of God. (The Hebrew *koyfer* is related to the Arabic word from which *kaffir*, applied to Negroes of South Africa, derives.) As used by orthodox Jews, both are terms of abuse, but Jewish *apikorsim* claimed to have some knowledge of the Torah and to have rejected it. They spoke of themselves as *veltlekh*, "worldly," or *fraydenker*, "free-thinkers." However, *apikoyres* and *koyfer beiker* are terms all too freely bandied about by various branches of orthodox Jewry without regard to fine doctrinal or ritualistic differences almost invisible to bystanders. Sholom Aleichem records with affectionate mockery the vendetta between two neighboring *shtetlekh* over the order of two prayers in the daily service; the length of a blessing or the brevity of a *kapote* could lead to a passionate exchange of *apikoyres! koyfer beiker!* For carrying a handkerchief in one's

218

pocket on the Sabbath instead of binding it about him, so as to make it an article of clothing instead of a forbidden burden, a man could be consigned to the limbo of the godless.

A *treyfnyak*, literally "one who eats *treyf* or unkosher foods," could in principle be called a *koyfer beiker* or an *apikoyres*, but there was a special offensiveness in the word, a connotation of disagreeable self-indulgence, or even hoggishness, literal or figurative. The self-indulgence need not, for that matter, be confined to or even include the pleasures of food. Just as *kosher*, from meaning "ritually pure" in the matter of food, has been extended to cover right behavior, so *treyf* extends to any reprehensible act, though without relinquishing entirely the noxious flavor of forbidden food. And so, to call a man *treyfnyak* was not to read him out of the synagogue but merely out of decency! Nevertheless, there were Jews who had lost every belief but who unobtrusively carried out the Law in the minutest detail. How did one know it? One didn't! It merely happened to be so.

Unbelievers, freethinkers, *apikorsim*, *fraydenker* had for their opposites appellations not less wounding and contemptuous. Perhaps the most satisfying of these was *khnyok*, which the Weinreich dictionary correctly but inadequately defines as "bigot, philistine, petty, unreasonable conservative." To get near the full force of *khnyok*, the reader must first of all be reminded of the pronunciation; like *treyfnYAK* and *paskudn-YAK*, and like the scorpion, *khnYOK* carries its sting in its tail, that is, in the last letters, which constitute a syllable uttered with venom. Moreover, in the case of *khnyok*, the preliminary guttural, choked off, vowelless, by the *n*, and issuing with a kind of spasm in *yok*, suggests an emetic, and really, one would have to add to all the above, without altering the basic meaning, that a *khnyok* is one who makes you vomit, almost literally. The *khnyok*, then, is primarily a species of an oaf crossed with what might be called the yahoo of *Yiddish-keyt*.

But while "bigot, philistine, petty, unreasonable conservative" are not incorrect, it must be remembered that these disparaging definitions, including particularly the last, can be turned against the irreligious leftist with equal justice—or injustice. The revolutionary doctrinaire, armored in intellectual self-assurance, intolerant of any deviation from his views, can be a perfect example of *khnyokishkeyt*. The *khnyok* may also be a man of much erudition, a Ph.D. whose all-absorbing specialty is the plumbing system of northern Ugarit or the vowel shifts in early Akkadian.

Much simpler is the *tsvuyak*, "hypocrite," which comes slightly diminuendo after *khnyok* in the weaponry of offense; then again a little behind is *gots kozak*, "God's Cossack," and *gots straptshe*, "God's attorney."

Especially odious in the eyes of the godless was the *bal tshuve*, the returner to the fold, the reformed sinner, who in the enthusiasm of his redemption outshouted and outsang the rest of the world. The Talmud is very tender toward reclaimed souls; it has a saying: "There where the *bal tshuve* stands, even the perfect saints cannot stand." The godless add bitterly: "Because of the smell."

CHAPTER THIRTEEN

Malediction and Benediction

1.

Robert Graves makes the observation that the more extravagant the curse the less venom there is in it. This is true whether we consider the curse in the pure sense, that is, a calling up of demonic forces, with intent to destroy, or in the less exact sense of descriptiveness, without invocation of evil. In either case excess defeats itself. Let us consider the case of Oswald, whom Kent, in *King Lear*, covers with extravagant abuse:

> A knave, a rascal, an eater of broken meats; a base, proud, shallow, beggarly, three-suited, hundred pound, filthy worsted-stocking knave; a lily-livered action-taking whoreson, glass-gazing, superserviceable, finical rogue; a one-trunk inheriting slave; one that wouldst be a bawd, in the way of good service, and art nothing but the opposition of a knave, beggar, coward, pandar, and the son and heir of a mongrel bitch, etc.

Such a composition of offensive attributes invites a burst of laughter; no person can contain one-half of the intent, and if the diatribe is continued, laughter is followed by wearisomeness and irritation.

The effect is equally self-contradictory when for the insult we substitute the curse. Graves lets go with a magnificent, all-round, sustained barrage:

> May the Father who created man curse him;
> May the Son who suffered for us curse him;
> May the Holy Ghost who was given to us in Baptism curse him, etc.

There is a shade of difference here; the treatment is formal and schematic, but the ultimate effect remains comical.

For sheer maleficence there is nothing to equal the passages we have described in the *toykhekhe*, Leviticus 26, and Deuteronomy 28. In these the punishments and rewards attending on the good and bad behavior of the Chosen People are set forth in the most exhaustive and exhausting detail. Formally speaking, the punishments or curses are so lurid, the rewards or blessings are so radiant, that if one were to sustain the reading the heart would alternately sicken and expand. But although every precaution is taken to solemnize the occasion, although it is considered a great debasement to be forced to follow the relevant Torah text in one's own name, monotony intervenes. Insofar as there is a difference between affirmation and negation, between blessing and destruction, it is the negative fantasy that carries the day, both by virtue of bulk and of intensity.

The extravagance of the ideas and images is entirely oriental, going back to prebiblical monstrosities. Arabesques of affliction and gratification dizzy the mind, their themes moving back and forth between the individual and the nation, between the flesh and the spirit:

I will send pestilence among you and you shall be delivered into enemy hands. . . . You shall eat the flesh of your sons and daughters. . . . I will lay your cities in ruins and make your sanctuaries desolate. . . . As for those of you who survive, I will cast a faintness into their hearts in the land of their enemies. The sound of a driven leaf shall put them to flight. . . . The Lord will strike you with consumption, fever, and inflammation. . . . with hemor-rhoids, boils, scars and itch. . . . with madness, blindness and dismay. In the morning you shall say, "would it were evening!" and in the evening you shall say, "would it were morning!"

Against this we hear the chant of the blessing:

> I will grant you peace in the land. . . . I will look with
> favor upon you and make you fertile . . . . I will establish
> My abode in your midst. . . . The Lord will ordain bless-
> ings for you upon your barns and upon your under-
> takings. . . . The Lord will establish you as His holy
> people. . . . The Lord will open for you His bounteous
> store, the heavens. . . . you will be creditor to many nations
> but debtor to none. . . .

In the relevant text the curses are three or four times as
voluminous as the blessings; benevolence is nowhere as nearly
inventive as malevolence; it loses itself in blandness. A similar
disproportion is to be found in the maledictions and benedictions of Yiddish, but the two fields of discourse are entirely
different. The Hebrew curse is entirely humorless; the Yiddish
curse, after achieving a monotony of literalness, breaks into
a genuine strain of humor. The Jewish people, being physically
defenseless, had two recourses short of suicide; it could contain itself in silent patience, devising every kind of ingenuity
to evade the world's brutalities, or it could vent its rage upon
the world in impotent intramural rages until it recovered its
balance and resumed its commerce with the world. It had
only faith and its wits to fall back on, the faith was deep, the
wits—and the wit—were lively. But the world was not uniformly brutal; there were interludes of normality and even
of kindliness, and the people developed correspondingly fertile
vocabularies of execration and gratitude. In the absence of
temporal power, the wish did service for the deed, and its
fervor was proportionate to its impotence, for good as well as
for evil. If there was more evil than good, the reason lay in
the circumstances. An interesting side issue was the subtle
satisfaction derived from cursing someone *in absentia* in a
language he did not understand; it was connected with a
mysterious potency.

225

But the end result would still have been a tiresome monotony if the element of inventive humor had not prevailed over repetitiveness. The curse, far more active and more manifold than the blessing, developed an artistic side in which attention to formulation became more important than the possibility of fulfillment. It became a form of choreography. I will not say that ill-will as such disappeared, but it was almost overborne by aesthetic and theoretical satisfaction. This was particularly true in the internecine or domestic use of the curse, when Jews cursed each other as a sort of exercise. They took a bittersweet pleasure in exaggerating their embroilments; if only they could have taken it out on the *goyim!* The correct delivery and appropriate formulation were not unappreciated by the recipient of the curses, while to the bestower they represented an equally important form of self-expression.

This area of the folk culture was largely the domain of the less instructed classes, and particularly of the women among them, which is understandable when we recall that women were excluded from whatever public activity internal Jewish life afforded, and their emotional tensions, more highly keyed than those of the men, were less frequently allayed. *Sheltn vi a mark-yidine,* "curse like a market-woman," catches perfectly the spirit of "fall a-cursing like a very drab."

2.

The common curse in Yiddish, or any other language, is usually little more than an expletive; it is a formalization which rarely corresponds to the literal intention. *Gey in drerd* (*der erd*), "Go into the earth," is simply the universal "Go to hell," and *ver geharget,* "Be killed," is the equivalent of "Drop dead." There are occasional flickers of warmth, such as *in drerd zolstu mir geyn!,* "May you be killed," but the

226

variation is easily exhausted. There is also the inverted curse addressed by a mother to her child: *zolst mir nit geharget vern*, "May you not be killed," a hasty last-moment substitution, a burst of helpless fury changed into a hasty retraction.

To acquire character of some kind, a curse must be apropos. *Khob* (*ikh hob*) *im in drerd*, "I have him in the earth," *i.e.*, "To hell with him," is unspecific, but *krenken zol er*, "May he be sick," or "May he be a sick man," narrows down the field of operation. We enter the range of the higher cursing with *zol er krenken in nakhes* (Heb), "May he sicken in satisfaction," that is, "gratifyingly, making a fulfillment or pleasure of it." It is a quiet curse, covering a gentle, insistent, unrelenting, and unviolent condition. *Oyskrenken zol er di mames milkh*, literally, "May he sicken out his mother's milk," probably means, "May his mother's milk sicken in him," or "May his mother's milk turn retroactively into a sickness." This confines the curse to a definite and clinical area. But *zol er krenken un gedenken*, "May he sicken and remember," or "May he sicken memorably," has no point of reference, no descriptive merit.

The sickness theme occurs in many forms, some general, some pointed. *Shraybn zol men im retseptn*, "May prescriptions be written for him," means anything and everything in the scope of pharmacology; the idea is one of continuing activity and anxious experimentation with the man's health. *Keyn dokter zol im nit helfn*, "May no doctor help him," sounds at first like "may no doctor want to help him," but on closer analysis reveals itself as "May no doctor be able to help him, may all doctors be helpless, may they be at a complete loss, with or without prescriptions." A *dokter zol im darfn*, "May a doctor need him," seems comparatively mild; but the offensiveness lies in its mildness. May a doctor need him for what? Diagnosis? An autopsy? Or perhaps the need is the doctor's—for a livelihood. Very sweeping is the all-round demoralizing *oyf doktoyrim zol er es oysgebn*, "May he spend it (all) on doctors," which need not imply anything more than imaginary sickness.

The anatomically focused curse carried a high degree of satisfaction. A *veytik im in boykh*, "A pain in his belly," or heart, or head, is free from vagueness or complications. In the same class are *a kramp im in layb, in di krizhes* (Slv), *di kishkes* (Slv), *di finger*, "cramps in his body, small of the back, bowels, fingers"; *shtekhn zol im in di zaytn*, "May he have stabbing pains in the sides"; *krikhn zol er oyf ale fir*, "May he crawl on all fours"; *zol im drikn in hartsn*, "May he have (physical) heaviness of the heart"; *zol im dreyen farn nopl*, "May he have a turning (dizziness) of the navel"; *varfn zol im hayzer hoykh*, "May he be thrown (by convulsions) housetop high"; *redn zol er fun hits*, "May he talk from heat," that is, from fever, in delirium.

Rhyme and rhythm augment the effect, sometime at the cost of intelligibility. *Geshvoln un gedroln zol er vern* rings powerfully, but while *geshvoln* means "swollen," *gedroln* is extremely rare, and has to do with varicose veins. On the other hand, *fargelt un fargrint zol er vern*, "May he turn yellow and green," is perfectly clear and gets its force from the alliterative *g*'s; also the two colors convey the complementary sufferings of body and mind, withering disease for the yellow, chagrin, envy, etc., for the green. Sometimes extravagance of expression, like vaulting ambition, o'erleaps itself and falls on the other side. Thus, *a mageyfe zol oyf im kumen*, "May a pestilence come upon him," and *a mabl zol oyf im kumen*, "May a flood come upon him," blunt the force of the personal misfortune by making it part of a general calamity, no distinction being established for special gratification. A *duner zol im trefn*, "May a thunderbolt hit him," and *a blits im in kop*, "A lightning stroke in his head," provide more satisfaction by singling out the target and not diffusing the effect in a universal misfortune.

As we have seen, some curses are merely generalized cries

228

of irritation; if they are at all specific it is by accident, the result of a passing whim. A *kholerye oyf im*, "A cholera upon him," *a fintster mazl* (Heb) *oyf im*, "Black luck upon him," *geyn zol er tsum tayvl, tsu al di shvartse rukhes*, (Heb) "May he go to the devil, to all the black devils, demons," and many more in that class are practically interchangeable. But a somewhat-out-of-the-way expression like *a ruekh in zayn tatn*, "A devil in his father," is not so much a curse as an expression of disgust or contempt or, at mildest, of disrespect. It also has a touch of quaintness. It is told of an extremely well-brought-up young man that his father was in the habit of bestowing upon him the severest tongue-lashings on the slightest provocation or none at all. The paragon of filial piety endured it all without a word until the verbal assault surpassed all bounds; then he ran out of the house and, encountering the first acquaintance on the street, burst out with *a ruekh in dayn tatn!* "A devil in your father!" Thereupon the amazed acquaintance responded with a hearty *a ruekh in DAYN tatn!* Vastly relieved, the model young man exclaimed, *dos hob ikh gevolt!* "That's what I wanted!"

The elliptical curse has the charm of a mock tactfulness. *Zayn nomen zol aheymkumen*, "May his name come home [instead of himself]"; *a kleyn kind zol nokh im heysn*, "May a little child be named after him," and *me zol shoyn nokh im a nomen gebn*, "It is time someone was named after him," gracefully avoid the mention of death (it is forbidden to name anyone after a living person); but the implication is gently poisonous. Also filled with kindliness is a locution like *ikh vel im bagrobn vi an oytser*, "I will bury him like a treasure," that is, carefully and lovingly, making much of him. Still elliptical, but more heavy-handed are: *me zol shoyn zitsn shive* (Heb) *nokh im*, "It is time they sat *shive* for him" (the prescribed days of mourning); *neyen zol men im takhrikhim*, "May cerements be sewn for him" (this could be premature; pious old Jews prepared their graveclothes in advance);

opkoyfn zol men bay zayn tatn di malbushim, "May his clothes be purchased from his father" (this last is particularly vicious).

Some curses have a large, generalized scope; they are carryalls of universal application. *Vos es hot gezolt zayn mir in klentstn finger zol oysgeyn tsu zayn kop,* "That which should have happened in my little finger should be directed upon his head," is somewhat metaphysical; it probably means, in the final analysis, "Let complete calamity come to him rather than that the slightest harm could come to me." Also somewhat unclear, but massive and lowering, is *vos es hot zikh mir gekholemt di nakht un yene nakht un ole nekht zol oysgeyn tsu zayn kop, tsu zayne hent un fis, tsu zayn layb un lebn,* "May that (evil) dream which I dreamt last night and the other night and every night be directed upon his head, his hands and legs, his body and life." This accumulation of sentiment must be spelled out slowly, like an incantation.

Some curses are intellectual constructions rather than emotional exercises. *Got zol im bentshn mit dray mentshn: eyner zol im haltn, der tsveyter zol im shpaltn, der driter zol im bahaltn,* "May God graciously send three persons upon him, one to hold him, the second to split him, the third to conceal (bury) him" (but this is half jocular, and depends entirely on the rhymes); *vifl yor er iz gegangen oyf di fis zol er geyn oyf di hent, un di ibrike zol er zikh sharn oyfn hintn,* "As many years as he walked on his legs may he walk on his hands, and for the remaining years may he push himself along on his behind." The next is a partnership curse, *vern zol fun dir a blintse un fun im a kats, er zol dikh oyfesn un mit dir zikh dervergn, volt men fun aykh beyde poter gevorn,* "May you turn into a *blintse* and he into a cat, and may he eat you up and choke to death on you, so that we would be rid of both of you"—the parties of the second and the third part are taken care of by the party of the first part. *Tsen shifn mit gold zol er farmogn un dos gantse gelt zol er far-krenken,* "May he own ten shiploads of gold—and may all of it be spent on sickness." This is a suspended and balanced pronouncement, the first half full of promise, the second, after a brief pause, extravagantly and superfluously malign, since it is inconceivable that there should be sufficient medical activity to exhaust in one lifetime, and no matter with how large a colloquium, ten shiploads of gold. Mathematically exact, but still beyond credible bounds, is the slowly develop-ing formula, *hobn zol er hundert hayzer, un in yedn hoyz hundert tsimer, un in yedn tsimer hundert betn, un der kadokhes zol im varfn fun eyn bet in dem tsveytn,* "May he have a hundred houses, and in every house a hundred rooms, and in every room a hundred beds, and may fever toss him from bed to bed." So extravagantly imaginative as to be lost in its own concept is *megulgl zol er vern in a henglaykhter, bay tog zol er hengen un bay nakht zol er brenen,* "May he be reincarnated as a candelabrum, to hang by day and burn by night."

One group of curses is directed at purely mental torment. *Hobn zol er a groys gesheft: vos me vet farlangen zol er nit hobn, un vos er vet hobn zol men nit farlangen,* "May he own a large business, and may he never have what is asked for, and what he has, may it never be asked for." The picture is one of dreadful and multifarious immobility, of frantic frustra-tion, but not of ill-health—at least in the ordinary sense—or of physical privation. Similarly, *got zol im helfn er zol tomid zayn gezunt un shtark, un shtendik fregn vos far a veter s'iz in droysn,* "God grant him that he be always healthy and strong and always asking what the weather is like out of doors," can only refer to a fixation—blindness, lunacy, and similar afflictions being ruled out. One curse, not loud but deep, indeed fatal, will be appreciated by all but fools: *got zol oyf im onshikn a nar,* "God send a fool to fasten on him."

All these are more or less fixed formulas, standbys, recognized courtesies; some are a little more elaborate and obscure than others, but they are not examples of pure improvisation. Indeed, they cannot be, for the moment they are recorded they are no longer one-time inspirations. The sudden squall of fury, the marketplace clash, the quick-witted improvisation round a word or phrase, is usually a feminine specialty. Myself no innovator in the field, I can only adumbrate the manner. Someone brings a report to Sore the vegetable-seller: *beylke di gendzlern hot gezogt az ayere tsibeles zaynen farfoylte*, "Beylke the goosewoman says that your onions are rotted"; at which Sore the vegetable-seller will snap back, *zog ir as s'iz shoyn tsayt az zi aleyn zol lign a farfoylte*, "Tell her it's high time she herself was lying rotten." And Beylke is being let off lightly if Sore does not add, *in eynem mit irn tayern man dem hikevatn un ire tsvey tsekrokhene tekhter vos se shlogt fun zey an ipesh*, "together with her darling husband the stammerer and her crummy daughters who stink a mile away." Or let the butcher send word *zog der mamem az khob (ikh hob) nisht keyn leber*, "Tell your mother I've run out of liver," and he will be informed or at least it will be reported in his behalf, *zol er blaybn on a leber un on gederem*, "May he be short of a liver and of intestines," not to mention other visceral appurtenances.

Sometimes a market-woman will call down upon herself the most hideous retribution to testify to her honesty or the quality of her wares, not forgetting, however, to add to the effect with a play upon words; *oyb ikh zog aykh a lign zol ikh lign mit di fis oysgeshtrekt tsu der tir*, "If I'm telling you a lie may I myself lie with my feet stretched out to the door," *i.e.*, dead. She will perhaps hang on to the verb for rhythmic prolongations: *zol ikh lign oyf gehakte vundn, zol ikh lign nayn eyln tif in drerd, zoln mayne kinder lign un tsen doktoyrim zoln zey nit kenen rirn fun ort*, "May I lie on bleeding wounds, may I lie nine ells underground, may my children lie and ten doctors be unable to get them to move"; to which she may add an oddly supplicatory note: *tate ziser!*, "Dear Father in heaven!"

What is true of the Hebrew counterpoint of malediction and benediction is equally true of the Yiddish—the negative far outweighs and outshines the affirmative. One limiting reason is that while the curse may work itself up into an absurdity while retaining some element of nastiness, that is, of genuineness, a blessing rendered absurd by extravagance becomes a self-defeating parody. There is a delicate line between praise and sycophancy. One may say to an oriental ruler, "O King, live for ever," but more satisfactory is even a hypocritical "Long life to you." *Lang lebn zolstu,* or *zolt ir,* "May you live long," *gezunt zolt ir zayn,* "Good health to you", *a brokhe oyf aykh,* "A blessing on you" (the last a little warmer), are courtesies, or friendly gestures. But the Hebraic *arikhes yomim,* "length of days," strikes a higher or more courtly note. We have seen that the limit is traditionally set at 120, and when one refers to the eventuality of death—as when a legacy will fall due, for instance—the phrase is *iber hundert un tsvantsik yor,* "after one hundred and twenty years."

However, benediction means more than mere longevity; one must consider the quality of the years. *Azoy fil gute yor zolt ir visn,* "May you know so many good years," is used to point up duration of recurrence, as in *azoy fil gute yor zolt ir visn vifl mol ikh bin geven bay ayer zeydn in hoyz,* "May you know as many good years as the times I have been in your grandfather's house." *Aza yor oyf mir,* "Such a year on me," in support of a statement, is a wish rather than a blessing, but *aza yor oyf im* is, unexpectedly, a curse or an insult. *Visn,* "to know," is a common vehicle for a benison, *ir zolt fun keyn shlekhts nit visn, visn zolt ir nor freyd,* "May you know of no evil, may you know only joy." *Lomir zikh begegenen oyf simkhes,* "Let us meet on joyous occasions," is a peculiar

233

phrase, amounting to "Let us know no more sorrow"; it is used when departing from a funeral.

The blanket *got zol aykh tsushikn vos ir vinsht zikh aleyn*, "God send you that which you wish yourself," is merely the familiar English "May all your wishes come true." *Got zol shoymer-umatsl* (Heb) *zayn*, "God guard and save," *got zol rakhmones* (Heb) *hobn*, "God have mercy," *hashem yisborekh* (Heb) *zol helfn*, "May the Blessed Name help," have their like in most languages; but extreme emphasis on children, their upbringing, and their successful launching into the married state, is peculiarly Jewish. *Naches fun kinder*, the special parental joy and gratification in children who have turned out well, is a haunting theme in the Jewish world. For a people living on its soil, the alienation of the young from the old is a personal affair; within the Jewish people it is also a national matter. The Jewish child that ceases to be Jewish cuts off more than the posterity of his parents; he diminishes the potential of his people.

Hence the proper education of the young has been the supreme worry of the Jewish people, and a successful outcome the first desideratum. We have noted the phrase *tsu toyre, tsu khupe un tsu maysim toyvim*, "to Torah, to marriage and to good deeds," as the prayer of pious Jews for their sons; it was their earnest blessing on each other: *ir zolt im megadl zayn tsu toyre, tsu khupe un tsu maysim toyvim*, "May you rear him to Torah, etc." Variations were, *ir zolt im gring dertsien*, "May you find his upbringing easy," *me zol trogn zayn droshe geshank*, "May the present for his wedding oration be carried about [in pride]."

But that "proper" education which was the focus of the tenderest blessings exchanged by Jews had the Jewish identity tacitly as its core. Unless so understood the blessings were not Jewish at all.

CHAPTER FOURTEEN

What Is Not German

1.

There used to be a popular saying, *vos far a yid farshteyt nisht keyn daytsh?* "What Jew doesn't understand German?" Satirical in tone for some, for others the saying was more than half serious. Those who set out from the other end, that is, knew only German, often assumed that Yiddish was nothing but a corrupted German, with odds and ends of Hebrew thrown in. Another saying, also jocular (this was long ago), ran: *di daytshn zaynen a fayn folk, nor dos loshn* (Heb) *harget* (Heb) *zey avek,* "The Germans are a fine people, but their language has been the ruin of them," literally, "kills them."

One can, by a careful choice of vocabulary, produce long, artificial passages in either German or Yiddish that will convey the same elementary meaning to anyone familiar with either language. There will be some trouble only with the grammatical constructions, the conjugations, and the declensions. But since there are large areas in each language not intelligible in the other, the choice of words in such passages would have to be made by someone thoroughly familiar with both languages. Moreover, special care would have to be taken about the words that closely resemble each other, or are even identical, but have by transformation come to mean something quite different. Anyone relying blindly on similarities will soon discover that he is talking nonsense.

Here are a few preliminary illustrations:

Warum in German (*pronounced varUM*), means "why"; *VOrem* or *VOrn* in Yiddish means "because."

The German *ich darf nicht* means "I dare not"; the Yiddish *ikh darf nisht* means "I need not."

because the doctor forbids it

237

The German *deswegen* means "on that account"; the Yiddish *fundesvegn* means "nevertheless."

The German *richten* means "to set, set up, turn (direction), pass judgment on, etc." None of these meanings is to be found in the Yiddish *rikhtn*, which is used only in the reflexive and means "to expect, anticipate, prepare for," as in *ikh hob zikh nit gerikht oyf aza enfer*, "I did not anticipate that kind of reply."

The German *trachten* means "to strive after, endeavor," the Yiddish *trakhtn* "to think"; the German *schmecken* means "to taste," the Yiddish *shmekn* "to smell." The German *kosten* has, as one important meaning, "to taste"; the Yiddish for "to taste" is *farzukhn*, which coincides with one meaning of the German *versuchen*, but not with others. To add to the confusion, the German *schmecken* and the Yiddish *shmekn* coincide in a phrase like *dos shmekt mir nit*, "I don't care for (fancy) this."

A master example of inversion is the German *Abscheu* (*b* as in *p*) and the Yiddish *opshay*; the first means "aversion, abhorrence, detestation," the second "respect, reverence, awe."

2.

A man complains in English, "I cannot sleep." In Yiddish he could say, *ikh ken nit shlofn*; in German, *ich kann nicht schlafen*. But he could also say in Yiddish, *es shloft zikh nit*, literally, "It sleeps itself not," which consists of Germanic words Slavic in content. The inability to sleep here indicated is total, unwilled, unconditional; it implies surrender, mood, helplessness. Nothing is keeping him awake, not toothache, nor noisy neighbors, not even a specific worry; only sleeplessness is there.

There are many examples of this impersonal reflexive,

and they have a flavor of their own, in which the Slavic mingles with the Germanic, and both sometimes take on forms of the Hebraic. *Ikh benk nokh a bisl frayntshaft,* "I long for a little friendship," is Yiddish and Germanic in construction (with some difference in the German *bange*); *es benkt zikh nokh a bisl frayntshaft,* "It longs itself for a little friendship, there is a longing for a little friendship," is impersonal in form, yet it makes a stronger personal appeal. The feeling of loneliness or estrangement, pervading all human relations, refocuses on the individual; it is the pathos of the species echoing in a single voice.

Es vil zikh fargesn in di tsores, "One would like to forget one's troubles," *es dakht zikh az der morgn vet zayn beser,* "One hopes, believes, opines that the morrow will be better," are again Slavisms in Germanic guise.

The Yiddish *gedenken,* "to remember," has a parallel in the same German word, but the Yiddish *a narishkeyt gedenkt zikh,* "A foolishness remembers itself," *i.e.,* "sticks in the mind," has no German parallel.

Of peculiar force is the popular idiom, *es redt zikh azoy,* literally, "it talks itself thus," which has a variety of interpretations: "That's what *you* say, it's easy to talk, that's just a manner of speaking." The tone is ironical or regretful or amused. Sometimes it rises to "That's a lot of baloney" or even (but without the vulgarity) "In a pig's eye."

Es regnt or *se regnt,* "It is raining," is exactly the same as the German *es regnet,* but the Yiddish *es regnt zikh azoy shtil* is meaningless to the German ear, having taken on a Slavic lilt; it can only be hinted at in English by "The rain is falling quietly, meditatively."

In a famous Yiddish love song of childhood, *"rayzele,"* there occurs the phrase *gey ikh mir a freylekher,* "I go me (along) a happy one"; the *mir* is dative, and the construction is called "the ethical dative." It is a detached *mir;* the singing boy is not relating himself to the act of strolling, he is simply intruding himself into the song, not acting any part in it. He is mentioning himself, he is calling attention to his existence, registering a mood. One can also say, in the pleasant colloquial style: *gey ikh zikh* (instead of *mir*) *a freylekher;* this again plays on both detachment and emphasis, "not me" and "me." There is nothing parallel in the German.

3.

The Yiddish interweave between the Germanic and Slavic verb prefixes has blurred their identities.

Taken as a preposition, the Yiddish *unter* is the same as the German; as a prefix it transforms the verb more often than not. The sense of "under" in English is clear in "undercut, undersell, understock," etc. But there is no longer an "under" sense in "understand, undertake, etc." In German and Yiddish the *unter* sense disappears much more frequently.

The Yiddish *untergeyn*, "to go under," *untershraybn*, "to (under)sign," *unterdrikn*, "to oppress" (*i.e.*, "press down"), *zikh untergebn*, "to surrender" (*i.e.*, "submit"), reflect the German; other Yiddish *unter* verbs follow the German, but have lost the meaning of *unter*, such as *unternemen*, German *unternehmen*; *unterhaltn*, German *unterhalten*. But now consider a whole series of *unter* verbs in which the German and Yiddish have nothing to do with each other:

Unterzogn means chiefly "to prompt, to convey information furtively," as to a student at an examination; the German *untersagen* is "to forbid."

The German *unterwerfen* is "to overthrow, conquer, subdue"; the Yiddish *untervarfn* has many meanings of which only one, seldom used, is parallel with the German—the reflexive *zikh untervarfn*, "to submit." The most commonly used Yiddish meaning is of Slavic origin, and comes near to

"planting something on someone"; the connotation is of slyness and underhandedness. In particular, the verb is associated
with an abandoned, or rather "planted" child: *untervarfn a
kind*, "Leave a child (on someone's doorstep)," or leave a child
to be picked up by chance. There is a different and more
sinister connotation in *untervarfn*. In the frequent cases of
Blood Accusation that have haunted the Jewish people, the
"planting," *untervarfn*, of a corpse was a traditional dodge
among certain types of criminal anti-Semites.

A curious development of *unter*, again completely alien
to the German, is its connotation of continuous and persistent
action, something done a bit at a time, in a minor key, as a
sort of accompaniment to something else. We may take the
verb *hungern* as example; it is both Yiddish and German for
"to hunger, be hungry." *Er hot gehungert* will do in both
languages for "He was hungry, he starved." *Unterhungern*,
which is choice idiomatic Yiddish, has no meaning in German.
It means "to be hungry much of the time, to get along, or
manage, by going short of food, to help oneself out by systematic undernourishment."

In the same way *untertraybn* (from *traybn*, "to drive,"
Yiddish and German), has meaning, in Yiddish only, "to
drive (the horses) a little from time to time." It also has
the meaning, "to urge (horses) on, drive (them) hard."
Vaksn, "to grow" (Yiddish and German), is straightforward
in meaning; as *untervaksn* it becomes circumstantial and non-
Germanic; it is used of children in the process of growing up,
but it is a continuous and unobserved growing up. *Dervayl
zaynen di kinder untergevaksen*, "Meanwhile the children
grew up," would be said incidentally about the tacit passing
of the years, "The children grew up on them, as it were."

These *unter* verbs increase in charm and subtlety as they
become more idiomatic. *Hustn*, "to cough," is Yiddish and
German; *unterhustn* is "to cough a little from time to time,
in a diffident way, continually, as an accompaniment to one's

241

talking." It might indicate a condition, and the effect could be sardonic but sympathetic, as if one were to say, "He does a bit of coughing all the time." *Tantsn*, "to dance," is Yiddish and German; *untertantsn*, "to dance after someone, dance attendance, toady to someone," is not Germanic; but much more interesting is the extension of *tentsl*, "little dance," which we have already encountered in the wedding ceremony. Now there is no verb *tentslen*, "to perform a little dance," but there is an extremely appealing *untertentslen*, which is trivial and comical, and denotes a restless hopping about, from nervousness, or servility, or a tic.

The temptation to read Germanic meanings into Germanic verb forms is, as we have seen, common. The Yiddish "expert" will take it for granted that *unterkoyfn* is from the German *kaufen*, "to buy"; but *unterkoyfn* is "to bribe," in German, *bestechen*. Similarly with *untershmirn*, which suggests to bribe," but can also mean "greasing one's palm" by way of tipping. A common folk locution, *az me shmirt fort men*, "If you grease, you ride," is no doubt *balegole loshn*, "driver's lingo," and is echoed in English by "Money makes the mare go." (The German noun *Schmiere* is "axle-grease," with no side connotations.) *Unterhern*, "to eavesdrop," seems by its form to suggest something like the German *unterhören*, "to underhear" (oddly enough it happens by accident to mean "overhear"), but there is no German *unterhören*; and *unterhern*, sound Yiddish as to form, is sound Slavic as to content.

Other uses of *unter* that are alien to the German content are *unterlekn*, "to toady"; *unterlenen dos harts*, literally, "to prop one's heart up," figuratively, "to take a little nourishment" (this last is a snivel phrase, a kind of cant); *unterhinken*, from *hinken*, "to limp" (Yiddish and German), with two meanings, one literal, as an extension of "to limp," the other figurative, as applied to an argument or a pretext. *Zayn enfer hinkt unter a bisl* is best rendered by "His reply doesn't hold water."

Comical, pathetic, rueful, apologetic, embarrassed, grinning, all in one, is *unterzindikn* (from *zindikn*, "to sin," German *sündigen*). It means "to sin in bits, from time to time, in installments, pettily, as occasions present themselves, but not grimly, viciously, or morosely"; a capsule description of Everyman, *l'homme moyen sensuel*.

Like most of the Germanic prefixes, *unter* can be attached to verbs with a Hebrew root and be just as Slavic in content as the other *unter* verbs cited. The Slavic prefixes are, however, rarely turned into Yiddish meanings. *Ganvenen* is a hybrid verb, "to steal," and borrows its form from the Hebrew; *unterganvenen zikh*, "to sneak up on," is Germanic and Hebrew in form, Slavic in meaning. To Sholom Aleichem is usually attributed the story of the village *melamed* who foresaw unexpected financial resources for one of the Rothschilds. "If I were Rothschild," he said, "I would be richer than Rothschild, because in addition to all that money *volt ikh a bisl untergeknelt*, I would put in a bit of teaching on the side."

4.

A Yiddish verb will often be an archaic or obsolete German form, without Slavic or other foreign origins. I cannot undertake to trace the evolution of such verbs, so for the most part I will only take note of some interesting cases. (I may without knowing it also stumble on Slavisms.)

The Yiddish *rikhtn* and the German *richten*, we have just seen, have certain resemblances and certain dissimilarities. This is also true of *aynrikhtn* and *einrichten*. To a German, *er hot zikh gut ayngerikht* would be acceptable as "He fitted himself up in good order"; but he would never guess that it also means "He soiled himself good and proper." Similarly, the German *verrichten* means "to perform, fulfill," while the

Yiddish *farrikhtn* is "to correct (an error), mend." *Farrikhtn dem tish* is good Yiddish for "to mend the table," but makes no sense in German.

Klingen is good Yiddish and German for "to ring," but whereas the German *verklingen* means "to die away" (of a sound), as in *das Lied verklingt in die Ferne*, "The song dies away in the distance," the Yiddish *farklingen* means "to fill with a ringing sound": *dos gelekhter fun di kinder farklingt dos hoyz*, "The laughter of the children sets the house ringing." The Yiddish *shmekn*, we have seen, means "to smell," while the German *schmecken* refers to taste: *di royzn hobn farshmekt dem tsimmer*, "The roses filled the room with their perfume," exhales the richness of the Yiddish word, but conveys nothing in German.

At the opposite extreme, offensively, is the Yiddish *farshtinken*, which does not resemble the German, and must be translated in a tortured English as "to bestink": *der gepeygerter koter hot farshtunken dem brunem*, "The dead tomcat stank up the well"; *farsarkhenen* (Heb), even more offensive, borders on the scatological. (*Peygern*, we have noted, means "to die," referring to an animal, but is an unpleasant word.)

Farkrenken has no German analogue and the nearest I can come to it in English is "to consume one's possessions in (the costs of) sickness." The adjective *krank*, "ill, sick," leads into a curious turn of phrase, *nit krank tsu zayn*, literally, "to be not sick," but taking on a sarcastic meaning, "not to be so sick as to . . ." It is a rather fishwifey way of saying, "He'll not die from it." If one were to state objectively that Reuben can afford to pay a monthly rental of five hundred dollars, the Yiddish would be *er iz imshtand* (or *in shtand*) *tsu batsoln finf hundert doler a khoydesh*, "He is in the condition, capable of, paying, etc." But if Reuben wants the lordliest accommodation and tries to get it on the cheap, the landlord may very well say of him: *er iz nit krank tsu batsoln*. The idiom is often put in the interrogative, with biting effect:

krank iz er, etc.? There is another, stronger shading. You learn that a man in good health and excellent physical condition, who is also hard up and in no particular hurry, is spending money lavishly on taxis. Now if it were any business of yours (*e.g.*, if you have been asked to contribute something toward his upkeep), you might ask, *krank iz er tsu forn mitn sobvey?*, literally, "Is he (too) sick to use the subway?" But the proper rendering would be: "What's the matter? Did he break a leg that he can't use the subway?" And there is a hint that for such impudence the fellow deserves to be sick or to break a leg.

Verbs in *far* with a Hebraic root naturally have no analogues in the Germanic. There are also other Germanic prefixes with Hebraic and Slavic roots: *farshikern* from the Hebraic *shiker*, "drunk," noun and adjective, begins with *shikern*, "to be a drinker, a drunkard." *Er shikert*, "He drinks," can mean anything from a toper to an alcoholic. *Farshikern* has two meanings: in the reflexive, *zikh farshikern*, "to get drunk, be intoxicated" (also figuratively, "be intoxicated with happiness"), and *farshikern*, transitive, meaning "to use up in drinking, to booze away," as in *er hot farshiktert zayn gehalt*, "He boozed away his salary."

The participle *farfaln* is a mournful and haunting word in Yiddish. Standing by itself it means "over and done with, irretrievably lost, alas, spare your tears, etc." *Farfaln vern* is "to disappear somewhere, without a trace, be swallowed up in the unknown." In these lines of Itzik Manger's, the melancholy words ring like a distant bell:

> *Harbstik royte bleter faln*
> *Un der kinig zitst aleyn,*
> *Se zingt der vint zayn alt geveyn,*
> *S'iz farfaln, s'iz farfaln.*
> Autumn crimson leaves are falling
> And the monarch sits alone,

The wind sings with an old lamenting,
"Dead and done with, dead and done with."

5.

Oyskrenken also has a rich deviation, "to incorporate
one's sufferings in the outcome of one's struggle." *An eygn
land ken men nit poshet oyfboyen, me muz es oyskrenken,*
"A land of one's own cannot be simply built up, it must be
agonized out, sweated out, bled out," was a saying of Chaim
Weizmann's. We have met the Yiddish *benken,* "to long
for"; *oysbenken* takes on the form of *oyskrenken,* and like it,
fuses suffering and fulfillment. When Tennyson writes

> O that 'twere possible
> After long grief and pain,
> To find the arms of my true love
> Round me once again. . . .

"after," as both time and process, hints at the effect of *oysbenken.* In the song of the Jewish partisans there is the line

> *Vayl kumen vet nokh undzer oysgebenkte sho . . .*
> For the longed-for hour will yet come for us . . .

where "longed for" must be twisted into "yearned into being,"
as if by intensity and persistence of yearning one had brought
about the fulfillment.

    Oyszayn, literally and artificially "out-be," has two con-
tradictory meanings according to whether we are dealing with
space or time, with *oyszayn a velt,* "a world," *shtot,* "city,"
etc., or *oyszayn di tsayt,* "time." *Oyszayn di shtot* is "to visit
every part of the city, to have been everywhere." *Er iz oysgeven*

gants poyln, "He visited (went searching throughout) all of Poland"; *vu iz der oremer bokher shoyn nit oysgeven?,* "Where has the unhappy youth not been in his wanderings?" *Oyszayn di tsayt* is "to disappear (as a willed act)": *eyder ir vet zikh arumkukn vet er oyszayn di tsayt,* "Before you'll have a chance to look around he will have disappeared (skipped, slipped away)"; *beyn minkhe le-mayrev* (all Heb) *iz er oysgeven di tsayt,* "Between the afternoon and evening prayers he was missing, was nowhere to be found."

We have met *tayne* (Heb) as "complaint, argument." As a verb, the hybrid *taynen,* "to argue, complain, hold the view, advance the opinion," is richly colored by the Jewish propensity toward speculation and argumentativeness, simple or complex. *Der yid taynet az me hot im farfirt,* is straightforward, "The Jew argues that he was misled." It can be rephrased as *der yid hot a tayne az me hot im farfirt,* "The Jew has a complaint that he has been misled." (It should be noted that when *yid* is used in this context, the Jewishness of the man has no ethnic connotation; he is simply a person.) *Er hot a tayne tsu mir* is somewhat more subtle; it is not quite "He has a complaint or claim against me." It is more like "He has put me in the wrong position, or in the position of a claimant. I have failed him in some respect, he has not squared accounts with me" (a compensatory claim need not be implied). But *taynen* is used in a wider sense. In a discussion touching a matter of fact, a point of law, or more particularly a problem of Jewish scholarship, the following phrases will be used: *ruven taynet,* "Reuben argues," *ober shimen taynet,* "But Simon counterargues"; *der brisker taynet,* "He of Brisk, the sage of Brisk, maintains, holds the view . . ." *Zikh oystaynen,* "to talk, argue it out (with someone)," can mean either a thorough discussion or an unburdenening of oneself. *Tevye der milkhiker hot zikh oysgetaynet mit dem reboyne-shel-oylem,* "Tevye the dairyman had it out with the the Almighty," presents Tevye as a kind of Omar Khayyam

247

"talking out" a full heart, convinced of the reasonableness of the Lord of the World if He only, with all due respect, gets off His Chariot, *i.e.*, His high horse.

6.

Optrogn (from *trogn*, "to carry," German *tragen*) overlaps with the German *abtragen* in several variations of meaning, but is entirely Yiddish and extremely colorful in the reflexive. *Zikh optrogn*, "to make off, beat it," has overtones of discontent and offendedness. *Zey hobn zikh opgetrogn*, "They left," would have to be followed by "in high dudgeon, their tails between their legs, disappointed," and the like. *Trog zikh up fun danen*, "Get out of this place," is insulting unless it is softened by a benevolent explanation, and then it is merely familiar or carries a danger signal, as in *trog zikh op fun danen, dos ort iz geferlekh*, "Begone from here, the place is dangerous."

Opkumen (from *kumen*, "to come," German *kommen*) has little in common with the German *abkommen*. The most widespread use of *opkumen*, "to get away with, to manage on," is well exemplified in such folk phrases as *opkumen mit shrek* ("fright"), "to come through a real or imaginary danger with nothing worse than a fright," and *opkumen mit a trukn shtikl broyt*, "to manage to get by on a dry crust," the idea being want, not discipline. *Opkumen far di khatoim* (Heb), "to expiate, atone for one's sins," is not looked upon as a voluntary act, but is nevertheless accounted as so much to the good, "account closed," as it were. Thence we reach *an opkumenish*, "an affliction, ordeal, tribulation," not necessarily with religious import, and sometimes not implying anything more than a laborious trial.

We met in an early chapter the expression *opshprekhn*

a beyz oyg, "to exorcise an evil eye." There is a simple phrase, Germanic in form but not in content, based on *shrayen,* "to cry, shout": *opshrayen a beyze gzeyre* (Heb), "to get an evil decree aborted or annulled." This phrase need not be associated with magic, although prayer may come under that heading; some kind of secular transaction will do just as well. Queer things have happened with the German *sprechen,* "to speak," and *Sprache,* "speech," and their Yiddish counterparts. Yiddish has no verb *shprekhn,* "to speak"; it uses *redn;* but it has, as we have seen, *opshprekhen,* unknown to German. *Shprakh,* on the other hand, is good Yiddish, so is *shprukh* or *shprokh,* "incantation."

7.

Onkveln, "to overflow with satisfaction, self-satisfaction, gratification," is a more intensive form of *kveln.* "Gloat" would fit, except as implying envy, or triumph over someone. *Kveln,* more familiar than *onkveln,* is one of those rich-sounding words assimilating Yiddish-speaking Jews hang on to, so that it crops up frequently where English is used almost exclusively. There is also some obscure confusion with the English "quelling," which has of course a totally different meaning. "You should have seen the mother *kvelling* at her son's *bar mitzvah,*" is a typical "Yiddish" expression. A delicate variant of *onkveln* is *onteyen,* which is "choice" Yiddish, and lends itself to various manifestations of quiet glee, including a smirk.

Onzogn, "to tell, charge, pass the instruction on," turns finely into "to presage." The nuances pass through time phases. *Ikh hob im ongezogt as er zol brengen dos kind aheym,* "I told him, charged him, to bring home the child," is a simple one-time order; *ikh hob im ongezogt er zol zikh nit mishn in yenems gesheftn,* "I told him not to poke his nose into other peoples' business," implies that the said person was not to have the habit of interfering, etc. A finer turn is *di shvere regns zogn on oyf a geretenish,* "The heavy rains presage a plentiful harvest," or better still, *di shvere regns zaynen an onzog oyf a geretenish,* "The heavy rains are a presage, etc."

One of the most sorrow-laden Yiddish phrases is *onkumen tsu,* "to have to apply for assistance, to be supported by, beg assistance from, be beholden to." It is at its most depressing in two forms: *onkumen tsu kitsve* (Heb), "to apply for public relief," and *onkumen tsu kinder,* "to be beholden (for assistance) to one's children," of which the latter is hardest to bear. This is not, at least necessarily, because of hardness of heart in the children, but partly because of the misery of the parents in being a burden, and partly because of the comedown in old age. *Oyf der elter,* "in old age," echoes the immemorial fear of the Psalmist: *al teazveni le-eys zikno* (all Heb), "Cast me not off in my old age."

Onheybn, "to begin, start," seems to have little connection with *heybn,* "to lift," German *heben,* unless we think of "to raise the subject." Here Yiddish and German overlap to a very limited extent. The reflexive *onheybn zikh mit,* "to start a dispute, quarrel, argument with, to go looking for trouble," is purely Yiddish. In my boyhood there was a *kheyder* joke about the Book of Esther: "Why is Ahasuerus the gentile the first one to be mentioned by name, and not Mordecai the Jew, or Esther? Because you should never start up with a Jew." In the locution, *heybt zikh nit on,* "doesn't begin to be so," neatly rendered by Weinreich as "nothing of the sort," the original force of the verb peeps through, as again in *heybt zikh on a mayse,* literally, "A story begins," meaning "Let's not go into *that*." The locution *heybn in himl arayn,* "to lift, exalt to the heavens," is perfectly echoed by "to praise to the skies."

CHAPTER FIFTEEN

Sampling Prefixes

I could amuse myself, if not the reader, for a hundred pages or so by listing constant verb-stems and trying out various prefixes on them. The results are much more interesting for German and Yiddish than for English, which compensates with the detached prepositions. We shall of course be meeting familiar prefixes, but I shall give them new forms.

Firn, "to lead," has, among other interesting variations, *unterfirn* and *iberfirn,* of which the second has as one important meaning "to spoil." *Ir kokhn hot mir ibergefirt dem mogn,* "Her cooking ruined my digestion [literally, stomach]"; *mit zayn shlekhtn aynpakn hot er ibergefirt di skhoyre,* "With his clumsy packing he spoiled the merchandise"; *mit ir nokhgibikeyt hot di mame ir ben-yokhidl in gantsn ibergefirt,* "With her permissiveness the mother completely spoiled her only son."

Unterfirn, "to accompany, give a lift to, conduct," takes a special turn as the noun *unterfirer,* approximately, "best man at a wedding"; but as a verb, *firn unter der khupe,* "to lead under the wedding canopy," does not correspond even remotely to the idea of "best man." A mother looks forward to the day *ven ikh vel firn mayn tokhter unter der khupe,* "when I will lead my daughter under the wedding canopy," but this is a happy figure of speech as well as a literal act. "Best man at a wedding" itself is only a substitute phrase; the *unterfirer* (plural) were those who brought the bridegroom in for the ceremony of the *badekens,* the "veiling (of the bride)."

Fargeyn, "to pass off, away, into a certain condition": *di zun fargeyt in flamen,* "The sun sets in flames"; *a yor nokh der khasene iz zi fargangen in trogn,* "A year after the wedding she became pregnant," literally, "passed into (child) bear-

253

ing"; *dos yingl iz fargangen in a geveyn,* "The boy melted into a fit of weeping." The saying *a patsh fargeyt, a vort bashteyt,* "A slap passes away, a word endures," may be freely rendered as "A slap flies past, a word stands fast."

Bageyn, "to commit," is used, like the English translation, with a reprehensible act; *bageyn an avle* (Heb), *a mord, a ganeyve* (Heb), "to commit a wrong, murder, theft." *Bageyn zelbstmord,* "to commit suicide," is considered a *daytshmerizm* by some modernists, but is widely used, *aleyn-mord* being rejected as an affectation. The reflexive *zikh bageyn,* "to do without," is very homey, and cannot be resolved intelligently into its component parts: *vilst nit? vel ikh zikh bageyn,* "You don't want? Then I'll do without."

Opgeyn, "depart (train, ship), lack, proceed": *di shif vet opgeyn genoy tsvelf a zeyger,* "The ship will leave exactly at twelve o'clock"; *es geyt im gornisht op,* "He wants for nothing"; *lomir hofn az di zakh vet glat opgeyn,* "Let's hope the thing will go off smoothly."

Fartrogn, "to endure, carry away": in the first sense it is used about persons, as in *ikh ken im nit fartrogn,* "I can't endure, bear him"; in the second sense it is used about some objects:

> *Ikh volt mayn harts*
> *vayt, vayt tsvishn dayne berg fartrogn.*
> I would carry my heart
> Far, far away among your hills.
>
> —Ch. N. Bialik

Untertrogn, "to keep bringing, serving up, to come bearing (obsequiously)": *di baleboste hot im untergetrogn tey, kikhlekh, ayngemakhts,* "The housewife served up [with a touch of zeal] tea, cookies, preserves"; *me darf dem nayem gubernater untertrogn epes a sheyne matbeye* (Heb), "We have to bring the new governor some kind of handsome present [literally, 'coin']."

Onzen zikh, "to be evident, stand out, be conspicuous, effective, look one's fill": *es hot zikh bald ongezen in shtub az es felt emetser,* "It soon became evident in the house that somebody was missing"; *in aza yam fun noyt veln zikh ayere por groshn koym onzen,* "In such an ocean of need your few pennies will make next to no impression"; *in di letste etlekhe yor hob ikh zikh ongezen a velt,* "In the last few years I've seen a whole world."

Onzen as a noun is close to the Hebraic *khshives,* "importance, standing, prestige," but while *khshives* can be used for objects and situations as well as persons, *onzen* is used only for persons: *ruvn hot shtoltsirt mit zayn onzen in der landsmanshaft,* "Reuben was proud of the esteem he enjoyed in the Old Country Association." The substitution of *khshives* for *onzen* would greatly enhance the sentence and Reuben's self-esteem; but in *di khshives fun zayn handlung iz gornisht optsushatsn,* "The importance of his action is beyond evaluation," *onzen* cannot be substituted. An *ongezeener gast* and a *khoshever gast,* both meaning "an important guest," are interchangeable; but *khoshever her goldberg,* "dear Mr. Goldberg," is merely formal, while *ongezeener her goldberg* would be, as a form of address, highfalutin; it can be used in the third person with dignity.

Oyszen, "to see, have the appearance of, to resemble, look alike": *es zet oys az mir veln muzn opleygn di nesiye* (Heb), "It seems we will have to postpone the journey"; *er zet oys vi der feter moyshe,* "He resembles Uncle Moses"; *er zet oys vi a barmenon, rakhmone-litslan,* "He looks like a corpse, God save us"; *er zet oys vi khoyzek,* "He looks wretched, horrible, ludicrous, a laughing-stock."

Khoyzek is a mysterious word, to all appearances of Hebraic origin (*cf.* the Hebrew *khazak,* "strong," used iron-

255

ically), but having no connection with it. Some authorities aver that one Khoyzek was a comical folk-figure round whom a number of stories had collected (*cf.* the famous Hershele Ostropolyer and Motke Khabad, as familiar in Yiddish lore as, say, Baron Munchhausen elsewhere), but this too is challenged. Nevertheless *khoyzek* is widespread and deep-rooted. *Makhn khoyzek fun emetsn,* "to mock, make fun of someone," and *es (er) hot a ponem fun khoyzek,* "It (the whole thing) (he) looks ludicrous, like a bad joke," are very common expressions. Professor Dov Sadan has a theory that *khoyzek* was a *shed* (Heb), "demon," and there is a locution, *khoyzek lozt grisn,* "regards from *khoyzek,*" when someone has been made a fool of.

Oysvern (so written to maintain the list, but properly written as *vern oys*), "to cease to be": *er iz gevorn oys dokter,* "he ceased to be a doctor," literally, "He became 'out,' no more, doctor." The force of *vern oys* is pointed up by the comparison between "to do" and "to undo"; the "undo" is a creative verb. The expression *iz gevorn oys dokter* is not merely a lapse into nonbeing, but a positive transformation into not-being; "He became a not-doctor." Thus we now have the descriptive "nonbook." We may imagine that the person in question was practicing medicine without a license and was exposed.

A popular locution, derisive, with a touch of *Schadenfreude,* is *er iz gevorn oys kapelyush-makher,* "He ceased to be a big-shot," literally, "hatmaker." The *kapelyush* (Slv) was a superior kind of hat, in the shape of a derby; the *kapelyush-makher* was, accordingly, a superior sort of craftsman. The phrase came to cover any kind of prominent person (*cf.* "brass hat"), and *gevorn oys kapelyush-makher* does not necessarily imply a major comedown; it can be and often is used of a very minor tragedy. If not for the touch of slanginess, a good translation of "Othello's occupation's gone" would be *otelo iz gevorn oys kapelyush-makhar.*

Bazetsn, "to seat, settle (a country), take possession of": *er hot bazetst di orkhim* (Heb), "He found places, quarters for the guests"; *di englender hobn bazetst oystralie in onheyb fun nayntsenten yorhundert,* "The English settled Australia at the beginning of the nineteenth century"; *nokh a langer balegerung hot aleksander mukden bazetst di festung,* "After a long siege Alexander the Great (of Macedon) took possession of the fortress."

A note of grace and solemnity sounds in *bazetsn di kale,* "to seat (enthrone) the bride." It is one of the high moments of the wedding ceremony, and the noun from this verb is *bazetsns,* reserved for this occasion and for this alone. One cannot use *bazetsns* in connection with, for example, *orkhim* (above), for *bazetsns* is a religious word. We have seen that *badekn* is simply "to cover." One can speak of *badekn di kale,* "to cover (veil) the bride," also *dekn dem tish,* "cover (lay) the table," while *badekns* is an exclusive and religious noun. In the same way *oysnemen,* with its various secular meanings, becomes refined by the addition of the *s* into the exclusive and sacred period of the Torah reading.

Tsuzetsn zikh, "to take a seat for a moment, sit down next to," is a prettily turned verb. *Es felt mir otem, ikh vel zikh tsuzetsn oyf a por minut,* "I'm short of breath, I'll take a seat for a few minutes"; *tsi meg ikh zikh tsuzetsn tsu aykh?,* "May I sit down next to you?"

Bashteln, "to place an order, surround (with objects)": *dem frak hot er bashtelt baym shtotishn shnayder,* "He ordered the frock coat from the city tailor"; *di poyerte hot bashtelt dem blumentop mit getshkes,* "The peasant woman surrounded the flowerpot with ikons."

Farshteln, "to block, disguise, conceal": *der oytomobil farshtelt dem aroysgang,* "The automobile is blocking the exit"; *in shomers a roman farshtelt zikh der raykher held for a betler,* "In one of Shomer's novels the wealthy hero disguises himself as a beggar"; *ikh vel zayn mit aykh ofn, ikh*

257

vel nit farshteln mayne kavones (Heb), "I will be open with you, I will not conceal my motives."

Onshteln, "to engage, set going, aim": *er hot ongeshtelt dem altn general far a lakay*, "He engaged the old general as lackey"; *nokh dem vos er hot tsugegreyt dem materyal, hot er ongeshtelt dem elekrishn vebshtul*, "After he had prepared the material, he set in motion the electric loom"; *er hot ongeshtelt di biks oyf dem tsilbret*, "He aimed the gun at the target"; *er hot ongeshtelt oyf ir a por oygn*, "He fixed his (big) eyes on her."

Untershteln, "to place under"; *der tish hot zikh geshoklt, hob ikh untergeshtelt a klin*, "the table wobbled, so I put a wedge under (it)." Figuratively and idiomatically *untershteln* has two widely different connotations: *untershteln a fisl*, "to put a leg (diminutive) under (someone), to trip up (figuratively), set a trap (slyly)," in the sense of putting an invisible object in someone's way. It parallels the Italian *dare gambetto*, "to 'give' a leg," which has passed into the chess term "gambit," thence into general use. The diminutive *fisl*, for *fus*, "leg," imparts a touch of gleeful malice to the phrase. *Untershteln zikh*, "to presume": *vi azoy hot ir zikh untergeshtelt optsufregn dem psak-din* (Heb) *fun aza talmidkhokhem?* "How did you presume to contradict the verdict of such a scholar?"; *vos shtelt ir zikh unter?*, "How dare you?"

Ophaltn, "to detain, deter, hold (a meeting, etc.), score (a victory), abstain": *ikh zeh az ir aylt zikh, vel ikh aykh lenger nit ophaltn*, "I see you are in a hurry, so I will not detain you any longer"; *er hot bedeye* (Heb) *gehat tsu koyfn dos bukh, nor ikh hob im opgehaltn derfun*, "He was of a mind to buy the book, but I deterred him"; *yenem ovnt hot di khevre* (Heb) *kadishe* (Heb) *opgehaltn an aseyfe* (Heb), "That evening the burial society held a meeting"; *bay der shlakht fun vaterlu hot england opgehaltn a historishn nitsokhn*, "At the battle of Waterloo England scored a historic victory"; *bay di kumendike valn vet di arbeter partey zikh ophaltn fun*

258

shtimen, "At the next elections the Workers party will abstain from voting."

Unterhaltn, "to support, bear out, amuse": *der khoyle (Heb) volt geven avekgefaln ven di kranken-shvester volt im nit untergehaltn,* "The patient would have collapsed if the nurse had not held him up"; *der khazn hot fartsoygn dem nign* (Heb) *un der khor hot im untergehaltn,* "The cantor prolonged the melody and the choir sustained him"; *er hot geshvoyrn az er iz unshuldik un der eydes* (Heb) *hot im untergehaltn,* "He swore he was innocent and the witness bore him out"; *ir megt geyn oyf dem ovnt, ir vet zikh gut unterhaltn,* "You can go to that evening (performance), you will find it entertaining (have a good time)."

Ongebn, "to announce, submit, apply for": *er hot ongegebn in der tsaytung az er iz a mitglid in der khevre* (Heb), "He announced in the paper that he is a member of the association"; *me bashuldikt mikh az ikh bin a kamtsn* (Heb), *muz ikh ongebn az in der emesn* (Heb) *bin ikh a groyser oreman,* "I am accused of being stingy, but I must submit that in reality I am a very poor man"; *ikh hob ongegebn mayn nomen oyf dem postn,* "I applied for the post."

Opgebn, "to deliver, return, turn in, devote"; *dos shikyingl hot opgegebn dos pekl,* "The messenger boy delivered the package"; *az er iz gevorn oys soldat hot er opgegebn zayn shverd,* "When he left the military service he turned in his sword"; *oyf der elter hot er zikh opgegebn mit kolishe inyonim* (both Heb), "In his latter years he devoted himself to communal affairs"; *ikh ken zikh nit opgebn mit ayere problemen,* "I cannot devote myself to your problems."

Oysgebn, "to spend (money), marry off (children), give out (pretend)": *vifl vilt ir oysgebn oyf a por shikh?,* "How much do you want to spend on a pair of shoes?", *zey hobn shoyn lang oysgegebn di kinder,* "They have long since married off their children"; *er hot zikh oysgegebn far a dokter,* "He gave himself out as, declared himself to be, a doctor."

Untergebn, "to keep adding small amounts, surrender"; *ven der tate volt zey nit geven untergegebn tsu bislekh gelt voltn zey oysgegangen fun hunger,* "If their father had not kept doling out little sums they would have starved to death." Here one can substitute *untershtupn* for the whole phrase *untergebn tsu bislekh gelt,* but thereby the sentence becomes condescending, even beggarly, if not grudging. It should further be noted that in *untershtupn,* the father does not, in this context, become an *untershtuper,* "a lickspittle subordinate," what the English call "an understrapper." *Di oyfshtendler hobn zikh untergegebn dem kinig,* "The rebels surrendered to the king."

Farforn, "to turn (drive) in, put up at, overshoot, head off, smash": *mir zaynen farforn in unzer alter akhsanye* (Heb), "We turned in at, put up at our old hotel"; *er iz farforn ergets keyn boyberik,* "he [lost his way and] drove, traveled, wandered on to the back of beyond" (*boyberik* is Sholom Aleichem's mythical village); *er iz undz farforn dem veg,* "he headed us off"; *aza buyan enfert men nit, er ken dir nokh farforn in di tseyn,* "You don't answer that kind of hooligan, he's liable to let you have it in the jaw." (*Farforn in di tseyn,* literally, "drive at your teeth," is part humorous, part slang.)

Iberforn, "to run over, overtake (vehicular transportation)." Somewhere I read a story of a rabbi who was asked by a young bride to interpret away a sinister dream she had had about her approaching wedding. In her dream the carriage in which she was traveling "had run over," *hot ibergeforn,* her brothers. "An innocent dream," said the rabbi, reassuringly. *du vest forn tsu der khasene* (Heb) *mit der gantser mishpokhe* (Heb); *tate-mame veln forn in eyn vogn un di brider dayne in dem tsveytn vogn, un dayn vogn vet iberforn dayne briders vogn,* "You'll be riding to the wedding with all your family; you and your parents will be riding in one carriage and your brothers in the other, and your carriage will overtake your brothers' carriage."

Aynredn, "to coax, persuade, delude": *vifl ikh zol im nit aynredn vet er ton dos zaynike*, "No matter how long I coax, persuade him, he'll do as he wants (do things his own way)"; *zi hot im ayngeredt az er iz a guter muzikant*, "She talked it into him that he is a good musician"; *zi hot im ayngeredt tsu farlozn zayne kroyvim* (Heb), "She talked him into leaving his relatives"; *er hot zikh ayngeredt az er shtamt fun groys yikhes* (Heb), "He deluded himself into the belief that he was of distinguished descent." A popular proverb has it that *an aynredenish is erger vi a krenk*, "A self-delusion, *idée fixe*, is worse than a disease."

Farredn, "to talk unthinkingly, becloud with talk": *ikh hob zikh farredt un gezogt a sakh narishkeytn*, "I talked at random and said many foolish things." *Farredn di tseyn*, literally, "overtalk someone's teeth," *i.e.*, "throw someone off the track, confuse and overbear someone with excessive talk": *keyn sibe* (Heb) *vet er aykh nit gebn, er vet aykh nor farredn di tseyn*, "He won't give you a reason but he'll talk you into a daze."

Araynfaln, "to fall in, fall into error, a trap, interrupt": *er hot zikh farmostn kegn dem khitren poyer un iz mies arayngefaln*, "He tried to match wits with (measure himself against) the crafty peasant and came off very badly"; *er iz arayngefaln in a more-shkhoyre* (Heb), "He fell into a fit of melancholia"; *zayt azoy gut un falt mir nit arayn in di reyd*, "Be good enough not to interrupt me." A widespread locution: *araynfaln vi a yovn in suke*, literally, "to fall like a Greek into a *sukkah* [festival booth]," *i.e.*, "to barge ineptly into a situation or conversation." The reference is to the Greeks of ancient times, but *yovn* also means a *goyish* soldier.

Aynfaln, "to collapse, cave in, become hollowed, occur (idea)": *der alter moyer halt baym aynfaln*, "The old wall is on the point of collapse"; *zayne ayngefalene bakn hobn eydes* (Heb) *gezogt oyf tayneysim* (Heb), "His sunken cheeks bore witness to his fasts"; *es iz mir keynmol nit ayngefaln az er*

261

hot mikh faynt, "It never occurred to me that he dislikes me"; *vos falt aykh ayn?* "What's the idea?" (in astonishment), "How dare you?"

Onfaln, "to assail (as aggressor)": *dem zibetn detsember, nayntsn hundert eyn un fertsik, iz der yapanisher flot ongefaln oyf poyrl harber,* "On the seventh of December, 1941, the Japanese fleet attacked Pearl Harbor"; *di yidine iz ongefaln oyf dem pedler mit a geshrey az er hot zi bashvindlt,* "The woman assailed the peddler with an outcry that he had swindled her." *Onfaln* is almost synonymous with *iberfaln;* as a noun, *onfaln* is linked with *onfal,* as *iberfaln* is to *iberfal,* also meaning "ambush," and *bafaln* to *bafal,* also meaning "mugging."

Araynleygn, "to put in, invest, lay oneself out": *ikh hob arayngeleygt di hant in kiln vaser,* "I put my hand into the cool water"; *der rov hot dem katself* (Heb) *arayngeleygt in kherem* (Heb), "The rabbi put the butcher under a ban"; *yeder shutef* (Heb) *hot arayngeleygt a dritl fun dem kapital,* "Every partner put in a third of the capital"; *er hot zikh arayngeleyt az der shidekh* (Heb) *zol bashteyn,* "He laid himself out to bring about the match."

Avekleygn, "to lay, set down, lie down": *erev yontef* (both Heb) *hot er avekgeleygt di makhshirim* (Heb) *un a gantsn mesles afile* (both Heb) *nit getrakht vegn zey,* "On the eve of the festival (or Sabbath) he put away his tools for twenty-four hours and did not give them a thought"; *er hot zikh avekgeleygt un iz shoyn mer nit oyfgeshtanen,* "He laid himself down and never got up again." A hearty colloquialism is: *der alter khazn* (Heb) *hot avekgeleygt a nesane toykef az di vent hobn getsitert,* "The old cantor 'gave out' with an *unsane toykef* [a New Year's prayer] that made the walls tremble."

Aynleygn, "to place on deposit as pledge, to destroy": *a helft fun dem nadan* (Heb) *vet er muzn aynleygen tsu di tnoyim* (Heb), "Half the dowry he will have to deposit at the betrothal"; *aynleygn a hoyz iz nit keyn groyse khokhme* (Heb) *oyfshteln a hoyz iz shoyn epes andersh,* "To pull a house down is no great trick, to put one up is quite a different matter"; *er vet aynleygn veltn un zayns vet er oysfirn*, "He'll turn the world upside down and he'll have his way." A colloquialism is: *lign ayngeleygt*, "to be quiet, keep one's mouth shut" (implying duress).

Farleygn, "to mislay, fold (arms), set (trap), set (one's heart on)": *ikh hob ergets vu farleygt dos bukh un ken zikh nit dermanen vu*, "I've misplaced the book somewhere and can't remember where"; *di froyen arbetn un di mener shteyn mit farleygte hent*, "The women work and the men stand by with folded arms"; *baym farleygn a pastke hit zikh zolst aleyn nit araynfaln*, "In setting a trap, make sure not to fall into it yourself"; *er hot zikh farleygt aribertsubrengen zayn bruder tsu zikh*, "He set his heart on bringing over his brother."

Oysleygn, "to set out (things), spell, lay out (money), interpret (dreams)": *baym oysleygn di skhoyre* (Heb) *darf dos shenste lign fun oybn*, "When merchandise is set out the finest must be on top"; *di hebreishe verter vern andersh oysgeleygt*, "The Hebrew words are spelled differently"; *zayt azoy gut un leygt oys di ershte ayntsolung far mir*, "Be so good as to lay out the first installment for me"; *er hot mir oysgeleygt dem kholem* (Heb) *tsum gutn*, "He gave my dream a favorable interpretation"; *di tsigayner haltn zikh far groyse mumkhim* (Heb) *in oysleygn kortn*, "The gypsies consider themselves great experts in fortune-telling by cards."

Unterleygn, "To lay beneath, plant (figuratively), assist": *unter dem tayern tsudek hot men untergeleygt eynfakhe zaklayvnt*, "Beneath the costly covering they laid plain sacking"; *di protestirer hobn gemakht a farshverung untertsuleygn a bombe bay der konferents*, "The protesters made a conspiracy to plant a bomb at the conference"; *oyb ir vet nit unterleygn an aksl vet zikh di unternemung nit rirn fun ort,* "If you will not put a shoulder to the wheel the enterprise will not budge from its place."

Farkern, "to consort with": *a frumer yid volt libersht*

263

farkert mit frume goyim eyder mit yidishe veltlekhe, "A pious Jew would rather consort with pious non-Jews than with secularized Jews." The verb *farkern* is slightly stilted and *daytshmerish,* but the adverb, *farkert,* "the opposite, contrary," is sound Yiddish: *vos ikh zol nit zogn tut er punkt farkert,* "No matter what I say he does just the opposite"; *ir zogt az er iz a kluger un ikh halt punkt farkert,* "You say he's clever and I believe the exact contrary."

Iberkern, "to turn over, overthrow": *kert iber dem medal un leynt di andere zayt,* "Turn the medal over and read the other side."

> *A foyst vu iz, vu iz a beyzer duner,*
> *vos zol zikh oprekhenen far ale doyres* (Heb),
> *mayn shtul, mayn kisey koved* (both Heb) *iberkern?*
> Where is a fist, where is a mighty thunder,
> Which shall take vengeance for all the generations,
> Overturn My Seat, My Throne of Glory?
>
> —Ch. N. Bialik

CHAPTER SIXTEEN

The Future of Yiddish

1.

I venture a guess that as much as half the Jewish population of America understands some Yiddish. And of course millions of non-Jews have picked up pidgin Yiddish, part of which may survive, first as slang, later as standard English.

But this is not the creative side of Yiddish. All over the country, small groups of Jews have been impelled to take up the study of Yiddish, usually as part of synagogue and center activity, but in no way motivated by strictly religious needs. A religious connection exists, but it is not formal and ritualistic; it has in it something of a natural piety, the memorialization of the generation which children and grandchildren cannot bring themselves to forget. It has in it the call of a sorrowful pride—"These are the unforgettable Sufferers, let not the language of their ultimate desolation perish altogether." There is also, in that pride, a strain of assertiveness, a declaration of the validity of Yiddish not merely as a Jewish language that happens to have existed, but as *the* language that Jews have a right to place as a living thing among the other languages of the world.

Now these are conscious impulses; they may be challenged as sentimentalities, or fads. More serious, and reinforcing the uncertain will, is a cultural resurgence rising from a deeper relationship to the Jewish phenomenon. The language factor is only one aspect of the national will. I have spoken of Yiddish as being organically intertwined with Hebrew in the spiritual as well as the linguistic sense; it is also proper to speak of Yiddish as a national phenomenon. Of all the curious turns of the Jewish cultural changes, none is more instructive than the rise of a lively response to Yiddish among

Hebrew-speaking Israelis. I recall the time, still fresh in my memory, when Yiddish was violently repudiated in the Jewish homeland by the pioneers and repressed in the name of a proud, exclusive Hebrew; I remember the vilification poured out on Yiddish as the language of the mean, the servile, and the cowardly. The linguistic revolution of the State of Israel is almost as astonishing as the political. The revulsion from the formerly despised ghetto language is of a complicated character, and will, I believe, have at least as much of an influence on American as on Israeli Yiddish.

I put on one side the original Yiddish still spoken by the old-time orthodox Jews of Israel as a protest against the use of everyday Hebrew; that, as we have seen, is the separate story of a petrified tradition. It is the modern, secular Israeli who is showing a sympathetic attitude toward Yiddish. Nor am I speaking only of academicians of the Yiddish faculty at the university in Jerusalem, or the established readers of a healthy Yiddish newspaper and the first-rate Yiddish quarterly, di goldene keyt (The Golden Chain), these last forming part of the residue of east European Jewry transferred to Israel. I have in mind the pervasiveness of a new relationship to the language. There are meetings, concerts, recitals, that are attended in part by sabras and half-sabras who have begun to "catch on." The holocaust has had its part in the process; the overemphasis on the passivity of the destroyed six million gave way to a more thoughtful perspective. That refusal to cooperate in complete death by hopeless violent resistance, that choice of partial survival in ignominy, was something more than personal; it was the last strategy of a people determined to survive at all costs for the sake of a precious charge. The rebirth of Israel was the slow, obstinate fruit of two thousand years of exilic ingenuity in pain. The sabra did not come into existence out of nowhere; nor did he survive in suspended animation. The sabra is the whole of the history of Jewry, in which the enormous Yiddish episode looms larger than all other historic episodes since the Destruction; and the *sabra* is becoming aware of it.

2.

The persistence of Yiddish must be seen in its proper evolving setting. We shall never again have monolingual Yiddish-speaking masses, or even small groups not thoroughly integrated into another, primary language. It is probable that considerable numbers of Jews will speak—or have an enjoyable reading knowledge of—three or more languages. A cultured Jew at home in his people's history and experience will be unable to dispense with Yiddish as the accompanying language. As a non-Israeli, he will need at least as much of a grounding in Hebrew as a four-year college student in French, with this difference: Because it is interwoven with Yiddish, and because it is becoming more and more a current mode of communication, Yiddish will not fade out as college courses in a language are apt to do. It will be—I am speaking always of the educated Jewish minority—a *needed* language, with its own intramural atmosphere, its sanctity in the midst of multi-colored secularity, international geographically but national in its appeal.

One hears passionately dedicated Yiddishists speak of an enormous upward leap in the possibilities of the language as a medium of communication. The slogan is: "Yiddish must be capable of reproducing in full the effects of any other great modern language. It must be equal to all the demands made upon it by all the scientific and linguistic wealth of languages like English, Russian, French, etc." Under "scientific," we are to understand, are subsumed the disciplines of physics, mathematics, psychology, biology, etc., and under "linguistic" the whole range of lexicography. Now there was a hectic interlude, in the Jewish Poland between the two wars, when Jewish national-cultural autonomy was given the kind of chance it had never known before, and a furious Yiddish activity developed in Yiddish schools and seminaries, in clubs and sports associations, promising to fulfill the program of the Yiddish maximalists. The physical liquidation of Polish Jewry put an end to the marvelous outburst of energy and inventiveness. Curious remnants of that cultural nova linger in corners, in forgotten books and pamphlets, but they are in fact only curiosities.

Exploring only one of the possibilities, I cannot conceive that any Yiddish-speaking Jews will use, or even recognize, the Yiddish technical terms of football, tennis, hockey, cricket, baseball, billiards, bowling, soccer, polo, etc., not to mention jackstraws and tiddledywinks. There will, of course, be a few happy fanatics inventing or recalling the more recondite details—but they are the least likely to apply them in use. In any case, sports terminology is being internationalized in its more general aspects; but the large residue that persists in local forms will not have its analogues in Yiddish.

If we take a wider view, the possibilities that have developed for Hebrew in physics, biology, etc. have practically no echo in Yiddish. There are, indeed, general terms, to which I shall refer below, but they are not even a beginning in, let us say, the vocabulary of a high school science student.

Much more urgent for the development of Yiddish is the pressure toward new words having the natural ring of the language. Neologisms must be used with care; there are new Yiddish words that are also new ideas in any language, and these are the least difficult to adopt, since they have no forebears. The badly needed Yiddish neologisms we have in mind are ideas already familiar in other languages, and taken over into Yiddish as awkward, sometimes ludicrous explanations or paraphrases. I have chosen a few examples out of a larger

number attributed by Yudl Mark to Professor Max Weinreich, in a 1964 essay:

"To dabble," *amatoreven*, could only be described by
tun epes oyf a laykhten, oyberflekhlekhn oyfn, "to do something in a light, superficial way."

"Chute," *aroploz multer*, literally, "let-down-trough,"
not a particularly happy invention, but a vast improvement on
the explanation, *aza ayngeboygene rine durkh velkher zakhn
vern aropgeglitsht fun oybn arop*, "a kind of curved groove
through which objects can be made to slide down."

"Elevator shaft," *shakht* (not in Yudl Mark), has become a standard absurdity as *dort vu der eleveyter geyt aroyf
un arop*, "the place where the elevator goes up and down."

"Ubiquitous," *umetumik*, was represented in the old
dictionaries by *iberal farhanden*, "to be found everywhere,"
and its parallel, *vos gefint zikh umetum*, "which finds itself
everywhere"; out of the sound Yiddish *umetum*, "everywhere,"
emerged *umetumik*, "everywhere-ish."

Another type of neologism is either fitted to recent de-
velopments or is a new expression of a concept familiar in
English. It is sometimes difficult to distinguish between the
two types.

Aylsho, "rush hour," had no Yiddish equivalent; the
compound Yiddish translates literally as "hurry-hour."

Beserveyser, literally, "better-knower," is perfect for
"smart aleck."

Bleyztants, "strip-tease," is made up of *bleyz*, "gap, blank,"
and *tants*, "dance."

Blishtshmeydl, "glamor girl," is made up of *blishtsh*,
"flash," and *meydl*, "girl."

Similarly, *dakhdire*, "penthouse," is "roof-apartment";
gantsdilik, "wall-to-wall," is "whole-floor," as compound
adjective; *her-un-tref*, "quiz program," is "hear and guess";
kush-vokh, "honeymoon," is "kiss-week"; *mendl un vaybl*,

271

"Mendl and wife" (I suggest "Mendel and Mrs."), is "hook and eye"; *omeyn-zoger*, "amen-sayer," is "yes-man," etc.

These happy inventions and hundreds like them are partly the work of Professor Uriel Weinreich, the son of Max Weinreich, and are to be found in *The Modern English-Yiddish Yiddish-English Dictionary*. So is the third variety of neologisms, those which belong to the scientific or technical field, of which a few are appended here:

Aroppluntsh, "splashdown," made up of *arop*, "down," and *pluntsh*, "splash"; *aviomuter*, "plane carrier," in which *muter* is Yiddish, and *avio* an international construct; *flivarg*, "aircraft," from *fli*, "fly," and *varg*, "equipment"; *atomkoyp*, "atomic pile," from *koyp*, "pile"; *impetveg*, "runway," from *impet*, "momentum"; *halevay gedank*, "wishful thinking," from *halevay*, "would that," and *gedank*, "thought"; *tshadnepl*, "smog," from *tshad*, "fumes," and *nepl*, "fog"; *trog-farhiter*, "contraceptive," from *trogn*, "to bear (child)" and *farhitn*, "to prevent"; *untervisik*, "subconscious," from *unter*, "under," and *visik*, "knowing"; *vifler*, "quotient," from *vifl*, "how many"; *vikltrep*, "escalator," from *vikl*, "wind," as verb, and *trep*, "stairs," etc.

Will these neologisms, apparently indispensable and for the most part extremely attractive, survive and weave themselves into a universal new Yiddish? Some undoubtedly will, overcoming the natural tendency of various Yiddish groups to break up into localisms. It is easy for the American Yiddish speaker to adopt *sobvey* for "subway," as the new dictionary does, but what will happen to the French Yiddish-speaking Jew, accustomed to *metro*? For him, and for Yiddish-speaking Jews everywhere, the "natural" word would be *unterban*, "under train," also suggested by the new dictionary, *unter* and *ban* being well established in Yiddish usage. *Vikltrep*, "escalator," as "winding-steps" suggests itself easily to all Yiddish-speaking Jews everywhere for a similar reason; and so with hundreds and thousands of word-formations being established, some to endure and some to fall away. But this is, so to speak, the mechanical aspect of the language. There are deeper problems that cannot be subsumed under a methodology.

3.

A group of neo-Yiddishists has appeared on the American scene, American-born, college-educated, who have taken in hand the task of the renewal of the language. In particular they have developed a campaign against the Yiddish of the established newspapers, with their often antiquated spelling and their laxity in the use of Anglicisms and Americanisms. The periodical of this group, *yugent-ruf, Call of the Youth,* is not particularly well written; the struggle to root or reroot itself in Yiddish puts one in mind of a similar struggle among the new devotees of Hebrew in the Palestine of fifty years ago. There is, however, a series of differences between the new impulse to Yiddish as manifested in this highly determined group and the impulse to Hebrew among the Palestinian pioneers.

These neo-Yiddishists are already divided. Some are Zionists and some are Diaspora Nationalists. The latter do not believe in the spiritual hegemony of Israel or in its political significance. But even the Diaspora Nationalists are divided, for while one subgroup believes in Territorialism, and is still looking for a Jewish homeland, or a series of Jewish homelands, in which to set up autonomous Yiddish-speaking groups, another subgroup believes that Jews should develop their Yiddish culture wherever they live. The Yiddish practiced by the Territorialists—originally seceded Zionists—has an old tradition; it is a rich Yiddish. The Yiddish practiced by the first group of neo-Yiddishists is often hard and raw in style. It is far more advanced than the Hebrew with which the *chalutzim* first struggled, but it is nothing like the ripe, colorful, idiomatic Yiddish of the best writers. To some extent it resembles, as a cultural artifact, Esperanto.

The neo-Yiddishists of all schools are an authentic sector of the Jewish will to live. They shrink from Jews who as not-Jews are spiritual zeros, as so many human beings are; they are saddened by Jews who have assumed valuable new personalities with no tincture of the old. But above all, they recoil with contempt from Jews who have made it a principle to suppress the Jewish identity as a progressive principle. This may take many forms in the present, as it has done in the past, but it has always had a curious universality: "Whatever else we do, let's get rid of the Jewish identity—and let's not jabber about distinctions and differences." The search for Yiddish self-expression, the stir toward a Yiddish revival, is one of the reactions against this Jewish self-destruction.

The revival of a language is not the same thing as a renewal of interest in a lapsed or forgotten language. The Renaissance witnessed a recrudescence of Greek in intellectual circles; we cannot call that a revival in the sense of a visceral resurrection. Between Plato and Erasmus—a better example would be the Greek Anthology—nothing developed; Greek was forgotten and then hauled back in the memory of the West. Yiddish, like Hebrew, was never forgotten; "revival" means in this case revitalization. It is revitalization by a minority, and its characteristic is the warming up of an ethnic relationship.

There is an interesting parallel between classical Greek and the ancient Aramaic. Aramaic was, as we have noted, the vernacular of the Jews of the Second Commonwealth, with branches in Mesopotamia. As the Palestinian vernacular it was accepted for daily use by the scholars who used Hebrew for studies and sacred discourse. Soon after the Destruction, Aramaic disappeared as a vernacular and—strange transformation!—turned into another sanctity. It was used in Talmudic study and—here is a stranger transformation—it was used by Cabbalists for the creation of the *Zohar*, the supreme book of mysticism. It has been stated on excellent authority that the Aramaic of the *Zohar* is phony! It is a pseudo-Aramaic, something like the pseudo-English of a modern imitating Edmund Spenser. But the *Zohar* is still read with reverence by the mystics, and what is harder to understand, the genuine Aramaic of early translators, made for Jews who did not know Hebrew, is read regularly by pious Jews side by side with the original Hebrew. It is the rule for an orthodox Jew to go over the week's section of the Torah on the Sabbath twice in Hebrew and once in Aramaic. But even these Jews do not write Aramaic any more. It is their Greek (though it is not Greek to them). It has endured two thousand years, and in the circle of the pious will endure indefinitely. It is understood and appreciated, but it is not a "revived" language. It does not keep on evolving, like Yiddish, and the enjoyment of it does not involve one in the laughter and sorrow of the *shtetl*, that is, in the emotions of grandparents, dead or living.

How long will Yiddish last? Languages with this sort of structure can be very tenacious and a particular tenacity attaches to certain Jewish experiences. Perhaps most relevant is the ongoing extraordinary effort, the creation of the *Great Dictionary of the Yiddish Language* by Yudl Mark and the late Judah A. Joffe. Conceived on the scale of the unabridged *Oxford Dictionary*, it is at present in its third volume, with seven more in prospect. I shall not attempt a description of this supreme expression of the Yiddish language. I only wish to note that it promises to gather into its pages all that has lived and still lives in the folk. That it should be in process of creation precisely at this hour in the history of Yiddish is a startling tribute to the people's vitality.

Index

Note on Use of Index

Many of the English words listed here are not to be taken as exact translations of the Yiddish. Their purpose is to invite attention to the more extensive treatment in the text of untranslatable variations and shadings in the language.